# the growing business handbook

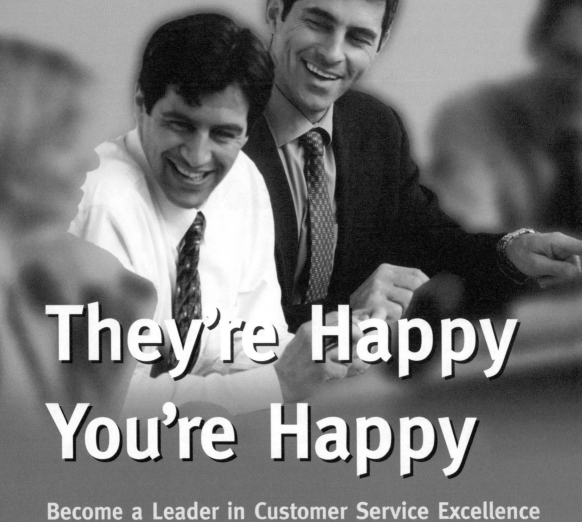

# They're Happy
# You're Happy

## Become a Leader in Customer Service Excellence

Enhance your reputation as an organisation that customers find easy to do business with. Organisational Membership of the Institute of Customer Service is a clear indication - both to your staff and your customers - of your commitment to achieve customer service excellence and offers you a key tool to sustain high standards of customer service professionalism throughout your organisation.

Join the Institute of Customer Service and help lead new standards in customer service professionalism.

For more information on Organisational Membership of the Institute of Customer Service call Robert Burdett on 01206 571716, email: membership@icsmail.co.uk or go to **www.instituteofcustomerservice.com**

Institute of Customer Service, 2 Castle Court, St Peter's Street, Colchester CO1 1EW

# the growing business handbook

### 8th edition

inspiration & advice from successful
entrepreneurs & fast growing uk companies

consultant editor: adam jolly

RECOMMENDED BY
INSTITUTE OF DIRECTORS

KOGAN
PAGE

London and Philadelphia

This book has been endorsed by the Institute of Directors.

The endorsement is given to selected Kogan Page books which the IoD recognizes as being of specific interest to its members and providing them with up-to-date, informative and practical resources for creating business success. Kogan Page books endorsed by the IoD represent the most authoritative guidance available on a wide range of subjects including management, finance, marketing, training and HR.

The views expressed in this book are those of the author and are not necessarily the same as those of the Institute of Directors.

**Publisher's note**

Every possible effort has been made to ensure that the information contained in this book is accurate at the time of going to press, and the publishers and authors cannot accept responsibility for any errors or omissions, however caused. No responsibility for loss or damage occasioned to any person acting, or refraining from action, as a result of the material in this publication can be accepted by the editor, the publisher or any of the authors.

First published by Kogan Page in 1997 as *CBI Growing Business Handbook*
Second edition 1999
Third edition 2000
Fourth edition published in 2001 as *IOD Growing Business Handbook*
Fifth edition 2002
Sixth edition 2003
Seventh edition published in 2004 as *The Growing Business Handbook*
Eighth edition 2006

120 Pentonville Road
London N1 9JN
United Kingdom
www.kogan-page.co.uk

525 South 4th Street, #241
Philadelphia PA 19147
USA

© Kogan Page and individual contributors, 1997, 1999, 2000, 2001, 2002, 2003, 2004, 2006

ISBN 0 7494 4424 X

**British Library Cataloguing-in-Publication Data**

A CIP record for this book is available from the British Library.

**Library of Congress Cataloging-in-Publication Date**

The growing business handbook : inspiration and advice from successful
    entrepreneurs and fast growing UK companies / [edited by] Adam
    Jolly. – 8th ed.
        p. cm.
    ISBN 0-7494-4424-X
    1. Success in business. 2. Management. I. Jolly, Adam.
    HF5386.G787 2006
    658--dc22

2005028463

Typeset by JS Typesetting Ltd, Porthcawl, Mid Glamorgan
Printed and bound in Great Britain by Cambridge University Press

# Contents

# SUCCESS<sup>m</sup>

*the power of financial management in business*

CIMA develops high quality professionals, whatever the size of your organisation. Our members and students work across all business sectors at all levels throughout the world.

Through a combination of skills, knowledge and the most relevant financial qualification for business the Chartered Management Accountant is at the forefront of their profession - driving business forward.

**Just some of the support we offer includes:**

**Certificate in Business Accounting** - More than just an entry route to CIMA's Chartered Management Accounting qualification, it provides a flexible approach to learning about business and finance with a stand alone set of modules, assessed exclusively through computer based assessment. Open access means all employees can study relevant elements of CIMA's highly valued syllabus as part of their personal development plans, providing solid financial training for financial and non-financial roles. Visit www.cimaglobal.com/cba for a full list of study modules.

**CIMA Training** - A no charge, quality assurance programme for employers of CIMA students to ensure the training of Chartered Management Accountants is delivered to a consistently high standard. CIMA has been voted the 'Best Student Body' by readers of PASS magazine presented in January 2005.
Visit www.cimaglobal.com/cimatraining

**CIMA Professional Development** - We provide lifelong learning support to members as they maintain their professional competence and ethical awareness. CIMA offers flexible CPD support to members as they work to enhance their professional development.
Visit www.cimaglobal/cpd

# "My business has the most demanding technology requirements – surely I can't just turn up and plug in?"

Businesses on the Isle of Man can make the most of an unrivalled telecommunications infrastructure ready and waiting to make competition on a global scale simply a matter of plug and play.

A fully digital network and a totally resilient, ring-fenced internet hub allows for 24/7 connectivity. Support services for ICT and e-Businesses, one of the fastest growing sectors in the Island, can be found locally.

With a zero rate of tax on trading profits proposed from 2006 for all businesses (e-Gaming companies already enjoy zero tax), and generous assistance and incentives, you can focus on your growth and development.

## You can on the Isle of Man

**Isle of Man**
Government

*Reiltys Ellan Vannin*

**Dti** To find out more about opportunities for e-business on the Isle of Man, visit www.gov.im/dti

# Let us assist you with your VAT affairs

## VAT Consultancy Services

The UK's Value Added Tax legislation can often appear complex, demanding and riddled with potential pitfalls. Drawing on many years of specialisation in the VAT field, with a first-hand understanding of how HM Revenue and Customs functions, our mission is to take the mystery and the worry out of your organisation's VAT affairs and maximise your profitability. Services for new business start-ups

Whether or when to register for VAT is always a key issue for new businesses. Every case is different and we will give you expert advice to suit your own particular circumstances and turnover projections. We will help you through the registration process and identify any key issues relevant to the products or services you are offering.

## Financial services providers

Recent changes to VAT legislation concerning financial services providers have highlighted the need to be fully abreast of which services are or are not VAT exempt and under which circumstances. Exempt supplies mean irrecoverable VAT, which affects the bottom line profitability. We are experienced in planning and negotiating with HM Revenue and Customs favourable structures, including special partial exemption methods that would maximise the overall VAT recovery and profitability of a partially exempt business.

## Overseas business

The basis of our service is our knowledge of VAT and our skill in guiding our clients through the maze of red tape involved in its compliance. Particularly for overseas businesses seeking to do business in Europe or build relationships with business partners, such input can mean the difference between success and failure in fully exploiting a business opportunity. The expert help that we offer will give your company a head start in entering or catering for the European market - and allow you to develop your business with confidence, to its maximum potential. As your VAT agents, we will act for you in all your dealings with the appropriate authorities, including completion and submission of the necessary returns. We can also assist in the recovery of VAT incurred outside the UK.

## Property business

Companies involved in the building, conversion, sale or rent of land or property need to be fully aware of their VAT obligations and plan ahead as necessary. Any company failing to do so could find themselves liable to the tune of thousands of pounds and even possible prosecution. Nevertheless, VAT relief is available for particular projects that meet specific and sometimes complex criteria. The Lysi team can advise you on whether your projects qualify for any kind of VAT relief and guide you through the process of securing relief.

## Why use us?

'Lysi' is the Greek word for 'solution', so it's the perfect choice of name for a company committed to providing independent specialist VAT solutions for clients across all forms of business. Our highly qualified team has long experience in looking after the tax interests of prestigious clients. The Chartered Institute of Taxation and the Association of Chartered Certified Accountants regulate us. We are also a member of the Confederation Fiscale Europeenne and are effectively part of a "family" of professional tax advisers established all over Europe. This gives us the ability to deal with all your European VAT issues in a professional and efficient manner.

We aim to provide a cost-effective alternative to large accountancy firms, without compromising on the same high standards of technical expertise. Our fees can be tailored to our client needs.

We look forward to working with you.

*Lysi*

VAT Specialists &
Chartered Certified Accountants

Conbar House
Mead Lane
Hertford
Hertfordshire
SG13 7AP

Tel: 01992 554 343 Fax: 01992 552 797 Email: enquiries@lysi.co.uk

www.lysi.co.uk

# Here's a tip from Royal & SunAlliance to improve your golf swing.

Golf coaches will tell you that a great way to improve your swing is to hold a beach ball between your knees when practising. This will stop your legs from collapsing and help your drive to become more accurate. And if you want to drive your business forward, our commercial specialists can help by providing a wide range of professional and financial solutions with different levels of cover.

For details of this and the many other ways that Royal & SunAlliance can help you please contact your broker in the usual way or log onto www.profin.royalsun.com

## We can't help helping.

ROYAL & SUNALLIANCE

Authorised and Regulated by the Financial Services Authority

Management Assurance (any combination from Professional Indemnity, Employment Practices Liability, Libel Insurance, Crime Insurance and Directors' & Officers' Insurance)
• Contingent Risks • Legal Indemnities • Charity Trustee Insurance • Personal Accident Insurance • Annual Business Travel insurance • Surety Bonds

...and in this country,
this is the bank for you.

International Cash Management is unique in each region.
That is why we select our ICM partners from the leading
banks in each country. This local strength combined with our
global connectivity allows you to increase business efficiency
by automating the management of your international funds.
To find out more about our ICM solutions and latest
product developments, contact our Director, ICM Sales,
Catherine Adair-Faulkner on **+44 (0) 20 7427 8096.**

Make it happen

www.rbs.co.uk/cbfm

## Part 11: Enterprise systems

mazars.co.uk

6'6"

6'0"

5'6"

# Have you got the right line-up?

5'0"

4'6"

4'0"

Looking for an adviser that can help take your business to the next level?

3'6"

We work with a wide range of entrepreneurs and owner managed businesses – including some of the fastest growing private companies in the UK. Whatever challenges or issues you face, we can make a difference to your business by providing a personal service backed by big experience.

3'0"

For further information, please contact Paula Gurney at growth@mazars.co.uk or telephone 01908 664466.

# MAZARS

**AUDIT • TAX • ADVISORY**

# Foreword

Taking a venture through a complete cycle of growth is a highly charged activity. The way each challenge is met and resolved holds the potential for creating or losing significant value.

Drawing on a wide range of professional expertise and commercial experience, this book gives a comprehensive insight into techniques and solutions for maximizing growth and controlling risks. With sections on marketing, funding, people, business technology, innovation, international expansion and property, it highlights potential new sources of value for enterprises to exploit.

It also stresses that achieving high performance is often complex and elusive. Costs can spiral out of control, cash can run short, customer service can flag, people can lose their way and innovative ideas can be copied.

Many enterprises discover too late that the skills that served them well as start-ups are different from those required to capitalize fully on their potential. No single formula for growth exists, of course, but rigorous planning has to be combined with an acceptance that markets and organizations are highly exposed to change. Flexibility and adaptability are becoming the norm in anticipating the demands of customers whose expectations are shaped by converging technologies and transparent global pricing.

This eighth edition of *The Growing Business Handbook* is designed to be a practical guide for entrepreneurs and managers as they confront decisive points in the growth cycle in the coming months. There are over 50 expert contributions: the IoD and Kogan Page are grateful to all the expert authors for sharing their experience and knowledge so freely.

*Miles Templeman*
*Director General*
*Institute of Directors*

## Plan Your Day And Life With The Performance Planner. Set, Measure And Achieve Your Goals Fast.

The key to your success is directed ACTION, which always follows the self-imposed discipline this **Performance Planner** is designed to create. You can make your future more exciting by using your **Performance Planner** every day to maintain that discipline and stay on track to reach your goals.

"Once you've established the goals you want and the price you're willing to pay, you can ignore the minor hurts, the opponent's pressure, and the temporary setbacks." – Vince Lombardi

### The Performance Planner Features:

- Goal Achievement Formula Charts
  - Seven Steps to Success
- Weekly Activity Record
  - Personal Performance Record
  - Your Daily Objectives and Activities Diary
- Important Meetings and Projects Journal
  - A Permanent Record of Notes, Thoughts and Action Ideas
- Monthly Activity Record
  - Appointments and Priority Activities
- Calendars and Holidays
- Birthdays and Special Events
- Address & Telephone Directory

With the **Performance Planner**, you can focus your time and energy on top priorities, which lead to the realization of your business and personal goals. Become a winner. Set and record your goals today. Visit www.brainybusiness.com or call 0800 011 2820.

---

# A. STEELE ASSOCIATES
## EXECUTIVE SEARCH AND SELECTION

A. Steele Associates (ASASS) was established in June 1998 and offers twenty five years experience in senior level Search Assignments across a wide range of general and senior management disciplines in sales, marketing, credit management, operations, support and technology. Our expertise has developed particularly in the identification of individuals for start-ups or re-organisations and the subsequent culture development and change processes.

Tel: 01798 815996
Fax: 01798 875817
E-mail: asteele958@aol.com

What vision does your
relationship manager bring?

That of a top international bank.

International success requires an international perspective.
As part of the sixth largest banking group in the world, your
local relationship manager has access to a network across
125 countries. To find out how we can help you operate
internationally, contact your relationship manager.

Make it happen

www.rbs.co.uk/cbfm

# Growth challenges

# Planning for growth

*Growth can make or break you, says Philip Verity, Head of Mid-Corporates at Mazars, the international accounting and business advisory firm*

Growing a business isn't necessarily as straightforward as it may seem: as the business evolves, the owners, managers and employees alike must all adapt to the, often substantial, changes that growth necessitates. These can be turbulent times for the organization – in some cases make or break – but with careful planning companies can manage this evolution, anticipate change and deal with the challenges that will inevitably arise, to achieve sustainable and profitable growth.

## Where are you?

The starting point in any growth plan is to have a thorough understanding and honest review of your business and your marketplace, including your customers, your competitors and your suppliers. There are various management tools that can help with situational analysis; some (such as SWOT and PESTEL) are not new, but still provide a very useful foundation for the analysis and a structure for the range of issues that should be considered.

Once a comprehensive understanding of the current situation has been established, the exciting task of looking into the future to describe where you want to take the business can begin.

## Where do you want to be?

As an entrepreneur or owner-manager, a key question to ask yourself is why you want to grow your business. For instance, do you want to grow your business to the extent that it provides a decent living for you and your family and is an asset that you can pass on to future generations? Alternatively, is your ambition to grow the company aggressively to maximize its potential and, possibly, sell it at some later stage, either to fund a new enterprise or to fund your retirement? The strategy you choose will have implications for you, your family, your employees and the business itself.

Having decided what you want from the business, the next stage is to set out your aims and objectives – what is your vision for the business? This vision will form the basis of your strategy and, communicated to other members of the team, may be used to motivate and engender their support and understanding of the future direction of the business and their role in it. Remember, it's good to set ambitious objectives; however, they should be challenging but achievable.

## How do you get there?

Once the starting and finishing points are established, the most important part of the growth plan is to set out detailed plans of how you intend to move from one to the other. Growth plans should include both short-term actions (six months to a year) and longer-term (three to five years or more), possibly staged, initiatives or changes that will enable you to build towards the objectives you have set for the business.

Your initial situational analysis will assist you to identify those issues, both internal and external, that could help you (such as opportunities in the market, regulatory changes or developments in technology) and those that may hinder or potentially derail you (new market entrants, problems in the supply chain or the loss of a key member of staff). Acknowledging all eventualities, positive and negative, will enable you to plan for them where possible, hopefully giving you the edge over your less proactive competitors.

At each stage of the process it may be wise to involve your accountants or advisers – they can offer unbiased advice and a sounding board for your plans. They will also bring a different viewpoint, fresh ideas and a reality check if required!

The following checklist provides an overview of some of the types of questions that business owners and managers should ask themselves when planning for growth.

### Vision

■ Why do you want to grow the business and what are your ultimate goals? Do you have an exit strategy?
■ As the business owner, how much control over the everyday running of the company do you want to maintain?

### Strategy

■ Is growth likely to be organic or achieved via a merger/acquisition? How do you intend to finance your growth?

∎ Do you have a formal strategic business plan (including budgets and medium- to long-term financial forecasts)?

∎ What do you consider to be the sources of your competitive advantage and are these sustainable? Who are your competitors and what are their strategies?

## Products and marketplace

∎ How attractive is your current marketplace? Are there likely to be any changes (legal, regulatory, etc) that will alter its attractiveness?

∎ Do you need to develop new products/services to meet market needs? If so, will this involve investment in research & development?

∎ Do you need to look for new markets? If so, might these be overseas?

## Customers and suppliers

∎ Who are your customers and what do you know about them? Are you dependent on any individual customers?

∎ What are your channels to market and do you need to find new channels to achieve the levels of planned growth?

∎ Who and where are your major suppliers? Are you dependent on any one supplier?

∎ Do your competitors also use the same suppliers? How easy is it to source elsewhere?

## Management and operations

∎ Is accurate information available to enable appropriate management and decision making? Have you set clearly-defined KPIs (Key Performance Indicators) for monitoring and measuring growth? Are you clear on the value drivers for the business, and do you have a system to monitor these regularly?

∎ Will growth require significant investment in premises, IT infrastructure, new equipment or distribution facilities? Are your business processes robust enough to meet the increasing demands of the planned growth? Will the controls that you have in place still enable you to keep the business on track?

∎ Is the business currently financially robust enough to support further growth (in terms of cash flow, profit margin, overheads, etc)?

## People and organization

∎ Who are your key stakeholders and what are relationships like with them? Will your stakeholders, or your relationships with them, have to change as the business grows?

∎ Does your current organizational and/or leadership structure need to change to facilitate growth?

∎ What skills and experience do you need within your team to help you achieve your growth plans? Do you need to recruit or train? How will you retain or incentivize key workers?

Philip Verity is a Partner and Head of the Mid-Corporate Market business line, at Mazars, the international accounting and business advisory firm.

Mazars acts for some of the fastest-growing entrepreneurial companies in the UK, offering a complete range of accountancy and business advisory services, including audit and assurance, tax advisory and compliance, corporate recovery and insolvency, consulting, forensic and investigations, corporate finance and financial services for private individuals.

For further information: tel: 01908 664466; e-mail: paula.gurney@mazars.co.uk; website: www.mazars.co.uk.

# Lessons of fast growth

*Jan Hruska, joint Chief Executive of Sophos, has built a £60 million global company from scratch. He discusses turning points in its creation*

When Jan Hruska started Sophos at his kitchen table in 1985, he never imagined it could become a company with sales of £60 million with nine subsidiaries around the world. In fact, he and his fellow Oxford PhD, Peter Lammer, thought it unlikely that they would be able to manage more than 10 people. Today, Sophos has grown into one of the world's top four developers of anti-virus software with 960 employees.

Twenty years ago in his front room in Kidlington outside Oxford, Hruska was looking for a fast-growing field in computer security. There were no computer viruses and he concentrated his efforts on data encryption. 'PCs were still in their infancy and were typically shared by three or four users, who had no way of separating their files and keeping them private.'

Sophos sold a few security packages, but Hruska admits that he would only be employing 12 people today if he had continued in this direction. 'Encryption is a beautiful and fascinating subject. People listened to us with enthusiasm, but didn't feel that they had to buy anything.'

In 1987, everything changed when the world's first PC virus was launched from a small computer shop in Pakistan. More followed, causing chaos for IT users. 'The phone suddenly started ringing with people asking whether we had anything to combat this new menace.'

Sophos's first product, which Lammer and Hruska developed together, was not virus-specific. It detected changes in a program, not its cause, but proved to be effective and precise.

With backing of £50,000 from Oxford Venture Capital in return for 20 per cent of their equity, Hruska and Lammer stopped doing everything themselves and started building the different functions of a company. 'We improvised as we went, but the whole organism quickly took on a life of its own.'

## The right DNA

In growing the company, Hruska has always insisted on recruiting only the best programmers. 'There are good ones and bad ones. The good ones are 10 to 20 times more productive than the bad ones. You can easily take on a liability. We've resisted recruiting someone for the sake of filling a place.'

Up to a year ago, he and Lammer undertook all the recruitment themselves. 'We could quickly see through people. We were recruiting the DNA for the company. We wanted good genes, not cancerous ones.'

'As companies grow, it is easy to recruit idiots, who then take on people less intelligent than themselves. It results in a collective lowering of the IQ of the organization. Recruiting intelligent people is a good insurance policy.'

## Outbreaks

When an outbreak occurs, Sophos's specialists take the virus apart and work out how it works, producing detection and disinfection, which then flows onto users' PCs. Technical support is then available around the clock through a global team of 120 people in Abingdon, Boston, Vancouver and Sydney.

From the start, Sophos has only worked in the business market, so instead of holding the hand of 30 million home users during a crisis, it can concentrate its resources on its customer base of 85,000 companies. 'They like it that we don't put them on hold for 30 minutes and play them Greensleeves,' says Hruska. 'Plus they can reliably download our anti-virus software without the web grinding to a halt.'

## Brutal reality

The focus on business users, who represent three-quarters of the anti-virus market, is giving Sophos a distinct advantage. Overall growth is currently 17 per cent a year, but Sophos is running well ahead at 35 per cent, allowing it to make ground on its main competitors, Symantec, McAfee and Trend.

A high proportion of new business leads are now coming through the Sophos website, which was mainly a source of technical information up until recently. It has now been redesigned to make it easier to download the software directly. Depending on the size of an organization, costs vary from £5 to £50 per user.

Because sales are by annual subscriptions, Hruska constantly faces the 'brutal reality' that users may or may not renew. 'Customers will soon find you out, unless your underlying technology is solid and good.'

## Swallowed pride

Three years ago, Hruska spotted a change in the pattern of renewals. IT directors were starting to expect to have anti-spam as part of their anti-virus software. 'We were developing our own anti-spam solution, but realized that we were going to be six to 12 months late, so we swallowed our pride and ditched our own product.'

Hruska looked around for who had the best solution and bought Active State, a Canadian company, for £80 million in 2003. 'We acquired the technology completely, rather than licensing it, as we want to guarantee continuous supply.'

Even though Hruska had read all the stories about the mess that companies can make of acquisitions, he still found it surprising how long it took to pull together as one organization. 'People resist change and you keep discovering pockets of resistance.'

## Short on space

Office space has been a constant concern for Sophos as it has steadily outgrown a succession of properties. 'We were always slightly lagging behind with premises,' says Hruska.

In taking Sophos' first 1,000 sq ft at The Quadrant in Abingdon, Hruska and Lammer relied on an enlightened landlord to recognize the company's potential and not to insist on an initial deposit of three times the rent.

They then bought a 10.4 acre site, which was a disused rubbish tip next to the Thames. 'We did not listen to the conventional wisdom that you don't buy or build property, you should rent it. We just could not find a property that was suitable.'

After putting up two buildings, they persuaded the council to sell them some more land to build 115,000 sq ft at a cost of £32 million. 'To attract the best people, we wanted them to come and say "Wow".'

It took three and a half years to build a showpiece headquarters, which has room for 600 people, but is already starting to get tight. 'We are nervously making projections about what we might need in three years' time,' says Hruska.

## Market entries

Sophos opened its first overseas subsidiary in the US in 1997. 'One of our first employees said we should be there, so we asked him to re-mortgage his house and invest some of his money in the subsidiary, which was remarkably successful. He looked at every pound spent and the US now accounts for more than a third of our revenue,' says Hruska.

In opening in other essential markets, Hruska, a native Croat who himself speaks five languages, does not follow a set formula. To find the right person to run the Japanese subsidiary, for instance, Sophos ran a language course for everyone in the company. Participants soon dwindled to five and one of these was chosen to run the new company in Yokohama. 'We wanted someone who speaks Japanese, as well as English, who is not shy about picking up the phone.'

Sophos has distributors in over a hundred countries, but growth in markets like the US and Japan relies on making a long-term commitment, rather than relying on the next sale to fund the business. 'Opening a subsidiary is a big commitment not just in people and property, but also in building an IT infrastructure.'

'We have a completely homogenous structure, which can only be achieved by being heavy-handed. It is essential that it is run as one company. Each department is transnational, working around the clock with people in different countries taking calls from wherever they are needed.'

### Liquidity

Investments in properties and systems have so far been funded out of cash. 'We make sure that we do things at the right pace, so that we do not over-extend ourselves,' says Hruska.

Like pharmaceutical companies, the risks in product development are high. 'We have a huge investment upfront to design the software and then have a low cost of production. If you get your design right at the beginning, then the rewards come at the end.'

After initial backing from Oxford Venture Capital, which sold three-quarters of its stake to build Oxford University's new physics lecture theatre, funding came first from 3i and then TA Associates, which now owns 26 per cent of the company.

Although Hruska's own preference is to stay independent, he realizes that venture capitalists expect to make an exit, so 'a liquidity event' will occur, which could be an IPO.

## Growing instability

Hruska is not taking anything for granted. 'The more you grow, the more unstable it becomes,' he says. 'Forty per cent is sustainable. After that the oscillations can become uncontrollable.'

'You are taking people on without enough time to ensure that they absorb the company culture,' he says. 'A growing company is a changing company. People don't always like it, even though they say they do.'

To make sure people's attitudes are more closely aligned with the interests of shareholders, a share purchase scheme has already been introduced and share options will follow shortly, even though Hruska is struggling with the rules governing how private companies offer them.

Along with Lammer, he remains in day-to-day control of the company, although a COO was appointed last year. In planning for the future, Hruska still thinks that every day is a risk. 'It is a case of minimizing anything which might spring from behind the corner. We want to make the company more resilient to any problems that might occur and we want to gain as much market share from Semantic, McAfee and Trend as possible.'

For further details: www.sophos.com.

# Entrepreneurial skills and behaviours

*Don't be fooled by the myth, argues Ignacio de la Vega, Instituto de Empresa Business School. Some entrepreneurs might be born, but many more are made*

Entrepreneurship is a fascinating domain. Everything to do with the activities and lifestyles of successful entrepreneurs attracts a great deal of public attention – we all know and admire people like Bill Gates (Microsoft), Richard Branson (Virgin), Jeff Bezos (Amazon.com), or other entrepreneurial tycoons. But the world economy is not only based on these high-flyers. It also depends on the efforts of millions of SME entrepreneurs, those valiant fighters that identify an opportunity and take it to the market by means of a start-up, a family venture, or an acquisition. And the entrepreneurship scenario would not be complete without corporate entrepreneurs, those executives and employees who use entrepreneurial tactics to achieve growth for their organizations and, of course, that new breed of entrepreneurs engaged in social and welfare activities, known as social entrepreneurs.

Is there any particular trait exhibited by all these groups? Are there any skills and behaviours that they have in common?

■ One of the most basic entrepreneurial skills is the development of an innovative attitude. The ability to identify business opportunities and transform them into winning business models. Innovation and creativity is an important asset here. Innovation skills start with the idea identification process, followed by the design of the business model (the more demanding and competitive the markets are, the more important it is to create value via innovation in the value chain). These are key skills for managing growth.

■ A second skill that defines the entrepreneur is the ability to secure the necessary resources to launch or grow the venture. Human resources, physical assets, capital, technology and licences, are all important resources that need to be identified, quantified, acquired and managed throughout the venture's life span. Successful entrepreneurs excel at this process and are able to convince others of the venture's potential.

■ A third, very important skill, which applies particularly to micro or small firms and high growth potential ventures, is the entrepreneur's ability to tolerate and manage risk. Every single business (and life) activity poses some kind of risk. The more dynamic the market, the higher the risk. Today's markets are very exposed to change. Change is the norm, not the exception, and while change augments risk it also makes for higher returns. Moreover, the more innovative the business model, the more dangers it entails. Yet, contrary to generally accepted opinion, the successful entrepreneur is not a good risk taker, but rather a good risk manager. Successful entrepreneurs are very well trained in the art of diminishing risk via continuous feasibility analysis, the adaptation of existing business models, excellent management practices and the capture and retention of the best possible business management team. The best entrepreneurs, those that achieve growth in competitive markets, are 'educated' in risk management and avoid anything that could possibly be compared to a 'gambler' attitude.

■ A fourth skill is related to the visionary abilities of entrepreneurs. The entrepreneur is usually defined as someone who is ahead of the market. Obviously, successful entrepreneurs do not have a crystal ball to see into the future. What they do have is information about the market and the changes taking place. They put a lot of effort into getting to grips with how the market is behaving, how customers perceive value and change their needs, and how competitors react. This information allows them to innovate and anticipate relevant changes in the markets. Hence the entrepreneur grows and changes in lockstep with market developments. The need to do this is also one of the main weaknesses of micro and small firms, which need to concentrate on managing their day-to-day business, and often have no time or knowledge to explore market trends.

■ A fifth skill that defines 'good' entrepreneurs is the way they manage their workloads. The seed and start-up phases of any new business, as well as the fledgling stages in the lives of SMEs, require enormous amounts of energy and long working hours. It is true that luck is a KSF for the success of any venture, but fortune favours hard workers! The scarcity of resources that is a feature of any new venture implies long working hours that continue throughout the life of the venture. Successful entrepreneurs are all hard workers, and only at the end of the journey do they begin to allow themselves more time for their own needs.

■ One final element or skill, often ignored by experts but a key trait of successful entrepreneurs, is the capacity to network. The ability to communicate and convince people around them: employees, suppliers, investors, authorities, customers, etc.

They need to be able to convince and motivate key potential employees to join unborn ventures, competing with safer offers in the market; they need to negotiate credits and better inputs with suppliers that do not know them; they need to convince venture capitalists, angels or friends and family to invest in their high risk ventures; and they need to get licences, permits or government aid. They have to excel in creating a powerful network of supporters in little time.

If we combine all these skills we can create a better definition of the successful entrepreneur, the type of entrepreneur that leads a venture through growth stages. We are talking about 'the individual or team that develops a business venture from an innovative concept of a product or service, acquiring and managing financial, human, technological and material resources, minimizing risk at every business stage through analysis, management and value creation, and employing a collective effort to obtain an adequate return on all employed resources'.

Identifying these skills helps us to understand just how wrong some of the major myths created by entrepreneurial literature are, including the following:

■ *Entrepreneurs are born.* Most of the above mentioned skills are 'learnt' through years of training, observation and management. Having said that, we can of course identify some born entrepreneurs, but there are not many in the market.

■ *All successful entrepreneurs in the 21st century start up with a breakthrough project, normally in technology-related industries.* Again, even if we can quickly identify a good number of high growth technology projects, most successful entrepreneurs do not have technological revolutions at the core of their business models. Some of today's major successes are ordinary ideas (with a great deal of innovation) managed in an extraordinary way.

■ *Only immediate financial success drives entrepreneurs.* Obviously, financial success is at the core of entrepreneurship, but high growth entrepreneurs seek medium to long-term financial returns. Hence they add value creation for society by means of job creation and the generation of collective wealth.

■ *High growth entrepreneurs have immediate and direct access to the venture capital industry.* Most successful entrepreneurs start by investing their own funds, often with a smart bootstrapping strategy, later moving on to friends and family funding followed by small informal angels. Only later on do they have access to VCs to fund expansion.

■ *High growth entrepreneurs base their success on their own knowledge, expertise and capabilities.* There is one main element that explains most major successes: a capable team. As markets become increasingly complex and competitive, high growth firms require the best multidisciplinary and complementary teams they can get. Even in the early stages teams are a key success factor, albeit in the form of advisers or sponsors. This is the real sustainable competitive advantage of high growth entrepreneurial companies.

Instituto de Empresa is one of Europe's leading business schools, dedicated to training entrepreneurs and corporate directors through its Master's degree and Executive Education Programmes. Instituto de Empresa is characterized by its global approach, its spirit of entrepreneurship and innovation, the design and implementation of applied research projects and the promotion of socially responsible initiatives. Instituto de Empresa currently has a network of 30,000 alumni that hold management positions in some 85 countries.

Ignacio de la Vega is currently in charge of the Direction of Strategic Development and of the International Centre for Entrepreneurship at the Instituto de Empresa Business School. De la Vega has been engaged in entrepreneurial activities as entrepreneur, investor, professor, consultant, corporate entrepreneur and government vice-minister for the last 20 years. De la Vega has published several books on entrepreneurship, and serves as visiting professor in several schools and universities around the world.

# Prospects for growth

*Having slowed over the past year, how quickly can the economy bounce back, ask Dr Andrew McLaughlin, Chief Economist, and David Fenton, Economist, The Royal Bank of Scotland Group*

## Overview

The UK economy turned in a good performance in 2004, but ran out of steam as the year wore on. Thus far, it has been unable to regain much momentum in 2005, with consumers seemingly reluctant to spend and companies similarly reluctant to invest. Lower interest rates should help to deliver a reacceleration in 2006 but, until then, UK companies will have to work that wee bit harder to achieve success. We are optimistic they will rise to the challenge.

## Reflections

First, the good news. 2004 was the UK economy's best year since the millennium. GDP grew by 3.2 per cent, up from 2.5 per cent in 2003. It was also the UK economy's twelfth year of uninterrupted growth. This represents an unprecedented period of stability for companies, individuals and the government alike. With volatility at a post-war low, and average economic performance high by historic standards, it is fair to say that the UK is enjoying something of a purple patch.

But the going got tougher as 2004 wore on. Consumer spending was the first area to soften, as higher interest rates pushed up households' mortgage interest payments. At the same time, the pick-up in oil prices and higher tax payments squeezed real take-home pay.

We started 2005 with two hopes for the UK economy. First, that consumer spending would bounce back from a sluggish end to 2004, and stabilize around its trend growth rate. Second, that other areas of the economy would take up the running. We had reasonably modest expectations for business investment that would, nevertheless, be sufficient to keep the economy ticking over in 2005–06.

By half-time in 2005 we were already 2-0 down on these hopes. Revisions show that while growth in consumer spending at the end of 2004 was not nearly as weak as originally estimated, it had ground to a virtual standstill in the first half of 2005. Companies on the high street were under greatest pressure, with retail sales slowing markedly. The housing market may have been a factor. Cash-terms spending on goods fell in Q1 for the first time since 1992, possibly reflecting the impact of a reduced level of housing market activity on big-ticket items, such as white goods and furniture. Spending on services has, thus far, held up somewhat better.

The shortfall in consumer demand is beginning to have an impact on companies' willingness to invest, which has fallen short of our relatively modest expectations. We had anticipated that, with balance sheets in good shape and profitability still reasonably strong, business investment would carry the momentum built last year into 2005. But after a listless performance around the turn of the year, it appears that this momentum has been lost. In cash-terms, business investment fell by 0.6 per cent in Q1, having fallen by 0.1 per cent in the previous quarter, the first back-to-back contractions for three years.[1] It's not that companies don't have the cash, or the appetite to borrow; but they seem reluctant to invest while the outlook for demand is so uncertain (see Table 1.4.1).

**Table 1.4.1** Constraints on investment

| Percentage citing... | Q4/04 | Q1/05 | Q2/05 |
| --- | --- | --- | --- |
| Inadequate net return | 52 | 47 | 42 |
| Internal finance shortage | 20 | 22 | 21 |
| Inability to raise external finance | 8 | 8 | 8 |
| Cost of finance | 3 | 2 | 1 |
| Uncertainty about demand | 43 | 49 | 54 |

Source: CBI Industrial Trends Survey (April 2005)

## Things can only get better?

There were some signs of improvement towards the end of the second quarter. Retail spending posted its fastest month-on-month increase since 2003 in June, and it looks like the manufacturing recession will turn out to have been short-lived. Regardless, the improvement in the data came too late to save Q2, which showed that growth was below trend for a fourth consecutive quarter. On this form, the Monetary Policy Committee (MPC) cut interest rates in August, for the first time in over two years.

But the monetary easing does not end there. The August rate cut, coupled with investors' expectation that there is more to come, has helped to push the pound back to where it was at the start of the year. At the same time, the FTSE has posted remarkable gains in 2005. The question is: will this easing in monetary conditions get the UK economy back on track?

Hopefully it will, but we would caution against expecting too much too soon. It takes about a year for interest rates to have their full effect on activity, which means it will be 2006 before companies start to see an appreciable impact on demand. In the meantime, it falls to a weaker pound to prop up the economy. This should provide some support to trade-exposed companies, via increased export demand and/or a boost to profit margins; it may also encourage tourists to spend more when visiting the UK.

The marked decrease in long-term interest rates during 2005, coupled with a steady increase in equity values, will also help to chivvy demand. But they are unlikely to prevent a below-trend performance from the UK economy in 2005. We expect growth of 2.0 per cent, which is well off the pace set in 2004 (3.2 per cent), though hardly a disastrous performance.

In 2006, the August rate cut will start to have an impact on growth. Again, we would caution against getting too carried away; a quarter-point cut will help to shore up demand but is unlikely to trigger a return to the boom days in consumer spending. Nor is it likely to fuel a boom in business investment; survey data show that the cost of finance is something of a red herring as far as constraints on capex are concerned.

We look for a mild acceleration in GDP growth to 2.4 per cent which is just shy of the UK's trend growth rate (see Figure 1.4.1). This is also some way short of the Bank of England's latest forecast (August), which looks remarkably optimistic to us. The Bank's forecast implies, among other things, that no further cuts in interest rates will

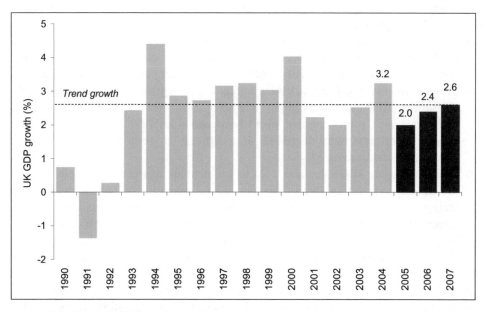

*Source*: DataStream/RBS Group Economics

**Figure 1.4.1**   Outlook for economic growth

be required to keep the economy ticking over. We are not so sure. We were never in the sub-4 per cent rate camp, but still think another cut will probably be required. This is unlikely to happen before 2006, however, with the MPC seemingly keen to let the dust settle on the August decision before it acts again. Time will tell.

## Risks and challenges

When an economy is on a downward trajectory, it is all the more vulnerable to economic shocks. This is the case with the UK economy at present. Shocks and their effects are, by definition, nigh on impossible to predict. Nevertheless, it is still worth outlining the key risks to the economic outlook; forewarned is forearmed, as they say.

As we see it, there are nine key risks to the economic outlook. For the benefit of those keeping score, six are to the downside and three to the upside. This means that, on balance, we have a nagging suspicion that the forecast outlined above may prove a tad optimistic. We then want to close this chapter by addressing a question we are frequently asked by customers and colleagues alike: in the current economic environment, is China an opportunity or a threat?

### Downside risks

■ *Policy impotence.* The assumption that the MPC will be able to sustain demand with looser monetary policy could prove over-optimistic. Lower interest rates might fail to stimulate consumer spending, if households choose to save the reduction in mortgage interest payments to, for example, offset the reduction in interest receipts earned on deposits.

■ *A significant fall in house prices.* The link between house prices and consumption is often overstated, but a house price crash would severely undermine consumer confidence. This would probably lead to lower spending and increased saving.

■ *Unemployment rises.* The UK labour market is still in good shape, but a few cracks are starting to show. For example, unemployment increased for a fifth straight month in June – something that hasn't happened since 1992. If the labour market were to deteriorate more decisively, it is difficult to see how a sharp economic downturn could be avoided.

■ *Global economy.* If US demand loses its momentum, and euro zone demand fails to build any momentum, British exporters would face difficult trading conditions in their two key markets. A marked rise in the value of the pound, possibly related to a correction of the US current account deficit, would exacerbate their plight.

■ *Oil price.* How long can the UK economy continue to absorb the higher oil price? If real take-home pay and profit margins continue to come under pressure, consumer spending and business investment will likely suffer further.

■ *A sharp pick-up in inflation.* Inflation pressures appear fairly well contained, but the surge in oil prices means a good old-fashioned bout of inflation cannot be ruled out. This would probably force the MPC to raise interest rates in response; we all remember what happened last time.

## Upside risks

■ *Policy overkill.* It is possible that the MPC will cut rates too far, too fast, leading to a surge in consumer spending and investment. This boom would be reinforced if the housing market were to reignite.

■ *Sterling depreciation.* Expectations of lower interest rates, and question marks about the outlook for the UK economy, have pushed sterling down against the euro and the Dollar. Further devaluation could lead to a marked improvement in the UK's net export performance.

■ *Wages pick-up.* Wage inflation has eased in 2005, as the labour market has softened. Still, unemployment remains very low and even if migrant workers continue to act as a release valve for the labour market, it would not take too much to stoke upward pressure on wages. Faster wage growth would, in turn, fuel faster consumer spending.

## China: an opportunity or a threat?

China has quickly established itself as the predominant topic of debate. Its arrival on the world stage, following years of economic reform, is the most visible manifestation of globalization. Its 9.5 per cent expansion in 2004 was appreciably stronger than expected. Further, this pace has been maintained in 2005, as export growth has continued to surge. Exports were 30 per cent higher in the first half of 2005 than the same period last year.[1] China's trade performance serves as a reminder of how unforgiving a process globalization can be, as UK companies have seen market share and profit margins exposed to the chill winds of competition.

But there is more to the Chinese growth story than exports. Retail sales are also growing rapidly. A rising share of labour in national income should support retail sales growth over the next few years. As a percentage of GDP, labour compensation rose from 50 per cent in the early 1980s to 68 per cent in 2003.[2] This trend will fuel the accumulation of household wealth and, in turn, consumption growth.

We would venture to suggest that companies should pay more attention to this dynamic in the Chinese economy, and view it quite properly as an opportunity. China's cost advantages mean it is displacing some activity from developing economies – just as Mexico did in the 1980s – but the global cake will be bigger for all of us. This is the long-term benefit that we all must focus on and respond to.

## Notes

1. National Statistics.
2. National Bureau of Statistics of China.

For further information, visit: www.rbs.com/economics. The Royal Bank of Scotland plc, registered in Scotland no. 90312, registered office: 36 St Andrew Square, Edinburgh EH2 2YB.

# Resilience for the growing business

*Ground lost to competitors during even a brief disruption can take years to regain, warns Martin Savage, Principal Continuity Management Consultant, Royal & SunAlliance*

When a business is growing rapidly it is all too easy to focus on opportunities and ignore potential threats. But any one of a huge range of events – including fires, floods, health hazards, regulatory or legal actions, staff defections, fraud, and power or systems failure – could result in highly damaging disruption to normal operations over a period of weeks, months or even years. Under the most extreme circumstances, the business may even succumb.

Business Interruption insurance offers protection against the direct financial consequences over a pre-agreed period of indemnity. But insurance will not address a number of other key factors of critical importance to the company's future – including loss of customers (beyond the indemnity period of the insurance policy), brand or reputational damage, and undermined staff loyalty. Business continuity management (BCM) provides a practical methodology for limiting and mitigating these risks.

It is often assumed that BCM – or business resilience, as it is increasingly commonly known – is a matter for large corporations and not something smaller business need consider. In reality smaller businesses are more exposed and more at risk from potential disruption to their normal operations than larger ones.

Smaller companies are more likely to have all their operations at a single site, have greater issues around cash flow, and lack the depth in human and material resources that their larger counterparts enjoy. Companies whose business depends on providing a continuous or 'just in time' service to customers are particularly vulnerable – as are those with a limited customer or supplier base they can ill afford to lose. Ground lost to competitors during even a brief disruption can take years to regain.

The downside of not addressing BCM should be obvious. But it is also worth stressing the positive benefits. Companies that can demonstrate effective continuity planning will be more attractive to investors, potential partners and customers – especially, but not uniquely, in industries such as food manufacturing, technology, engineering and financial services. An informed and proactive attitude to identifying and managing business risk can also help to secure more attractively priced insurance premiums.

In addition to building resilience into a business, the continuity management procedures described in the remainder of this chapter can also help to uncover more efficient and secure business processes and practices. For all of these reasons, it is well worth any growing business allocating the time and resource to identify and plan against potential threats to its operations. It is, after all, an investment that could make the difference between survival and failure.

Business continuity planning for any growing company need not – indeed should not – involve microscopic analysis of every last aspect of its operations. The process of preparatory review and the resulting business continuity plan (BCP) should be 'appropriate' – to borrow the Financial Services Authority's terminology – to the nature, scale and complexity of its operations.

There is little benefit in going through an endlessly exhaustive process that results in a huge tome of a BCP that will quickly date as the business continues to evolve. It is also neither rational nor helpful to expect that everything can carry on exactly as before a business-interrupting incident. Realistically, any small business must accept that some things will have to give. The important thing is to identify and prioritize the most critical aspects of the business's operations.

There are two key BCM stages involved here: business impact analysis and risk assessment.

Business impact analysis focuses on itemizing the various processes and activities carried out within each area of the business and ranking them in terms of how critical they are. Initially this exercise can be carried out directly by key people within each department or function – but should subsequently be validated by someone higher up the organization who is able to take more of a helicopter view across the business as a whole.

For each business-critical activity identified, a rating should be defined, say from 1 to 5, or even simply 1 to 3 for a smaller business, reflecting its relative importance to the company's ability to continue functioning. In each case, management should identify the interval of time after which the inability to perform a particular function would begin to cause major problems.

It is also important to clarify what resources would be required to restore or replace crucial lost capabilities to the point where the business can continue functioning to the minimum level identified. This analysis will create a frame of reference for determining an appropriate business continuity strategy.

In parallel with the business impact methodology described above, there is the opportunity to carry out a risk assessment exercise. At the same time as considering what is crucial to the business – in terms of people, functions, premises, equipment, business records, utilities, suppliers, materials and so on – risk assessment techniques can identify ways of building additional resilience into these areas through appropriate loss prevention measures.

Risk assessment is a required procedure for health and safety in the workplace – and a similar methodology can be applied to business continuity. The four main aspects of risk assessment are: identifying risks, reviewing existing controls, implementing additional controls to minimize these risks, and assessing the impact should one of these threats materialize. The objective of the process is to ensure that suitable loss prevention and damage mitigation arrangements are in place.

Having completed the process of business impact analysis and implemented whatever measures arise from the risk assessment exercise, the business is in a position to formulate a meaningful strategic plan for business continuity. Understanding what would be crucial in the event of an incident makes it possible to formulate practicable plans for coping with the aftermath.

When planning for recovery, there is no point in trying to second-guess 'loss scenarios'. It will be something different! In essence, when considering the recovery strategy, plan for circumstances where you are unable to make use of all or part of the facilities (for whatever reason) for a period that would require alternatives to be brought to bear.

These plans will need to include a range of strategies for keeping the company in business – depending on the nature and severity of the incident. This could involve provisions for contracted assistance, alternative premises and/or equipment, secondary suppliers for key materials or services, and so on. The key thing is that the strategy must be sufficiently flexible to allow for whatever combination of circumstances may arise.

There are two key thoughts to keep in mind at this stage: 'What if' and 'Never assume'. The first underlines the importance of thinking outside the box to anticipate risks posed by less obvious threats. The second should remind management decision-makers not to take anything for granted. The one thing you can guarantee about business-threatening incidents is that they will not conform neatly to any predefined pattern.

The strategy adopted then feeds through into a BCP document. This will be the bible when any trigger event materializes. It should be obvious therefore that it must be accessible, available in more than one location, continuously reviewed and updated as the circumstances of the business change – and that everyone who will be required to act upon it should be fully aware of its existence, availability and contents.

Part of the provisions of the BCP should be the clear identification of teams or individuals responsible for key activities, including invoking, controlling and directing the plan's implementation; internal and external communications; emergency response (evacuation, damage assessment, etc); facilities and technology recovery; and business recovery. However small the business, adequate provision must be made for deputization should any of the key individuals not be available when an incident occurs.

As noted above, the BCP should be appropriate to the nature and scale of the company's operations. The BCP should ideally cover a clear statement of aims and objectives, the team structure, specific procedures for recovery, and directions for communicating with both internal and external audiences. The very minimum requirement would be a list of contact details for all employees, customers, suppliers, emergency service providers, investors, banks, insurers and so on. Timely and appropriate communication is absolutely crucial following an incident.

Staff need to understand what has happened and what role they should now play. Customers and suppliers need to understand the nature of the event and how their interests will be affected. The media need a story – if management does not provide it there is every chance the press will make up something more damaging. Above all, each of these audiences needs to understand that the situation is under control.

Once the plan is in place, it should be tested on paper, ie through group discussions re-asking the what-if questions and making any adjustments necessary, by testing communications cascades, and in walk-through rehearsals. Ideally any fallback IT provisions should also be tested. The key consideration is that the BCP should always be seen as a work in progress. The circumstances and priorities of any growing business are changing all the time. The BCP must continually evolve to reflect this.

In a sense, this is nothing more than applied business common sense. The extra dimension is maintaining the discipline required to fully understand your business, its critical points, its vulnerabilities, and the measures required to guard against these – and, of course, a willingness to continue challenging any assumptions in your BCP and asking those what-if questions. The last time a company needs to discover the deficiencies in its business continuity planning is when an incident has already occurred.

Royal & SunAlliance is one of the world's leading multinational general insurance groups focusing on all major classes of general insurance. Royal & SunAlliance currently transacts business in some 130 countries looking after 20 million customers and the group employs around 28,000 people worldwide.

# Improve the atmosphere at work with this absorbing tip from Royal & SunAlliance.

NASA have found that placing plants in the work environment is an excellent way of absorbing toxins from the atmosphere. And here's another breath of fresh air. At Royal & SunAlliance we've enhanced our Enterprise product range for small businesses by adding three specialist insurances: Directors' & Officers' Liability, Professional Indemnity and Personal Accident/Business Travel. As with all our Enterprise products, they are backed by a service that will help provide you with the right solution for you.

To find out more about our complete range of Enterprise products and our service proposition for small businesses, please contact your usual broker.

## We can't help helping.

ROYAL &
SUNALLIANCE

Authorised and Regulated by the Financial Services Authority

Enterprise consists of: Business. Shops. Offices. Contractors. Properties. Clubs. Van. Business Car. Small Hotels. Directors' & Officers' Liability. Professional Indemnity. Personal accident.

**2**

# Exploiting ideas

# The innovative enterprise

*Your best weapon is systematic, radical innovation, argues Peter Ives at Business Dynamix*

The only certainty in business is that change is the only constant. There is more change all the time and it is coming faster and in more complex ways than ever. Innovation is the only sustainable solution. Yet I still hear business people saying, 'I understand that to grow I need to innovate but at present I'm just trying to survive, not develop new products'. But there are only two ways for any business to improve its profits and that's either by increasing sales or reducing costs.

> The DTI defines innovation as 'the development of new ideas and their economic application as new products or processes. Businesses and other organizations engage in innovation when faced by problems or when they perceive profitable opportunities. Innovation provides opportunities for productivity growth through the development of more valuable products or services or the development of new processes that increase efficiency. It also drives improvements in people's lives through changes to the environment in which they live and work.' (DTI, *Competing in the Global Economy – The Innovation Challenge*)

Innovation is typically thought of as creative ideas developing a new product or service that will sell. But it can also transform a business when applied to processes and models. Innovation is not just about marketing and sales but is about rethinking everything that you do in your business. It's about challenging the how and why:

- Can I do it better?
- Can I work smarter not harder?
- Is there a better way to service a market?
- Is the present business model out of date?

Innovation is as much about improving your business processes as it is about developing new products and services.

We all get into our 'comfort zones' and continue to do repetitive processes that we've always done. Often the value of ICT is not realized in businesses. Question what you do and ask:

- Are there processes that I do on a regular basis?
- Do I need to do them?
- Can they be automated?
- Can I redevelop the process so that my customer does more of the work?

Businesses need to concentrate on their core business and the effective use of technology can help people to spend more time doing what is profitable. With the advent of the 'network' business more and more businesses are staying small in numbers and outsourcing many of their cost-centre tasks.

Innovation is just as important in the way that businesses work with their suppliers. For many years major companies have used supply chain management to improve their stock holding (cost containment) whilst optimizing new product development (sales income).

Much of our business thinking has been based on the manufacturing processes with control, hierarchy, diligence, efficiency, replication and quality being some of the virtues that we have acquired. But in a world that seems committed to faster and faster change, business structures and models can no longer afford to be 'set in stone': flexibility and adaptability are the key strengths of the new economy. Imitate the style of the great boxer Muhammad Ali and 'float like a butterfly and sting like a bee'.

In too many companies, real business innovation seems to be the exception. Innovation is safely channelled into R&D or new-product development, where it can't infect the rest of the business. Many organizations seem hostile to innovation, barriers seem to be everywhere. But, just as innovation is about the 'How can we...?' rather than the 'Why we can't', there are usually ways to unblock the blockers. Innovation is more about a state of mind than a skill or technique. It is easy to get sucked into the inactivity of bureaucratic processes.

Innovation can really make a difference when it is applied to your target markets. You just can't grow revenue significantly unless you really excite customers. That's not easy, particularly if all of your energy is focused on day-to-day survival. Radical innovators don't accept markets' norms, or the 'that's the way we've always done it' mentality. Markets can be changed, whether it's Dell questioning the need for dealers to sell its PCs, Easyjet selling budget flights via the internet and cutting out the frills, or Vodafone having the nerve to take on the incumbent market giant, BT, and taking the mobile phone market from under their nose.

When most people think about the future, they typically think of how they can improve existing products and processes, but what they should be looking at is, are customers looking for something new? Customers will always make room for something that is new and offers extra benefits. DoCoMo, the Japanese company, developed an internet-enabled mobile phone, attracting 30 million customers in 30 months to its i-mode service, proving that phones are no longer just about voice traffic. Radical innovation can change more than just buying habits: it can change customer expectations.

Remember that the benefits the industry has been promoting are not always the ones that connect with the wants of their customers. Traditionally, PC producers have banged on about speed but customers are now realizing that there is more to their buying decision than just getting the fastest; it's often more about a machine that lets me do what I want, where and when I want.

Markets are being changed for ever and the convergence of technologies is decimating what were thought to be safe industries. How could a telecoms provider five years ago have anticipated the threat the internet posed to its voice traffic business model through Voice over Internet Protocol (VOIP) services?

Innovators are not inventors. They rarely have Eureka! Moments; their focus is on business improvement rather than invention. One of my favourite examples of the difference was when Sir Clive Sinclair and Alan Sugar were negotiating the sale of Sir Clive's computer business to Amstrad. Negotiations were hitting a problem over the amount on offer. Sir Clive implored Sugar to pay the full price, citing that the products contained 'state of the art technology' to which Alan Sugar responded that if it was run on elastic bands and that was what the market wanted, then that would be what he would produce. Sugar's approach was that of the innovator who looks to address/ stimulate needs that a market has yet to fully appreciate rather than that of the inventor who believes that their 'baby' is the important factor.

Sometimes the innovation comes from being willing to accept outside help. One area where we often get involved is when additional funds are needed to enable the business to grow. The majority of businesses have followed the 'norm' by going to the bank for finance. This means that they are often locked into short-term debt that is likely to mean that the bank will find that it becomes over exposed through loan and overdraft facilities and will be forced to refuse further funds, leading to the cry, 'My Bank doesn't understand my business'. Funding for innovation requires a 'package' of funds approach, using a 'staged' mix of grants, awards, debt and sometimes equity and other specialist financing tools.

Remember: never be afraid to look at things in a different way. Not through 'rose-tinted spectacles' but by daring to think perhaps there is a better way to achieve what is wanted.

So, innovation is not the domain of 'creative types'; it is for all of us as long as we are prepared to accept that we must constantly challenge the norm, looking for better ways of doing business. Sometimes it will be an uncomfortable ride, with challenges from others, but the burning belief will take you through, and there is no business feeling that I know of that can come anywhere near the feeling that comes from the success of achieving a 180 degree change in addressing a market.

Business Dynamix focuses on releasing the innovation within a business, working to develop a culture of continuous improvement designed to maximize returns from all assets, both physical and intellectual. Its accreditations include the National Business Link Consultants Register, the SBS Investigating an Innovative Idea programme and High Performance Coaching for the Academy for Chief Executives. Peter Ives is managing director and has spent some 15 years in supporting innovation. For further details: tel 01992 704506, or visit www.businessdynamix.co.uk.

# Innovation for SMEs

*Smarter thinking, knowing your market and engaging your customer are requirements when your business is looking to pursue radical improvements in its products and services, says Lincoln Lewis at London Innovation*

Businesses that introduce new products and services or significantly improve business processes and practices are almost twice as likely to increase turnover as those that don't, according to the London Business Survey (2003).

However, innovation is not a golden elixir and is inherently associated with risk, and should therefore be underpinned by the hard reality of commercial viability. A misconception arises from a lack of comprehension of what innovation really is or, even more worrying, the widely perceived notion that unless it's technology, it cannot be innovation.

Innovation can be defined as exploiting new thinking in the shape of a product, process or service. Strictly speaking, business innovation should enable an entirely new set of performance features; improvements in known performance features; and/or a significant reduction in costs. Richard Leifer sums this up in his definition of radical innovation as a product, process or service with either unprecedented performance features or familiar features that offer potential for significant importance in performance or cost.[1]

The lettuce in a plastic bag invention is often used as a very good analogy for both service and product innovation. This invention revolutionized the highly perishable food sector, removing the need for fully trained chefs to ensure product freshness prior to service. The then innovative process and product packaging meant that supermarkets could keep their products on the shelf a lot longer and attract more sales while reducing operational costs.

# only seeing the barriers?

If your business is struggling to introduce new products or services, we may be able to help. Get a JumpStart from London Innovation.

Be inspired. Visit:
www.london-innovation.org.uk

 London innovation

 PART-FINANCED BY THE EUROPEAN REGIONAL DEVELOPMENT FUND

LONDON DEVELOPMENT AGENCY

Innovation tends to rely heavily on the creativity, skills and knowledge at the SME's disposal and typically follows a traditional implementation cycle. It is essential for innovation to succeed that a culture of fresh thinking, challenge and adaptation is engrained within the business ethos. Innovators have traditionally been perceived as being counter-productive, non-compliant, and troublemakers who are difficult to manage and politically naive. However, when managed within a climate conducive to creative criticism and ideation, innovators become constructive agents for change. When implemented, an innovative culture can enable SMEs to deliver an improved product, service, business process or practice.

Business innovation should aim to increase productivity and reduce costs, leading to increased competitiveness within local and global markets. The threat to businesses from globalization in the product and service markets is accelerating. As a result, SMEs face increased competition not only for sales, but also for technical know-how and skills. In this environment, competitiveness at the company level depends crucially on the speed to market of new products or services and the time to implement new cost-saving business improvements. Similarly, the creation of wealth and employment depends to a large extent on the speed with which innovative breakthroughs are converted into a commercially viable product or service.

Innovation requires much more than the ability to turn a new idea into a working product. An efficient pipeline of new innovations is not enough; it is only through the application of the innovation in the marketplace that measurable gain will be achieved within the business. It is therefore critical that before investing company resources into innovation, a business has a thorough understanding of its marketplace, the customer base, and fully investigates the expected impact of the innovation on the market.

## Smarter thinking

Ideas are the lifeblood of any business, whether it's creating new products and services or improving on existing business practices. It is essential that businesses embrace a culture of innovation, and give themselves the time and space to come up with and act upon new ideas and better ways of conducting their business.

Ideas need space to flourish, but commercial pressures often limit the amount of time available for innovation and creativity. There are simple ways of making space within your business for ideas:

■ hold regular ideas workshops;
■ train managers to listen;
■ win buy-in from staff;
■ reward contributions.

## Know your market

Guaranteed success for every new venture might seem a futile dream, but there is a way of bringing it closer. Knowing your customers and market inside out will give new initiatives the best chance for success. Research is the bedrock of market understanding. But market research is not just about reading the occasional report: it's about continually assessing the market, keeping up to date with the changing landscape of your competitors and customers.

An understanding of customer values and requirements is crucial to ensuring their satisfaction. 'Knowing your customer' is critical to the creation, expansion and retention of the customer base. This understanding allows you to target customers, sell effectively, compete and spot new opportunities.

For many companies customer service is an afterthought. It is important to get to know your customer and understand the experience they want and the experience they are currently having. Make sure that your workforce is passionate about serving the customer and use innovation in customer service as a differentiator so that you stand out from your competitors.

## Think about where your business is going

You've decided to embrace the challenge of change. But how do you ensure the momentum is still there and you're not stuck in a different rut in six months time?

Constantly look for new opportunities, new markets and new ways of doing things and encourage everyone around you – including supply chain partners and even customers – to do the same.

Opportunities and threats are just as likely to present themselves on the other side of the world as round the corner. Constantly revisit your business plan and strategy to ensure it is still relevant.

No one knows what the future looks like. Seeking and incorporating knowledge and ideas will ensure you are better prepared for it. But only by building agility into the organization will you be able to pre-empt customers' changing demands. The only certainty is change. Embrace it within your organization, and continually evaluate your offering.

## Note

1. Richard Leifer *et al, Radical Innovation,* Harvard Business School Press, 2000.

The London Development Agency is the Mayor's agency for business and jobs. It prepares the Mayor's business plan for London and mobilizes the support and resources of hundreds of partner organizations to help build a thriving economy for London's people, businesses and communities. The LDA is dedicated to improving sustainability, health and equality of opportunity for Londoners.

The London Innovation programme was created by the London Development Agency with the aim of increasing awareness of the potential benefits awaiting the capital's businesses through the introduction of an innovative culture within their organization. For more information, case studies and practical advice on innovation within business in London, visit www.london-innovation.org.uk.

# A wealth in ideas

*Turning ideas into wealth depends on IP, says Jacqueline Needle at Beck Greener*

Do you believe that intellectual property (IP) rights, and patents in particular, are:

■ expensive;
■ irrelevant to small and growing businesses; and
■ difficult, if not impossible, to enforce?

If these are your views, you are in accord with the majority (70 per cent) of non-patent holding smaller companies that took part in 2000 in a research project investigating the value of IP. The research established that only 30 per cent of smaller companies in the UK, France, Germany, Italy, Spain, the Netherlands, Sweden and Finland had ever applied for a patent.

However, James Dyson founded a company which, because of his successful use of the patent system, was enabled to manufacture and sell vacuum cleaners particularly profitably, and in the process he became a millionaire. Dyson licensed his patents to companies in other countries, most notably to a company in Japan, such that the worldwide manufacturing capacity for his cleaners was enhanced. Dyson was also able to keep versions of the vacuum cleaner made by competitors, most notably by Hoover, off the market.

In recent years, Mandy Haberman's company has made and marketed the 'Anywayup Cup' profitably, and success in enforcing her patents has seen a competitive children's drinking cup from Jackel International removed from the market.

## Difficult and expensive?

Individuals and companies can succeed and make money without involving themselves in IP issues. However, such an approach is not risk- or expense-free. There are many examples of companies that have ignored IP completely only to be accused of patent or trademark infringement. The champagne at a product launch party can taste very flat if an unexpected court injunction stops the launch in its tracks. The expense of dealing with such accusations, especially if the product has to be removed from the market, will be significant. Even worse, this unexpected expense could probably have been avoided.

Most IP does cost money, and if the issues are not understood, it can appear difficult. However, without IP, creativity cannot be captured and protected and it is this protection which enables ideas to be turned into wealth. The difficulties disappear with knowledge and Mandy Haberman, amongst many others, has criticized SMEs for not having at least one person in authority who has been educated in IP.

Not all IP rights cost money. Copyright and unregistered design rights arise automatically. A company needs to keep the original software or design documents in a systematic way so that the date of origination can be established, and the creator or author identified. The company also needs to ensure that it owns rights it uses in its day-to-day business. For example, a company commissioning a logo design for its own use will not automatically own the copyright in the resulting logo. A specific agreement will be required to transfer the copyright from the designer to the company.

Patent Office records can be freely searched on the internet for information about the trade marks that have been registered. A company can avoid conflict problems by ensuring that its proposed trade mark or logo is not already registered by someone else.

It does cost money to pay professional patent attorneys to register trade marks and to draft and file patent applications, but the potential rewards are high. For the price of one full page advert in the *Daily Telegraph* it would be possible to cover the fees arising over a five-year period to obtain grant of a patent for a new invention in a selection of four or five European countries, in the United States and in Japan. The newspaper may be in the bin within 24 hours, whilst the patents could provide a platform for profitable trading for 20 years.

## Irrelevant for SMEs?

All businesses, regardless of their size, trade, have competitors, and seek commercial advantages over those competitors. A small company coming into conflict with the rights of others does not have the commercial 'muscle' that large corporations can use to force a settlement. IP rights might be the only weapons an SME can deploy in the event of a conflict. Effective use of IP could be vitally important to SMEs.

An SME using IP *effectively* will:

■ have a person in authority who has adequate knowledge of IP issues;
■ have routines in place to safeguard rights; and
■ seek professional assistance when required.

### Have a person in authority who has adequate knowledge of IP issues

Conflicts can arise, or rights can be lost, if appropriate action is not taken during the timescale of a project. A knowledgeable owner or executive can identify, and then avoid, any risk of conflict by undertaking searches. During any project the executive can also decide whether any of the ideas are so commercially valuable that protection should be sought.

### Have routines in place to safeguard rights

Any proprietary information of commercial value should be identified and kept confidential. Employees should be made aware that such confidential information must not be divulged. Measures can be taken to restrict the availability of confidential information within a company, and departing employees should be reminded that their duty of confidentiality will remain even after they have left. Both the recipe for Coca-Cola and the exact composition of the batter for Kentucky Fried Chicken are still known to only a handful of people.

A majority of those made rich with the assistance of IP, such as James Dyson, have had ideas or inventions that have been patented. A patent can only help if it is valid, and a valid patent can only be obtained if the patent application is filed before there has been any public disclosure of the invention. It is essential that any new idea of potential worth is kept totally confidential to the company during the early stages of design or development. At some time a positive decision should be made as to whether patent protection is likely to be required. If it is decided that patent protection is not warranted then public disclosure can be made, but it should be realized that putting the idea in the public domain also dedicates it to the public, as the right to obtain patent protection in most countries has been given up.

### Seek professional assistance

It is important to get the patenting decision correct, especially if a project is thought to be of potential value to the company. Not only must an invention be new to be patentable, it must also be non-obvious compared to what is already known. However, many inventors will wrongly define the final result of their labours as obvious, perhaps because they see it just as the consummation of days or weeks of everyday work.

The patentable invention also has to be of industrially applicable subject matter and not in the list of entities that are explicitly excluded from patent protection. The inexperienced are often heard to exclaim with certainty: 'You can't patent that.'

If the invention has taken time and money to develop, will take further resources to get into the market, and is forecast to have a future, it would be wise to take professional advice. In such circumstances there is a very high chance that the invention will be patentable. Even if the patent attorney advises that an invention is not generally patentable, other protection options may arise. For example, the significant differences between European and US patent laws mean that products which cannot be patented in Europe can be patented in the United States.

Alternative forms of protection, such as a Community registered design, may also be available and might be commercially useful.

## Are IP rights difficult to enforce?

It is commonly said that patenting an invention is a waste of time because the company will not be able to afford to enforce the patent. However, less than 1 per cent of all patents are involved in any dispute, and it is the existence of the patent, rather than of the invention, which provides the wealth-generating opportunities.

If a product newly on the market is successful it will soon attract the attention of competitors. They will want to provide their own versions and thereby share in the potential profits. If the product is not patented, the competitors are free to use the idea, although they cannot make a slavish copy. Domestic, electrically powered air fresheners were put on the UK market one September some years ago as the 'new, ideal Christmas gift'. By October there were in excess of 10 competing devices available such that the originator's Christmas market was literally decimated.

If the new product is patented, or is the subject of a patent application, the majority of businesses will pause before rushing to develop rival versions. Even large business is reluctant to get involved in patent litigation without good commercial reasons. It may be that a competitive product can be developed that 'gets around' the patent, but that will require the competitor to spend time and money with no certainty that it will succeed. When Xerox introduced the first generation of copying machines, it had a worldwide monopoly for the 20 years for which its patents existed without having to take action for patent infringement. As soon as the patents expired numerous competitive photocopying machines were launched.

The competition is attracted by success, and so infringement actions are generally about inventions that make money. This profit stream alone might be enough to enable a patent action to be funded, as was the case for both James Dyson and Mandy Haberman. It is also possible to take out legal expenses insurance to fund such actions.

In the past, patent infringement actions in the UK had to involve three types of professionals, namely patent attorneys, solicitors and barristers, and were therefore alarmingly expensive. The Patents County Court was set up to provide affordable patent litigation. It has enabled costs to be reduced considerably by allowing a patent attorney to act alone, and by requiring more focus on the issues.

More recently appropriately qualified patent attorneys, referred to as Patent Agent Litigators, have been given rights allowing them to litigate in the mainstream English courts, up to and including the House of Lords. This reduces the numbers of professionals needed in a case. There have also been changes in practice in these courts that have streamlined procedure and required the issues to be simplified. We are now in an era where patent infringement actions, whilst never cheap, can be undertaken for a much more reasonable cost.

Jacqueline Needle, a partner of Beck Greener, is a graduate in electrical and electronic engineering. She is a Chartered Patent Attorney, a European Patent Attorney and a Registered Trade Mark Agent. In 1997 Jacqueline was awarded, with distinction, an LLM in Advanced Litigation and since then has become a Patent Agent Litigator. Thus, Jacqueline is one of a handful of British patent attorneys who are able to undertake litigation in intellectual property matters in the English courts.

Beck Greener is a firm of patent and trade mark attorneys based in the heart of London's historic legal district. Beck Greener provides a comprehensive service covering all aspects of intellectual property, namely patents, trade marks, designs and copyright. It is the aim of the firm to provide robust and commercially relevant advice.

For more information, contact: Beck Greener, Fulwood House, 12 Fulwood Place, London WC1V 6HR; tel: 020 7693 5600; fax: 020 7693 5601; e-mail: mail@beckgreener.com; website: www.beckgreener.com.

# Building and managing an IP portfolio

*A company's value often rests on its IP, say Tessa Bucks and Kelly Virdee-Crofts of Boult Wade Tennant*

As can be seen from the recent case of the MG Rover Group, intellectual property (IP) is often a company's number one asset. In this particular case, Shanghai Automotive Industry Corporation paid £67 million for just a part of the Rover Group's IP portfolio. The Rover Group's other largest asset, the MG trade mark, has been priced at a whopping £50 million! This is in stark contrast to the mere £57 million that was paid for most of the Longbridge site.

In the IT sector, IP mainly comprises software rights, trade marks and registered domain names. Think of the Easy Group. How many IP rights does it own? It has over 100 trade marks registrations and applications in Europe alone, and that does not include other IP rights, such as patents, domain names, copyright or rights in other territories. The Easy group has a virtual monopoly on the prefix 'easy' for certain goods and services and has successfully prevented many others from trading under this particular trade mark in its business sector.

In the engineering sector, the emphasis is usually on patents and designs and less on trade marks.

In many cases the value of a company rests entirely on its IP portfolio. Thus a strong IP portfolio can increase the value of a company. It provides the means to defend your market share and, through protecting innovation, to further develop and expand. Registered IP can also prove a useful deterrent to competitors, making them

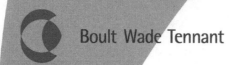

less likely to tread on your toes. Even IP rights that are not currently being used can provide a source of income, through licensing or even selling. Such rights could, for example, be design rights or patents for products no longer being manufactured, or trade marks no longer being used but which still have substantial goodwill.

An IP portfolio can also help to attract investment – if you've secured a monopoly on a wonderful new product, others will want to invest in your company.

## How to start an IP portfolio

Most companies already own IP, some without knowing it. What about your company name and logo as trade marks? If these have not been registered as trade marks, they should be! Do any of your products have distinctive names or logos? If so, these should ideally be protected through registration. Although one may have common law trade mark rights in the UK without registration, these are expensive to defend and are not necessarily available in other countries. Registration, on the other hand, does give a clear cut case for preventing others from using your marks. So carry out an audit and see if there are any rights that ought to be protected and are not.

## Building your portfolio

A manager should be appointed to ensure that the IP portfolio overall is built in a way that makes economic and commercial sense. A strategy for filing applications needs to be decided early on, so that the right markets are targeted. Few companies can afford to obtain protection for their IP in every country in the world. It is better to have strong patent, trade mark and design protection in a few key countries where your markets are based, rather than just a few rights in a wide spread of countries. Always file applications in the countries where your manufacturing bases are, as well as those countries where you sell your products or processes. Obtaining IP rights in your home country is an essential first step.

Good IP advice is crucial to secure value-for-money protection for the most promising IP. For example, product or apparatus patents and designs are far more valuable than process or method patents. In terms of other parties infringing your rights, it is usually easier to detect infringing products than processes or methods. Competitors can be very reluctant to invite you onto their premises for inspections!

The IP manager also needs to review competitors' rights and plan for dealing with any conflicting rights. It might make better sense to settle out of court, rather than sue a competitor. Court actions are very costly and the winner can only be guaranteed to receive at most 70 per cent of the cost of suing someone. On the other hand, if you are a small entity, it is not always sensible to let the big guys off. This can eradicate your market share, leaving you with nothing.

## Wooing inventors

The key to building your portfolio lies with your employees. Your research and development team needs to be educated about IP so that they recognize when they have invented something that is patentable or worth a registered design right. They also need to know about confidentiality so that patentable ideas are not lost through careless disclosure. The use of confidentiality agreements is vital when discussing innovations with investors or buyers.

In the engineering sector, many engineers are employed to manufacture products, rather than invent. They therefore need encouragement to investigate new possibilities and to spend some time in developing and improving products and processes.

A typical incentive for inventors is the provision of a reward for each IP right that is established. Some companies give an award of, say, £1,000, for each patent application that is filed. If there are several inventors then perhaps they can share a slightly larger sum, for example, £2,000. A rewards dinner or party once a year to recognize key inventors provides a further incentive for employees to invent.

## Brain-storming sessions

Not all innovations for products or processes are created by sole inventors; brain-storming sessions can help target particular problems for which solutions need to be found. Regular sessions can yield good ideas for new IP rights. The sessions should comprise not just the research and development team or engineers from a particular department or area, although these are valuable in finding solutions to a problem particular to a certain sector. Mixed sessions, including sales or service personnel, can provide the opportunity for a wider group to interact and can provide ideas for a more general and overall IP strategy.

## Internal infrastructure

A good internal infrastructure ensures that ideas are reported to the correct personnel and are not lost. Such an infrastructure for the reporting of ideas should include employees being able to communicate through an intranet, via e-mail and through personal contact with the IP manager. IP managers should not be strangers to the inventors, as people often fail to communicate their inventions. They are not always aware that the incremental improvement that they have made is actually worth anything, so all too often they remain silent rather than pick up the phone. A lack of communication between the IP manager and the inventor can be especially tricky if they are located at different sites. Thus an IP manager needs to pay as many visits to the site of the research and development personnel as possible.

An invention disclosure form can help to focus the inventor's thoughts so that all the information that is required for the drafting of a patent specification is recorded. This ensures that communication between the IP manager/patent agent and the inventor is cost-effective and trouble-free.

## Good documentation

All ideas should be documented well, thereby helping to avoid the loss of valuable IP rights. It is well known that companies work hard to find a solution to a problem and, through poor documentation, lose the solution, only to encounter the same problem in later years and invent once again. As an example, a well-known company asked the UK Patent Office to conduct a search for the solution of a stable paint for aeroplanes. The Patent Office very quickly found a patent disclosing the solution – a patent belonging to the company in question, dated half a century earlier!

## Keep the inventor's interest

It is easy to entice and encourage your staff to invent with the promise of a monetary reward when a new application for an IP right is filed, but it may be difficult to keep their interest during the often long period of prosecution of the patent application. A good incentive is the provision of a further reward once a patent is obtained in a key country. If a particular invention is key to the success of a product, the inventor should be recognized. It makes good sense to reward and continue to reward good inventors – after all, a company's fate rests in the hands of such individuals.

Through such innovation a company can expand, and through the registration of IP it can defend its position, deter competitors and generate income.

Tessa Bucks is a Patent and Trade Mark Attorney and Managing Partner at Boult Wade Tennant. Kelly Virdee-Crofts is a part-qualified Patent Attorney.

Boult Wade Tennant is a firm of Chartered Patent Agents and European Patent and Trade Mark Attorneys. The firm advises on all aspects of intellectual property protection, management and enforcement in the UK, Europe and worldwide. Website: www.boult.com.

# 3

# Customer service

# Becoming customer friendly

*Actively encourage feedback and complaints to make yourself more profitable, says Mark Bradley at Customer Service Network*

## Satisfaction? Is that the best you can do?

If you haven't already seen the compelling evidence proving the link between excellent customer service and the bottom line, then you haven't been paying attention! Study after study, research programme after research programme and, most persuasively, actual UK company experience tells you that if you understand what's important to your customers and you consistently exceed their expectations when delivering to them, their support and your future are guaranteed.

So, for a growing business, it seems fairly straightforward. Yet my experiences of UK retail service demonstrate that, sadly, it's far too straightforward for some.

The problem starts with the word 'exceeding'. Wasn't it customer satisfaction we were supposed to be focusing on? But the word 'satisfaction' implies varying degrees of arousal according to the prevailing context. In football terms a manager may complete his post-match interviews with a cursory 'I was pleased with the performance'. Only trouble is, that doesn't necessarily mean his team won. Your partner may have spent hours preparing the evening meal, but if you answer 'satisfactory' to the question, 'How was it?' the evening's entertainment may end right there. It's only later into the evening, when your charms have redeemed you, that the term 'satisfaction' actually represents peak performance.

So, to avoid the anaemia of the uncommitted, you need to establish what your customers want from you and, according to the business you're in, it could be any number of things. Start by inviting some customers to a discussion and ask them for their perceptions of your business. Customer service is too elusive a term to be simply conveyed – you need to know what specific element is most important to them. Encourage story telling and don't limit the range of discussion – because their perceptions of you could have been created long before they did business with you. Keep in mind your ideal customer transaction (what it looks like when everything works perfectly) and see how close their experiences are to this imagined benchmark. Do this well, in conducive surroundings, perhaps even with an incentive, and you're in a strong starting position. Fail to do this and it's like trying to corral cats. Unfocused and uncertain, you're in danger of bypassing satisfaction and going straight to *dissatisfaction*.

## Don't stifle complaints!

But, console yourself, because dissatisfaction isn't as bad as it used to be. For many organizations, having systems and processes that make it easy to generate customer feedback (including making it easy to complain) is a direct element of their profit strategy. For small businesses that can be as simple as making sure the MD takes every complaint call and, for larger enterprises, allowing simple recording of customer feedback on the company intranet. Some businesses have found that switching the emphasis of their customer surveys from satisfaction to dissatisfaction (ie, tell us what we're not doing well and need to improve) generates a strong return in retention, repurchase and advocacy. Some organizations mistakenly believe that a reduction in the number of complaints is a critical success factor. It is if you're focusing on reducing the number of root causes to the problems, but if you're performance managing your team on reducing complaints, they will! You'll miss out on the opportunity and your customers will soon lose interest.

## Focus measurement on customer priorities

So to my next question: do you know how interested in you your customers are? The best and most effective way of doing this is to use the outputs of your customer discussions to produce a list of questions for your customers. Let's say 'willingness to help' emerged as their biggest priority and let's weight the scoring to ensure that it's performance in that respect that people focus on.

Make sure you get an overall rating of service so that you compare the answers to the various preceding questions with it to better understand what 'drives' perceptions. Give your customers space to let you have their verbatim comments, as they will provide the detail and insight required to make practical, meaningful improvements to your products and services. Make sure you find out what's important to your business (re-purchase, retention, advocacy, franchise protection, etc) and include these 'persistency' questions. Whether you do this by e-mail, web, post, face-to-face or telephone, just make sure you do it regularly – or at least at a frequency that matches the intensity of the business transactions they experience.

One last thing on measuring customer perceptions: please include your own team when publishing these results. If the people providing the service are involved in the process (and this means giving them the freedom to analyse the data and introduce and suggest their own performance improvement ideas) then the likelihood of those changes being sustained is increased. However natural the instinct to take a central command and control approach (it is, after all, your business), you need to devolve leadership to all of your cohorts, especially the ones closest to the customer.

## Treat employees as valued customers

Just how you do this takes us to the importance of building a successful team in your business. Now, naturally, pay and benefits are very important and you need to constantly review these elements to hang on to your best people. However, it's rarely this factor alone that leads to peak performance, as history and, curiously enough, Dilbert have told us it's the 'engagement' factor that matters. I recently read that the happiest job anyone can have is that of hairdresser. It's a profession, with skill, precision and style, but it's a job with variety, with social contact and a central place in the community. Maybe it's the benchmark against which every role should be compared (so, Nigel, increase your sales of ISAs, focus on savings retention and let's see if we can't improve on your *flat tops*). But it does bear scrutiny, so it's vital you understand what your own employees' priorities are. When you do, you'll no doubt quickly uncover one of the great truths of modern business: the better people feel about themselves, the better they will perform and the higher your customers' ratings will be.

This then implies that if your customers want to feel like you have their best interests at heart, you should do the same for your employees. There are a variety of ways to do that, but none can match the potential and practicality of management behaviour. That is to say, whatever the organizational structure, managers who practise encouragement, coaching, honesty and leadership will create similarly enthusiastic teams. Managers who rule by remote detachment and resource control will generate more of the former in their acolytes. And whether it's in response to customer feedback or in general performance improvement, you'll find that imposing solutions on your teams is generally a self-defeating hobby. Many businesses will reward effective management endeavour generously and most will base performance management around certain key criteria involving sales, retention and cost control. Those who dare base at least some part of reward on activities such as observation, coaching, recognition, problem solving and devolution are at risk of outperforming their competitors.

## Let the team lead

'But how do I get my team to take responsibility?' Fair question, as the best 'self-managed' teams do not constitute themselves because their managers told them so. Ownership is key, so coaching has to focus on identification of 'gaps' and personal/team commitment to closing them. Many of the sports coaching models work on this principle, with the team member selecting the area for discussion, and then identifying an organization where it's delivered really well. Once they've identified the 'gap' they have, in effect, taken ownership and they can, by and large, be expected to be more committed to addressing it than if it were simply imposed on them by a well-meaning boss.

But life isn't usually like that and most service improvement endeavours founder on the rocks of convention. We'll do what we've always done and, as I'm sure you know, doing what you've always done and expecting different results is the first sign of insanity. To pinch a cliché from football, it's a big 'ask' but there are problem-solving tools out there and, funnily enough, they solve problems.

## Continuous improvement

So, when you're next looking at customer feedback, or holding a team meeting, or in a one-to-one with a key employee, think about the following, take a deep breath and... use one of them.

*Brainstorming:* a popularly badly managed tool whereby the manager seeks ideas ('Say anything you like, nothing's going to be ruled out') and then routinely prioritizes the suggestions according to his or her own view of the world. Get them all down and then group them according to the most appropriate headings. This process of *affinity grouping,* whereby you group suggestions according to their general category, will make the process of producing an actionable idea all the easier.

*Force field analysis* sounds suspiciously painful, like undergoing some unnatural electronic interventions in a tank of water. In reality, it's a process whereby you articulate your objective and then consider the barriers (those things that are stopping you achieving the aim) and the supports (those things in place that could help you). Rather than focusing on realizing the objective, the process forces you to think about mitigating the restraining factors and maximizing the supportive conditions.

One thing that does appear to involve a tank of water is *fishbone analysis* – and this is, again, an ultimately simple way of dividing a problem into bite-size chunks and is very conducive to team meetings.

And we haven't even started on *SWOT, PEST* and *negative brainstorming* (the latter being a particularly effective way of introducing humour into the process – by simply asking, 'What would do the opposite to what we want?')

And finally, *leadership.* Is this what I see practised by the UK senior manager who, on responding to press criticism of his employees' inflexibility, said, 'It would be irresponsible of us to give our front line staff discretion'?

You may have read about *values* in business books – and how they're replacing strategy as the basis of top performing organizations. Simply put, they are a set of uniformly understood principles upon which the business is designed and which are visible in the processes and practices encountered by employees and customers alike. The point being that if there's a problem, the values should offer you a solution. But you have a business with 15 employees and Derek, your night security guard, suspects that values will shortly be followed by mass tree hugging exercises in the Yorkshire Dales.

You've guessed it, the values are *you*. What you believe, what you say, the consistency and transparency of your behaviours and attitude, the preaching what you practise, the walking the talk and, most important of all, your continued reiteration of what's important to customers and how this supports the business and the employees' well being and prosperity. This would, if practised correctly in the majority of large organizations, render the term 'values' obsolete.

The power of leadership and control has always been a key factor in the establishment of businesses, but it's in the *letting go* that the enterprise thrives and, in taking an integrated approach to identifying what you want, you're more likely to exceed your customers' expectations.

Therefore, to summarize:

■ Don't rely on 'satisfaction' as an indicator of success: strive to exceed expectations and delight your customers.
■ Open up the feedback channels and find out what causes dissatisfaction.
■ Make sure you're focusing on what's important to the customer – never make assumptions.
■ Treat your employees the way you would like them to treat your customers.
■ If you're open and honest about business challenges with your customer-facing teams, then learn to let go – and they'll drive your customer service forward.
■ Problem-solving tools are not dry, academic anachronisms – they work, so try them out.

Mark Bradley is director of best practice at Customer Service Network, as well as a writer and speaker on organizational excellence. He recently published *Inconvenience Stores: One year in UK customer service* (www.ardrapress.com).

Customer Service Network is the UK's leading service excellence networking organization. It brings together managers and directors responsible for customer service to allow them to exchange views and share experiences with their peers. Membership is corporate, which means any representative from an organization can attend any event on the calendar that interests them.

Our main activities include interactive networking days, site visits and workshops, supported by a range of membership services including education, customer and employee satisfaction measurement, service excellence audits, mystery shopping, complaint management, research and benchmarking.

To find out more about the benefits of membership, please call us on 01902 311641 or visit www.customernet.com.

# The top 20 questions about customer service

*Paul Cooper, Director of the Institute of Customer Service, answers the questions that he is most frequently asked about customer service*

As I travel all over the country and overseas, I see an enormous amount of interest in customer service. People everywhere, at all levels in organizations, clearly want to improve what they do for themselves, their colleagues, their organization and their customers. As a result I am often asked what are the key issues in customer service today, and what are the most frequent questions asked. So I thought that I would put together the top 20 or so questions that I and my colleagues seem to get asked everywhere, and see if we can start a debate, as I'm going to give you my answers too!

Just like on the TV then, here are *The Top 20 Questions*.

## 1. Of course I believe in all this service excellence stuff, but how do I convince my bosses/board?

Easily number one and I guess a symptom of the modern business world. I tell people to start trying to make a difference themselves to prove the case, especially the point that giving great service usually costs less than giving poor service, if you measure it right. Even bosses can be convinced occasionally by facts and an overwhelming business case. We are getting more and more solid research results that show that it is service excellence that really leads to strong financial performance (see the Service Excellence=Reputation= Profit research by Bob Johnston, ICS, 2003).

## 2. How do I reduce my headcount turnover?

I believe that this is a combination of the right recruitment practices, induction, training and culture. We have a rapidly growing body of evidence that organizations that are actively developing their people using qualifications like NVQs or the ICS Professional Awards are seeing reduced headcount turnover as one of the early, significant organizational benefits, along with increased employee satisfaction.

## 3. How can I get my complaints down?

By stopping asking the wrong question! In the initial stages it's not a matter of getting them down but: 1) ensuring that you are hearing about all of them; 2) resolving brilliantly the ones you get; 3) stopping them being repeated; and 4) learning lessons and passing these on to others. This might even lead to a short-term increase in complaints, but this is an illusion – you always had them but didn't know about it. In the long term complaints will probably go down, but as long as every new one is different to the old ones, what does it matter – you're still learning.

## 4. Is a call centre/CRM system/outsourcing/offshoring a benefit to improving customer service?

The classic yes and no answer. If any of these things are being done/introduced *primarily* to reduce costs, then I would doubt whether real improvements in service levels will be gained, especially in the long term. If they are to be considered as an integral part of a strategy that is about improving customer service, one or more of them could be useful. There are *no* quick fixes in improving customer service, but there can be some quick wins. The main factor is to never outsource what you don't fully understand, just because you can, as you'll then never be able to properly monitor your provider's performance. I would close with one key cautionary note to anyone. Make sure you are really comfortable with the answer to this question: Does it *really* make sense for you to lose some or all of your control over your most important long-term asset – your customers?

## 5. Why isn't my CRM system working to my and my people's satisfaction?

Join the 70-plus per cent of organizations that apparently are currently asking this. In my opinion it is likely to be two basic things. First, the whole thing was put in with little or no reference to the people who would be using it – the front-line professionals in customer service, sales, etc, who know what they actually need. Secondly, you have mixed up the importance of the words in 'CRM'. Customers don't want to be managed, but they are usually perfectly happy to have a relationship with you. Put the emphasis in the process on building long-term relationships with the customer rather than trying to manage them.

### 6. How can I maintain a long-term service excellence strategy when every five minutes the organization introduces its latest change programme?

First, get used to it; it's always going to be that way. Secondly, be an active advocate that any change must presumably be to make the organization more profitable, and we all know that this comes from improved service excellence and reputation. The only way to get this is to be more customer-centric and so this must be core to the change programme. QED.

### 7. Why isn't customer service as good in the UK as it is in the United States and Australia?

You know in many cases it is. It's just a problem of perception. If we have one bad experience with a call centre, suddenly all call centres, and the whole process, are awful. The UK has as many great organizations, in many sectors, that are as good as anywhere in the world. In the United States, the whole service thing is often money driven – I'll give good service because I'm expecting a massive tip from you. I accept that in some stores, hotels, etc in the UK there is a poor staff attitude to serving the customer. But I don't think it's endemic. The reasons are usually the same across the board; they are hiring the wrong people – often part-time, short-term cover – not training them, and not trusting them. What else do they expect? A true customer service professional in the UK, trained and recognized for what they are, is as good as or better than, their equivalent anywhere in the world. It's an attitude of mind, and pride.

### 8. We're in the public sector/a monopoly – why should we have to care about giving good service?

Aren't you a customer too? What if it was your mum? Don't you have any pride in your work? Do you want to work for an organization that has a bad reputation? Why would you get up in the morning? Customers now compare you with other organizations in your area regardless of sector – how do you perform? How long have you got – I've got hundreds of reasons!

In many sectors, especially the public sector, both government requirements on reorganization/restructuring and regulators' involvement are also making a customer-centric approach pretty much compulsory, or some may be restructured out of existence. Not the best method of persuasion perhaps, but a reality.

### 9. Can you give me a definition of customer service – what does it look like?

*Customer service* is the sum total of what an organization does to meet customer expectations and produce customer satisfaction.

*Customer satisfaction* is the feeling that a customer gets when he or she is happy with the customer service that has been provided.

*Customer expectations* are what people think should happen and how they think they should get treated when asking for or receiving customer service.

And we've got loads more!

## 10. Should I be doing any benchmarking and will it help?

Another yes and no, but mainly yes. Comparing yourself with the best is a good way to learn how to improve as long as you get the whole story, not just a perception of it. Learning from other sectors can often be much more beneficial than same-sector comparisons, as you may all be doing it wrong, and one can see new ways of approaching issues and problems. Measuring and comparing the same things over time is much better than just a one-off view/comparison, as trends can be observed and lessons learnt. Remember, all of you in the private sector – there are a lot of excellent things nowadays coming out of the public sector – tap into it and get good ideas that might work.

## 11. What should I measure?

The right things, not the easiest things. There are many systems out there today that will literally measure everything that can be measured, but ask yourself – will it get looked at, will it lead to actions being taken, is it really relevant? There is a current trend in contact centres to take out much of the traditional call time, etc. Measurements and results seem to show that productivity and satisfaction go up. There's a message there somewhere. The two things that you should always do in some way are to measure employee and customer satisfaction/delight. But the true question is – are you doing it to give yourself a warm feeling inside, or to see where you have to make changes? You get what you measure, so what are you really trying to achieve?

## 12. What are the biggest things getting in the way of developing a service excellence culture?

Financial and strategic short term-ism and a lack of vision at board level. There is just not enough proper leadership from the top setting out clearly, and living, the values of the organization, communicating these to others, and then galvanizing everyone's efforts around the same objectives. This is not rocket science but it needs consistent effort and application. People, and particularly front-line people, need to know that the organization means what it says and they need to feel that they are a full part of the enterprise and that their efforts, skills, etc are recognized.

## 13. People who are great at customer service are born not made, aren't they?

Although there is a certain element of truth in this, as can be demonstrated by psychometric testing, people's performance can be improved significantly with the right developmental training, improved attitudes to work and their organization, and constant reinforcement. There is good evidence that the gaining of formal recognition, through a qualification like the ICS Professional Awards, or an NVQ, especially reinforced by membership of a professional body, makes a significant difference to a person's commitment and attitude to work as a whole, and their organization.

## 14. So what constitutes this whole 'customer service industry', then?

We believe that there are many ways through which good and bad customer service can be delivered, but these are all sub-processes of customer service, not industries in their own right. Retail/high street, contact centres, CRM, e-service, help desks, etc all form part of the whole thing, and the ICS has a responsibility, and involvement to support them all. Can you think of a job that doesn't include an element of customer service, internal or external?

## 15. Where does the customer service message sit with sales and marketing?

It is actually the underlying support to their whole being. With no customers to sell or market to, a commercial organization has little purpose. Great customer word of mouth in many cases can be at least as important as a sales force, and excellent organizations realize that retaining and maximizing existing customer loyalty is even more important than gaining new customers. On the marketing side, for a long time product was 'king', and an organization built its reputation on this. Nowadays there is a growing push for service quality to be recognized as the real builder and retainer of reputation.

## 16. Is it time we had a Customer Service Director?

Maybe. It depends on what the person will be responsible for and whether, as a result, everyone else on the board will abrogate their responsibility for customer service to the CS Director. The important requirement is that any CS Director should have responsibility for internal customer service as well as external, so that processes are aligned and departmental responsibilities are clearly defined. The ultimate CS Director is always the MD/CEO, which is where the real responsibility for customers must lie. It can't be delegated.

## 17. How can we tell the world how great we are as an organization at customer service?

The first point is that you have to be. This is not a product that you can market the hell out of and hope you can get away with it. The customer, internal or external, will see through that one very quickly. The second point is that you must get your timing right and the external customer must come second, after you've got everything right internally. You see, if you increase the customer promise without improving things internally, all you breed is resentment and worsen employee satisfaction and relations, which leads to higher turnover, recruitment problems and disaster.

## 18. How do I get consistency of service across the whole organization?

The key is great internal communication linked with an excellent induction and training programme and culture that encourages empowerment, but sets standards, processes and procedures. The key phrase is 'joined-up', and this also requires consistency in approach to employees. It has been said that the real problem is that employees *do* listen to what you tell them, so mixed signals, or no signals at all, lead to problems. Praising good practice and passing it on is invaluable, and ensuring that all of the support controls, such as processes and procedures, are well known and always up to date are far too rare.

### 19. How can I get my people to handle out-of-the-ordinary customer situations appropriately when bending the rules a little?

There are of course sometimes some regulatory issues here, and these must be taken into consideration. However, the general answer has to be getting them fully on board with the culture and working within a trust, not a fear/blame culture. If small mistakes are made, this is part of the learning curve, not a reason for chastisement and blame. Learning from other, more experienced people through mentoring and coaching is essential, and the development of self-assurance will all lead to them, and you, building confidence. A manager's job is not to accumulate power, but to develop others.

### 20. How can I keep my staffing costs down?

Research shows that more than 25 per cent of the annual salaries bill of many organizations goes in advertising for staff, recruitment, temporary labour, induction training, absenteeism, and lost revenue for a missing person. The short answer therefore lies in reducing this to a minimum, primarily by hiring the right people and then concentrating all efforts on minimizing headcount turnover. This should be directed at staff recognition and development programmes in their current jobs so that they will feel engaged and competent, which will almost certainly lead to a major improvement in their discretionary effort. This should then continue to include continuous development programmes that will help determine potential, and a well thought out career plan structure. These are all key factors in getting a significant and permanent improvement in employee satisfaction, and we already know how important that is, don't we?

The ICS is a not-for-profit institute dedicated to the improvement of customer service in companies throughout the UK. The ICS has developed a national awards programme for all customer contact staff which provides independent qualifications at three different skill levels, leading to membership of the Institute. Around 5,000 people have already registered for this programme.

We were incorporated in 1997, and already have the backing of nearly 260 major organizations in the UK. There are six different levels of organizational membership – council, corporate, business, associate, regional and international.

The Institute has an established and very active regional network which encourages networking, study visits and best practice opportunities.

The ICS has a comprehensive ongoing research programme. We also have available a wide range of publications on many aspects of customer service and produce a quarterly magazine, *Customer First,* and a quarterly newsletter for members.

We are also very active at seminars, conferences and exhibitions and also in magazines and other media, with a wide-ranging number of customer service related topics on which we will make presentations, speeches, or write articles. We are also always ready to make presentations in-house within organizations to promote good customer service.

For further information, contact Paul Copper, Director, Institute of Customer Service, Institute of Customer Service, 2 Castle Court, St Peter's St, Colchester, Essex CO1 1EW; tel: 01206 571716; website: www.instituteofcustomerservice. com; e-mail: paul.cooper@icsmail.co.uk.

# Creating customer focus

*Gaining new customers costs more than keeping your old ones happy, and loyal customers generate more income. Ted Marra of Marra Quality Inc argues that companies should stop talking about becoming customer focused and just do it*

It is possible that the birthplace of meaningful organizational change based upon customer focus was Canada during the mid-1980s. Many organizations around that time launched significant programmes for organizational change around the customer. In fact, it was Dave McCamus, then president of Xerox Canada, who set the tone and direction when he drew a diagram, in the presence of the group of executives charged with transforming Xerox Canada to a truly customer-focused organization; see Figure 3.3.1.

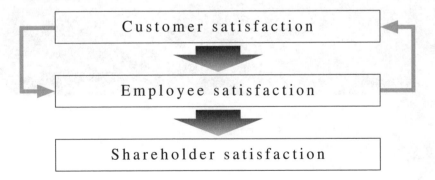

**Figure 3.3.1**   The leap of faith

# IQA
# COMPANY
# MEMBERSHIP

## JOIN A GLOBAL NETWORK

**Why join?**
IQA Company Membership gives a powerful message
to customers, suppliers and stakeholders that your organisation
has a commitment to quality.

**What are the benefits?**
- discounts on courses and products
- access to publications, information and news
- free introductory quality seminar
- use of 'Commitment to Quality' logo
- significant networking opportunities and events
- support from IQA's global partnerships and alliances

For more information contact IQA on
t: 020 7245 6722

Institute of Quality Assurance
12 Grosvenor Crescent
London
SW1X 7EE

T: 020 7245 6722
www.iqa.org
email: khitchins@iqa.org

What he proposed was a longer-term approach to running the business. His philosophy was that customer and employee satisfaction were inextricably linked, and more recent research has convincingly confirmed this hypothesis. By taking care of the customers and employees, the shareholders will be taken care of as a result of the higher revenue, profitability and market share value being realized.

So, what has happened since the mid-1980s? Not a great deal, disappointingly. The reality is that there is more talk about customer focus and its virtues than action. The result is that in a survey done as recently as 2000 by the EFQM regarding critical strategic issues facing organizations, senior executives said that the number one issue facing them was how to become more customer focused. The reality is that when the going gets tough, anything to do with the customer (and staff for that matter) drops off the table or is put on the backburner.

## Focus on change

Focusing on the customer is the fastest, most positive way to create and sustain meaningful change in an organization. Today, to be truly successful, organizations must look externally, focusing more and more on gathering real-time information about customers and competition. The value of the customer-contact functions and the engagement processes (sales, delivery, technical support, etc) where organizations interact with their customers have become critical success factors. Research has shown that a 1 per cent increase in customer loyalty equates to an average 9 per cent increase in overall organizational profitability. It costs six times as much to attract a new customer as to keep an existing one. Do you know how many positive references your current customers give your organization?

Organizations are waiting for a clear understanding of the requirements necessary for becoming customer focused. A good starting point for identifying these requirements is the Baldrige and excellence model criteria. Both of these best-in-class management systems contain significant elements directly or indirectly related to the customer. In fact, if all the customer-related components were added up, they could easily represent nearly 500 points. In addition, both models contain customer focus as either a 'core value' or 'concept of excellence'. Figure 3.3.2 highlights some of the primary customer links within the excellence model.

## The cat's whiskers

What would you hope to find in a truly customer-focused organization (see Figure 3.3.3)? You would first find a customer-focused culture in operation, and an organization in which people at all levels had a deep abiding belief in the importance of the customer and where management at all levels were aligning their actions and behaviour with their words by making the necessary investments, setting priorities, engaging customers and allocating resources that clearly communicate to all (customers and employees alike) their resolve to satisfy customers.

This customer-focused culture would then influence the nature and content of the organization's vision, business plan and key business objectives. From the business

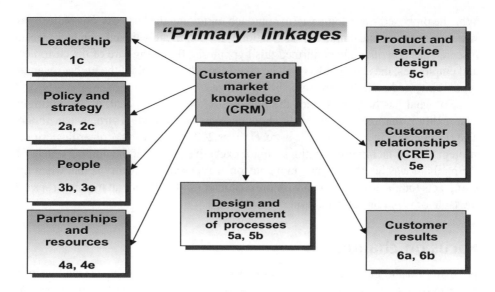

**Figure 3.3.2** A customer-focused organization (EFQM)

plan should then flow customer relationship strategies targeted to those customers you want most. Companies must ask themselves: 'Where do we want our relationship strategies to have impact?' It seems logical that this is where your organization engages the customer. Research by Bain & Company indicates that it is not unusual for organizations to lose 20 per cent of their customers annually if they do not pinpoint these customer-crucial areas.

Customer-sensing processes can be thought of in much the same way as whiskers on a cat. Without whiskers, cats behave erratically and are unable to judge distances effectively. It is the same with organizations, as often these 'sensing' processes tend to be dysfunctional – not providing the right information in a timely manner. While there are potentially a number of 'sensing processes' the following should be considered to be chief among them:

■ an enquiry, problem and complaint management process;
■ a customer satisfaction/loyalty measurement and management process – with the emphasis as much on 'management' as 'measurement';
■ a customer contact process – call centres, customer service or support operations.

## The CRM bandwagon

CRM systems are too often viewed as a quick technological fix, but usually they do not live up to the software provider's promises.

The reality in many organizations is that their implementation of a CRM system has absolutely nothing to do with their inherent belief in the importance of the customer in a relationship sense – only an economic sense. Also, many of the organizations

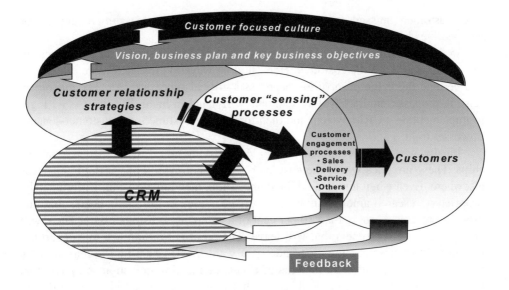

**Figure 3.3.3** The customer system of an organization

in which CRM systems have failed to reach their potential lack any well-defined customer relationship strategies. The adage, 'If you don't know where you are going, any road will get you there' holds true here. The problem is that after spending a considerable amount of money on a CRM system, organizations get down the road and find themselves arriving at an undesirable destination – one where the cost/benefit is dramatically and negatively out of balance. Further, the customer-sensing processes of many organizations are often dysfunctional. They provide poor quality information regarding customers which is then utilized to drive poor decisions. In fact, the CRM system simply accelerates the use of poor information to make poor decisions even faster.

There are four distinct phases in the relationship with a customer. First is the 'attraction' phase – identifying and attracting what the customers want most. Unfortunately, many organizations fail to capitalize on the opportunity of gaining two types of information during this phase. These are: a) understanding the customer's motivation for buying from an organization as well as their expectations; and b) gaining competitive intelligence in those cases where the customer has been dealing with a competitor.

Next is the 'new' customer phase. 'New' customers have unique needs that are often not met by organizations. As a consequence, 'new' customers are forced to follow a trial and error method to find the easiest way for them to get what they want from you – particularly so in the business-to-business environment. If the learning curve for 'new' customers is too long and steep, they may go elsewhere. If they leave after two years, an organization will lose money on the deal. During this phase, the customer-sensing processes are critical for monitoring complaints, satisfaction and the enquiries or requests for service, allowing a business to respond to the changing needs of its customers, missed opportunities, product, service or process improvements, or competitive challenges.

In the mature phase, there is often a need to bring new energy or excitement to the relationship with the customer. Here, finding ways to cross-sell more effectively or fine tune the value proposition becomes a critical success factor. The customer-sensing processes and a CRM system can work hand in hand. But there is no logic to implementing a CRM system and then forcing the dysfunctional customer-sensing processes to fit.

Finally, what most organizations should be striving for is creating secure relationships. These are ones where the customers would not even think of doing business elsewhere. Even when tempted by the competition, they remain loyal. Unfortunately, proprietary research among a number of organizations in Europe indicates that this group represents no more than 10 per cent of a company's customer base. There will always be some customers that will leave. The point is to minimize this departure, particularly if these are the customers you want most. Examine the reasons why customers leave and identify patterns of events that lead to defection. A system that can detect 'at risk' customers will allow a business to intervene and preserve the relationship. The longer the customer remains with you, the greater the revenue and profitability of that customer.

Customer focus? Easy to say, but more challenging to do. First, understanding the requirements is a key. Building a customer system that is sensitive to all the stages in the relationship lifecycle with customers comes next. Avoid the urge to jump to a quick fix such as a CRM system before you have your relationship strategies well-defined and your customer-sensing processes functioning effectively.

---

## Assess your current practice and behaviour

Rate your organization on a scale of 1 to 5 where 1 equals 'We don't do that around here', and 5 equals 'We have a world-class approach to this issue'. See how you compare:

■ Management's actions and behaviours are always consistent with their words regarding the importance of customers.
■ Customer and market data and information are key to our policy and strategy formulation.
■ The skills and knowledge critical to building and sustaining customer relationships have been identified and training has been conducted for all of our customer-contact employees.
■ We rate our suppliers based upon the value add which their input (eg, materials, components, information) provides to our customers.
■ Our organization has a comprehensive approach for ensuring that customer requirements are translated into specifications for new products and services.

- Our organization has an accurate, realistic and comprehensive overview of the total complaint level (verbal and written) as received by all areas and all functions within the organization. Our data indicate a steady decline in overall complaint volumes over the past three years.
- We experience a level of turnover and absenteeism among our customer-contact personnel that is so low, our organization is considered 'best-in-class' in our industry.
- Management ensures that clear, complete disclosures of relevant information are provided to customers and other stakeholders, such as communities, on a regular basis.
- We track supplier problems that impact on our customers and work with those suppliers to prevent reoccurrence. There has been a steady decline in these types of supplier problems over the past three years.

### Some questions to ask about your customer-sensing processes

- How good are your engagement processes?
- Where are your people having difficulty satisfying the customers they interact with?
- Where is the competition doing a better job?
- What are the basic needs and the wants (those things the customers would really like you to be doing that you are not) or ways of adding value (providing a tangible or intangible benefit the customer recognizes)?
- What are your internal process effectiveness indicators saying?
- Are you delivering service excellence across the scope of your engagement processes?

For further information about the Institute of Quality Assurance please contact iqa@iqa.org. For general enquiries contact Ambica Mehta, IQA Marketing Manager; e-mail:amehta@iqa.org.

Ted Marra is president of Marra Quality Inc, which focuses on performance and relationship excellence. He has concentrated on the design, pilot testing and full implementation of customer complaint management processes.

# Gaining market share

# Winning new business

*Business growth is a matter of personality, says Renee Botham at DMO, the business growth specialist*

In your business growth initiatives, what you do has to be matched equally with what you represent for your prospective clients. Given that you are offering a product or service that is, in the main, similar to those of your competitors, why should an organization choose your company to work with?

At one time, DMO represented two extremely large PR firms; they both offered international capabilities, they were both top 5 worldwide agencies. If you were to list their skill sets, they would be largely the same. Yet they were as different as chalk and cheese and what made them so was their 'personality'. You could pick it up from the moment you walked in to their offices. One had a slightly more formal feel, the other, more relaxed. It was in their literature and how they described themselves. It was there on their website. They pitched frequently for the same business and I suspect that choice was often made by the way you *felt* about the company.

What you need to keep in mind when considering your business is not so much a hunt for its USP (unique selling point), rather, what are you evoking as your company's brand image. Here are a few thoughts for you to consider.

## Trust

They trust you to deliver what you have promised when you pitched for the business; on time, at the price you gave them, and they like you. They believe that whatever problems were to arise, you will sort it out. Too many companies today promise too much, go in at a rate that is impossible to keep to and don't listen to their clients' needs.

## Personality

A business has a personality that is usually a reflection of the people who run it. It is there in all they say and it is consistent in all their corporate material. Here is a simple exercise for you. Look at your website, look at how you write your letters, especially your sales letters; now imagine that instead of your company name it is that of your competitor. Can you spot the difference? Is there a style that someone who knows your business would say, 'No, that's not them'? When you write anything that is going out from your company it must reflect your business personality. Your presentation material must be the same; in fact all touch points of your business must show that same personality. Think about companies you admire, think about what they mean to you and why. Virgin, Easyjet, Top Shop, Intel: they evoke something for you and whether you like them or not is inconsequential – you know what to expect from them.

## Price

You will have thought carefully about the charges for your products/services, realizing that it is important to be competitive in your marketplace, but this is not a reason for selling on price alone. You must lead by example and if you *value* your business and what you deliver, you can justify your charges. There will always be a prospective client saying, 'You are more expensive than x'. It is your role to demonstrate that what they will be getting is the best and that is beyond what your product or service is actually doing for them, it's a 'package' of goodwill, trust and partnership. It is your faith in what you can deliver that is most likely to convince them. I think it's wonderful that Chanel can state that its perfumes range from £500 to £45. Whatever end of the price range you are aiming for, the sentiment remains the same.

## Corporate pride

To me, corporate indifference is the eighth deadly sin. Anyone who is working with you and I mean *everyone*, has to display the same passion and pride about your company. Receptionists, switchboard, the often forgotten accounts department are as important as your sales team and 'front men'. Do you want to work with a company that has secretaries displaying an arrogant nonchalance, a front desk that is dismissive and a general air of 'I ain't bovvered'? What is unattractive on the surface is likely to be hidden decay on the inside. When you are planning your business growth, who else knows about it beyond your directors and the sales team? Are you communicating to everyone the values and plans for the company they are working with? You may well have a drive to succeed but you can't do it alone; you need everyone to be pulling in the same direction and this goes beyond a salary. People care for things *that matter to them.*

# Preparing your new business growth plan

Your what?

Well, you have completed your business plan so where's your map showing how you are going to reach the ambitious plans you have set for yourself and the business?

If your plans are to seek out all those people who have promised to help you, trust me, a time will come when you will have exhausted the 'friendship' and it becomes difficult to go back to ask about the promised project that wasn't the right time when you spoke last.

What about the direction of the business? It may be that you are selling in to one market and you feel a need to move in to another. Where are your strategic plans to do this?

For all these reasons and more, you need a new business action plan so that there is momentum and a pipeline. When you are too busy with the work of today are you setting yourself up for a 'famine/feast' scenario?

Here are a few tips to help you:

■ When you won your last few projects, what made your clients go with you beyond price and product?

■ Think laterally about what you are providing and ask yourself, what other industries have the same or similar issues?

■ Look at your product/service and question yourself and your team about how else you can make your clients happy, as a springboard from what you are doing already.

■ Use your team to come up with suggestions about your business – you are not the sole source of all great ideas. Allow your people to take responsibility and then once you have discussed it with them, allow them to run the campaign.

■ Be ahead of your competition – do you know what they are offering? Once you do, don't just replicate it; instead, think about how you can be ahead of them.

■ Are you working with all the touch points within your clients' company? It's a lot harder to be sacked if you are working for more than one division.

■ Timetable your monthly activities so that as you are in to one month, you have research and plans starting for the next. With a six-month plan you can always shift things around should you win business that precludes your attacking your next months' targets.

■ Keep to your core offerings. Too many companies fail through ideas that don't play to their core strengths. A company needs to understand what you do.

There is nothing to me that beats the high of winning new business. It's not complicated you know. It's about being strategic, keeping things simple and an absolute belief in what you do. The rest is contagious.

Renee Botham is managing director of DMO, business growth specialists.

DMO has been supporting its clients to achieve an increase in revenue through new business wins for over 16 years. It works across a wide range of sectors including financial, pharmaceutical, marcomms, IT and telecomms. From strategic new business plan to meeting the key decision-makers, DMO succeeds by employing only senior execs to support its clients' plans for growth.

For more information please contact Renee Botham or Gill Green, tel: 020 8385 3800; website: www.dmo.co.uk.

# Network marketing

*Pursue the relationship, not the sale, says Andy Lopata, Managing Director of BRE Networking*

Both the local and the global economy are changing rapidly. One in four people across Britain are currently running or considering starting their own business. This is confirmed by the report published in 2004 by the Small Business Service, an agency of the Department of Trade and Industry.[1] As I travel around the UK to networking events, I meet more and more business people who have left corporate life to either set up on their own or to work with others in much smaller businesses.

The next big change in the world economy will be the growth and rapid industrialization of the Asian economies, particularly those of India and China. As Asian industry grows, we will also see the downsizing of large business in the Western world. The new global economy will mean that small businesses in the UK will find themselves subject to ever increasing competition.

Corporates now recognize the potential provided by freelance consultants whom they bring in on a project-by-project basis rather than employing people full time. This will inevitably mean an acceleration of the growth in the number of small businesses in the UK as more people are made redundant or voluntarily leave their jobs.

For people who have set up their own business, or who find themselves competing in a very busy marketplace, 'networking' suddenly takes on a great importance. Few of us are taught about or ever have to rely on networking whilst working in larger businesses or industry but it is the lifeblood of many growing businesses, ensuring that they survive and prosper.

The reliance on networking will not be restricted just to smaller businesses. As larger businesses become more streamlined and confront a more competitive economy, they will look outside their own walls to gain an advantage in the marketplace.

## Pursue the relationship, not the sale

When talking about networking, however, it is important to dispel a few myths and mis-conceptions. Networking is not new. People have been exchanging information, ideas and contacts for centuries. Most companies will look to recommendation and referral as their primary source of new business, but very few companies have a strategy in place to encourage the growth of positive word-of-mouth about their services.

The first thing to do when deciding whether to pursue a proactive networking strategy is to look at why you want to network and what are the outcomes that you are looking for. Traditionally, businesses have looked to networking as a source of direct sales and have approached formal networking events in that vein. However, these businesses will have struggled to gain much in the way of sales and moved away from networking very quickly without ever recognizing what benefits they could have realized.

If you have attended a networking event with a view to increasing your sales, the chances are that most of the other people at that event have the same goal in mind. If that is the case, then they are in 'selling mode' and not in 'buying mode'. As a result, they are not in the right frame of mind to buy from you, thereby reducing your chances of success.

Instead of focusing on selling to everyone you meet, consider what else you can gain from networking. If sales are your key objective, what would be the best way to achieve them? I am not saying that networking will not increase your sales, just that you should be looking at it as a part of an overall word-of-mouth marketing strategy – a way of getting people to tell others about your business.

## Getting to market

With the growth of the small business economy, the traditional routes to market now play a smaller and smaller role. Advertising for small businesses can be expensive and there is more competition for valuable PR coverage in the press and on the radio. There are a growing number of exhibitions to display at but not all of them achieve the type of footfall to guarantee success, and the ones that do tend to require a substantial investment. We are becoming swamped with 'junk' e-mail and now have spam filters to remove unsolicited messages before they reach our inbox. And, with increasing regulation, cold calling, in its many forms, has become a less attractive option than it was before.

Effective networking becomes a real benefit as it provides a more cost-effective route to market. It offers the advantage that, through the people you meet, you are gaining access to others who may well have a need for your services at the time of the discussion and who are more likely to buy from you. After all, if someone is speaking about you the chances are it is because they think the other person needs your help. And people do prefer to act on recommendation rather than seek out services in the phone book.

# It's not what you know, it's who you know... and who knows you!

Once you have accepted that networking can increase your sales not by selling to people you meet at events but by referral to their clients, suppliers, friends and family, you can move away from the direct approach that restricts so many people. When you meet people through networking, make sure that you banish preconceptions about who you are talking to, what they do and how you think that they can help you, and focus instead on building a relationship with the people with whom you develop a rapport.

It is very easy to find yourself scouring attendee lists and looking at people's business cards and name badges and deciding immediately how much you need to be talking to them. And yet the psychologist Stanley Milgram showed in his experiments in the late 1960s that we are only six steps away from anyone in the world, leading to the much quoted theory of 'Six Degrees of Separation'.

Most people in business will have several hundred contacts, ranging from senior politicians to business leaders and from celebrities to local entrepreneurs. Unfortunately they do not carry their contact lists around with them and will not invite you to pick the connections you most desire! Such valuable connections will only be made as they build trust in you and understanding of the service you provide and the people you can help.

I have benefited personally from a referral from a seemingly unlikely source at a networking event, having been introduced to a director of British Airways by his uncle, a sole practitioner working in Henley. I have also seen a member of one of our groups introduced to the HR Director of one of the largest hotel chains in the world by a fellow small business, and even been aware of one member being given a route through to President Putin of Russia when requested. You are unlikely to meet any of these connections at a local networking event!

So, build relationships with people who you meet through networking, find out about their business, look to connect them to others in your network and make friends. As they grow to like and to trust you, make sure that you clearly communicate how they can help you and who you need introductions to and they will be far more receptive and willing to help than when you had just met them. Networking takes time and needs your patience and perseverance, but the rewards are often worth the investment.

# Working together

A business's balance sheet is not one-sided, however. As your business develops in an increasingly busy marketplace, you need to maintain a competitive advantage in as many ways as possible. Through people you meet at networking events who are in complementary, almost competitive businesses, you may find opportunities to develop synergies and work together or cross-refer. This can allow you to meet clients' needs in ways you were unable to before, and even tender for larger contracts than were previously possible.

Barry Nalebuff and Adam Brandenburger covered the importance of working this way in their book *Co-opetition*, encouraging businesses to identify producers of 'complements' to their own product or service. 'A complement to one product is any other product that makes the first one more attractive. For example, hardware and software, hot dogs and mustard, cars and car loans.'

Members of the Reading Business Referral Exchange (BRE) group are working and pitching together on several major contracts with national organizations. Paul Voakes, a member of the group who is at the heart of these initiatives, says, 'The individuals need common understanding, goals and beliefs as well as a wish to contribute to the development of the solutions across the board, not just their own part of it. This diversity drives innovation and a consistent mood connecting the range of services. The aim is to find a lean and scaleable model, to exploit the opportunity, and emotional tie to the client. All good brands are based on emotion. In our common language we describe this as mood and model. If we have both we may well differentiate ourselves from the competition'.

The world's largest companies are also working together to gain a competitive advantage through networking. The Geneva Car Show in March 2005 saw the launch of a groundbreaking collaboration between Toyota and Peugeot-Citroen, with a joint production venture at Kolin in the Czech Republic. Jean-Martin Folz, Chairman and Chief Executive of PSA Peugeot-Citroen Group, said, 'This type of partnership between independent companies is the most appropriate response to increasingly global markets. These win-win agreements allow us to share development and production costs without renouncing our independence, to pool skills and expertise.'

By building relationships with a range of different businesses, you can also realize substantial supply benefits, not just by achieving reduced costs but also by dealing with trusted suppliers who are more likely to 'go the extra mile' for you, particularly if you have a relationship built either on trust or on mutual referral.

One of the biggest benefits of networking is one of the least publicized, and that is a peer group, and the support, advice and input they can provide. For many people, going from a corporate culture where they have been surrounded by people at a similar level, to one where they are working on their own or with a small number of colleagues can be quite a culture shock and a very lonely experience.

It can be easy to disappear into a shell, with no one to share problems and ideas with at work and, for some people, a family at home who do not understand the issues involved. Networking can give you access to a peer group who have gone through the same problems and with whom you can share your ideas, expertise and experience.

## The networking network

Whatever you are looking to achieve from networking, you need to plan your strategy. There are many networking organizations, from the IoD and BRE to local Chambers of Commerce and industry-focused organizations. You can network at breakfast, lunch and dinner. You can attend meetings with your competitors there or with your competition excluded. You can now also network from the confines of your own office with online networks such as Ecademy, Kickstart-Connect and Linked-In.

Networking opportunities are there for you to learn, develop your industry, grow your contact base, enhance your profile or build referrals. It is for you to try the different organizations and decide which ones work for you.

Whichever route you choose to take, you need to take a step out of your comfort zone, to make it happen. Remember, what you get out of networking is proportionate to what you are prepared to put in. Therefore, ensure that you choose which ones you can commit to without affecting your core business by over-committing.

As the global economy changes we are facing more competition from the rising nations of the East and from new businesses emerging all the time. We will need to rely more and more on working together for mutual success. Get ahead now by building a networking strategy for your business.

## Useful links

Business Referral Exchange (BRE) – www.brenet.co.uk
Ecademy – www.ecademy.com
Kickstart-Connect – www.kickstart-connect.com
Linked-In – www.linkedin.com
NRG Business Networks – www.nrg-networks.com
British Chambers of Commerce – www.chamberonline.co.uk
Junior Chamber of Commerce – www.jciuk.org.uk
The Missing Link – www.misslink.co.uk
Federation of Small Business – www.fsb.org.uk

## Key networking tips

Plan what you want to achieve from your networking.
Build relationships with people you 'click' with.
Commit to the networking organizations you join.
Be courageous and take opportunities that come your way.
Communicate clearly what you want and how others can help.

## Types of networking organization

Referral generation.
Network building.
Educational.
Professional development.
Synergy building (related professions).
Social.

## Benefits of networking

Build trust and understanding in your business.
Grow your contact database and take a step closer to anyone in the world.

Boost your reputation.

Generate referrals and high quality leads.

Develop relationships to enable you to enhance your service or product.

Be in a position to connect others in your network.

Improve your confidence and presentation skills.

Gain access to suppliers you can trust.

Receive support, advice and input from your peers.

Build your knowledge.

## Note

1. The SBS Household Survey of Entrepreneurship, 21 July 2004.

Andy Lopata is one of the UK's foremost speakers and trainers on business networking. He is the Managing Director of BRE Networking, one of the UK's largest referral-focused networking companies and has developed successful tips and tools for building networks and referral-based marketing strategies.

Andy is the co-author of two books about networking published in 2005: *Building a Business on Bacon and Eggs* and *...and Death Came Third*.

BRE groups are based in towns and cities across the UK where members meet on a regular basis to develop trust in each other, understanding of their respective businesses and focus on generating referrals for each other.

For more information, tel: 0845 100 4822 or visit the BRE website at www.brenet.co.uk. Should you wish to contact Andy for advice on networking effectively, you can e-mail him at andy@brenet.co.uk.

# Online ads bring quick results

*Danny Meadows-Klue, founder of the internet industry's think-tank the IAB, argues that there's much more to online than websites and that businesses of all sizes and sectors are missing a trick if they are not reaching their customers through online marketing*

If the last time you thought about online was six months ago then it's time to take a fresh look. This is a medium that does anything other than stand still and the reason it remains the fastest growing marketing channel is the power of its results. Every firm has a website these days, but web advertising is proving to be the key tool for connecting customers to that site or even persuading them to pick up the phone. The web has become the new way we research purchases and by failing to appreciate this, firms miss out to their competitors.

Companies of all sizes and sectors have integrated online marketing into the rest of their marketing plan as simply another channel, and any surf on the web demonstrates the results: cars are promoted with lavish online films and microsites; food and drink manufacturers remind customers of their products before lunch; holiday brokers sponsor travel editorial; and professional service firms use niche online business media. Even local plumbers and taxi firms now buy their keywords on Yahoo and Google. Some sectors – such as jobs and finance – made the switch faster than others, but every year investment grows because savvy executives have realized that this is where their customers have gone.

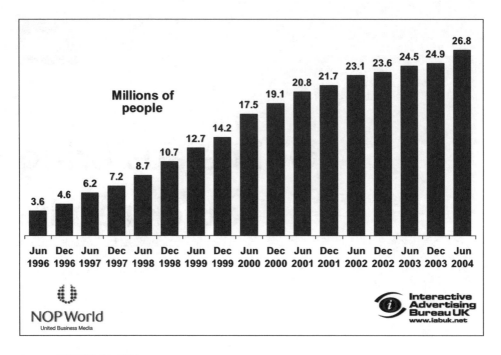

*Source*: NOP World, 2004

**Figure 4.3.1**   UK internet audience growth

During the past three years a new digital media mix of tools has emerged that can help marketing budgets of all sizes work harder than they do in traditional channels alone. Whether your campaigns are to build brands or generate direct response, more and more marketers have turned to online, upweighting its role in their media mix and putting in place simple mechanics that accurately track its performance.

### *Free resources online*

- How online advertising builds brands
  www.IABuk.net/BrandImpact
- Award-winning online creative
  www.CreativeShowcase.net
- Direct marketing techniques and examples
  www.IABuk.net/DirectMarketing
- Latest news about online marketing
  www.IABuk.net/News
- Latest advice on privacy and online marketing
  www.AllAboutCookies.org

## Because this is where your customers are

The internet has come of age in the last five years and the majority of Brits now enjoy easy access. The amount of time they each spend online is also growing and the internet has become their second most used media channel after TV, accounting for about 20 per cent of all time we spend with media. Among many demographics it has leapt even further to become the must-have tool they cannot be without and a staple part of their lifestyle, providing the answers for everything from entertainment and shopping to keeping up with the news and chatting with friends. In the UK we already make almost 6 per cent of our purchases online and in some sectors like travel it may be more than twice that. It's hard to imagine an area in which the internet cannot play a role.

The reason many firms miss out is because the pattern of media consumption has undergone a seismic shift since the end of the 1990s and some executives are yet to appreciate the scale of the changes. However, against a background of media fragmentation, it's no surprise that growth of online audiences proves particularly attractive to large advertisers. Dig deeper, however, and there are even more compelling reasons:

■ *Daytime is primetime* – with the internet now the key business communication tool, audiences that could never before be reached are available and attentive.
■ *A medium of a thousand niches* – online combines exceptional lifestyle and interest targeting with a mass reach that matches press or television.
■ *Lord Leverhume's challenge has been answered* – the era of never being sure which elements of your advertising were being seen or working is over because there is no wastage in interactive campaigns: marketers only pay for adverts that are called by their audience's computers.

And this is just the start. There are dozens of further reasons that explain why the online marketing industry is growing 75 per cent every year: from the ease of international media planning to the way customers can be connected to a brand's online store, and from the powerful creative impact online messaging can have, to why online has become the first port of call for customers searching for holidays, new cars or financial products.

## Ten to 20 per cent of media spend: a good start

In 2004 the online ad market was already accounting for more than 4 per cent of media spend (over £500 million pa in the UK). It overtook the size of the cinema ad industry first, then radio at the end of 2004, reflecting the scale of change in the behaviour of leading marketers. But this is only part of the story. Scratch beneath the surface and you still find a chasm between firms that have learnt where the internet fits in their business and the others who are yet to even start.

Whether their customer base is business or consumer, whether the transactions are large or small, whether the product can be bought online or not – the web has a critical role to play.

**Figure 4.3.2** Examples of online advertisements

The latest research into media-neutral planning has shown that the optimal role of online advertising in brand campaigns is at least a tenth of media budgets. Campaigns with only token online elements are failing in their objectives. 'Even for the low involvement brands like a bar of soap like Dove or a hot snack from McDonald's, 10 to 15 per cent of media campaign budgets should be online', explains Rex Briggs from Marketing Evolution, one of the pioneering research groups exploring how marketers can get the most value from their media. Many marketers are clearly still missing out.

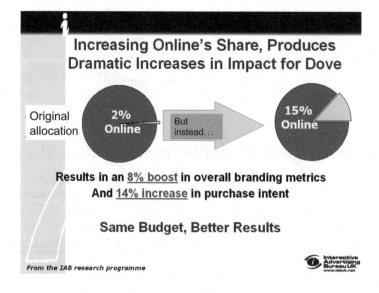

**Figure 4.3.3** The impact of online advertising

## Easy to buy

Another change in the last few years is the sudden growing-up of the industry. The core products in online marketing have been defined and then refined, culminating at the end of 2003 when the IAB reached agreements with hundreds of British websites to roll out a core group of four new ad shapes. This Universal Advertising Package has become so widely adopted that it is likened to the internet's equivalent of 'half page' or 'full page' press ads and because exactly the same shapes fit so many websites, there are no costs in resizing artwork.

## Web advertising

The marketing model from traditional media has also transferred online, but with three important twists. First, the low cost of online advertising allows many firms to align their brands to premium newspaper or TV media in a way they could never have offline. Secondly, the internet gives companies a way to target exceptionally specific groups of customers because the vast variety of websites and the rich depths of the specialist channels within the large sites allow firms to find the very precise editorial environment they want to be seen in. This is a medium of a thousand niches, creating a perfect place for every brand. The third twist is price. The entry cost has stayed exceptionally low and although audiences have risen at a meteoric rate, there are cheap and easy ways of launching test campaigns to learn about what works for your firm.

---

### Key questions

- Is someone in your team responsible for exploring interactive marketing?
- Do you have an experienced agency or media owner partner?
- Is your interactive marketing integrated with your traditional marketing?
- Are your online campaign objectives clear and is there a mechanism in place to precisely track the effect?
- Do you know how much value investment in marketing through traditional channels brings you?
- Have you tested the water with simple banners and search marketing?

---

## Getting started with search

Most small firms typically begin online advertising through search and directories. Those Yellow Pages and Business Pages are now routinely accessed online and your firm needs to retain its rightful place. Hot on the heels of directories are the search engines and in particular their paid-for listings services that guarantee your message will stand out even though there may be thousands of websites with similar products.

Google and the other search engines take your message to a customer the very moment they express the greatest interest in your services. The old approach direct marketers would use of customer profiling (demanding extensive demographic information about your prospects) is turned on its head, because with search the customer seeks you out. It has been a revolution for marketers because this advertising comes with no wastage: only those overtly interested ever see the sales message and it has become exceptionally popular with small businesses. It is also becoming a revolution for finance directors because the rigid cost controls allow companies to set, and stick to, an acquisition price per customer. Not surprisingly search has been embraced faster than any other form of marketing and with campaigns starting from £50 and bookable with a credit card it's not hard to see why.

## Takeaways

Online is the active ingredient in everyone's marketing mix. It adds powerful value to the total campaign and can be tested to prove its effect. Smart companies have shifted their spend into online and are benefiting from faster business growth as well as enjoying a lead over their rivals. If the last time you looked at online was six months ago then you will be in for a surprise.

---

### *Free information*

For more information about internet audiences, IOD members can e-mail or call the Interactive Advertising Bureau team (CallCentre@iabuk.net, 020 7886 8282) and ask for our free research papers and guides including:

- IAB introduction to internet audiences
- IAB guide to getting the media mix right in brand advertising
- IAB introduction to search engine advertising
- IAB tricks of the trade for search engine marketing
- IAB Universal Advertising Package of key shapes

Danny Meadows-Klue is Chief Executive of the Interactive Advertising Bureau (Europe) and the co-founder of IABs in seven countries. In 2005 he launched the first digital marketing training specialist and can be contacted through Danny@ DigitalStrategyConsulting.com.

# Search engine marketing

*A properly implemented search engine marketing programme can provide huge volumes of traffic and resulting sales leads, says Phil Robinson at Clickthrough Marketing*

Over the last few years, search marketing has become big business and an increasingly important part of the marketing mix. In particular, the Google IPO in 2004 has generated huge awareness in search marketing.

If you are a growing SME then your market coverage, brand awareness and marketing budgets may be more limited than your larger established competitors. As a result, you need to be more creative in how you spend your marketing budgets and access new customers.

Have you considered a focused search engine marketing campaign to drive qualified leads and sales from your website? If not, and when you consider that 85 per cent of all searches online are done via search engines – then the question to ask your marketing department is, why not?

A properly implemented search engine marketing programme can provide huge volumes of traffic and resulting sales leads. Your competitors that are running active search marketing programmes are winning business by being listed in the search engines for relevant search phrases.

Many businesses have already switched huge proportions of their marketing budgets to search marketing because the returns outweigh traditional offline methods so much that it's almost a no-brainer.

Search engine marketing is tailor-made for SME growing companies because it offers an opportunity to access a huge pre-qualified marketplace on a level playing field with competitors, and most importantly at relatively much lower cost than traditional marketing campaigns

# Search marketing options

So, what are the options in search engine marketing? There are two. First, there is *Pay Per Click (PPC) advertising,* a search engine marketing technique that requires you to pay a fee every time someone clicks to your website from an advert you've placed in a search engine's results. Therefore, you only pay each time someone visits your site. Second, there is *Search Engine Optimization (SEO),* the art of fixing, improving and optimizing your website so that there is a good chance your web pages will appear at the top of natural or free search engine listings for your selected search phrases. Effective SEO goes much further than meta tags and titles, and should involve search engine approved methods.

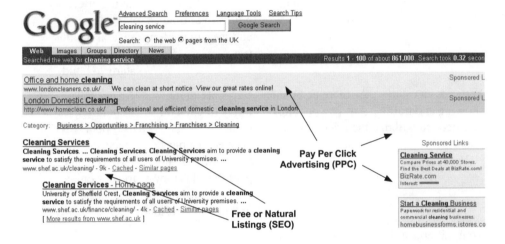

**Figure 4.4.1**   Google

## *Search Engine Optimization (SEO)*

Effective SEO is a complex and time-consuming process. Some people do not bother with SEO because they argue it is too difficult to achieve natural listings on search engines. It is difficult, but if done correctly the benefits can be huge and long lasting.

Because of the complexity and time-consuming nature of doing SEO properly, most companies that take SEO seriously employ a specialist agency. Many web design agencies and webmasters will experiment or say they offer SEO, but the majority are not SEO specialists and only scratch the surface of what is possible.

### The risks

If done poorly, SEO can have serious side implications for your business – a worst case scenario being that your corporate website is dropped by the search engines, meaning that your internet presence becomes virtually invisible to your online target market.

**Table 4.4.1** Pros and cons of PPC and SEO

| Pay Per Click (PPC) | | Search Engine Optimization (SEO) | |
|---|---|---|---|
| Pros | Cons | Pros | Cons |
| You can set up a pay per click campaign yourself with a credit card | Once you stop paying the traffic stops immediately | It does not cost you each time a user clicks on your link | Implementing SEO is a hugely complex and time-consuming process |
| You decide and control your daily, monthly or weekly budget | Doing it yourself requires you to manage bids and adverts on a daily basis | If your site maintains good SEO practices the resulting traffic builds over time and lasts in the long term | Results usually take a minimum of 4 weeks to start taking effect and can take up to several months before traffic really starts to build |
| Your ads can start showing and traffic is generated within hours | As more companies start pay per click, the price of bids is rising | Users are more likely to click on natural listings because people know they are not paid for, plus they are more prominent in the search results | An agency or webmaster that uses poor SEO practices can cause serious damage to your online presence |
| Your ads appear for the search phrases you have chosen | Click fraud is an issue for businesses that have unethical competitors that wish to use up your budget | | |
| Can be used as a temporary measure before SEO begins to show results | Can under-perform and become expensive if not monitored and managed by a professional | | |

This has happened to numerous company websites and will continue to happen while there are webmasters and agencies willing to drive traffic using unethical methods.

If you are looking for an SEO agency, get them to be very clear on the methods they adapt and look for statements, white papers and articles on their website that discuss their best practice ethical approaches.

### How do I know if I need SEO?

If you run occasional searches on relevant phrases to your business then you will already have a good idea how well your site is ranking. Most good agencies will offer a free website assessment on some of the key indicators such as link popularity, search engine inclusion and positions.

## Pay Per Click (PPC) advertising

Over recent years PPC advertising has grown strongly; however, in 2004 expenditure on PPC engines grew exponentially as an increasing number of web-based businesses began to realize the returns available. By 2008, online marketers will spend an estimated £15.6 billion on PPC advertising (Forbes).

PPC marketing offers an excellent alternative to achieving natural free listings on search engines through SEO. Implementing effective SEO can be time-consuming and can take several months before you start seeing results.

In simple terms, with PPC marketing you decide which search phrases you want your adverts to appear for and you only pay each time a visitor clicks on your advert to your website. The cost per click depends on how many of your competitors are already bidding for phrases, and can range from 10p to £5 per click in highly competitive sectors like credit cards.

Popular phrases like 'accountancy services' are more expensive than other more specific phrases. For example, 'accountancy services in Birmingham' may be 60 per cent cheaper than 'accountancy services'.

### How do I know which PPC engine to use?

The PPC engines serve varying geographical markets and have different percentage shares of the global search market. The major PPC engines are Google Adwords and Overture.

The best engine to use depends on your chosen geographical target market, budget available and marketing objectives. The two main UK pay per click search engines, Google (www.google.co.uk) and Overture (www.overture.com), own a huge 90 per cent of the UK search market. Overture feeds adverts to Yahoo, MSN and many other engines.

# Offline marketing vs search marketing

*Consider this:* a mailshot sent second class to 2,000 people would cost £420, excluding stationery costs. All these people have not asked for the mailshot, so only a tiny percentage of these people will respond.

If you spend £420 on pay per click marketing, based on a cost per click of 20p, this would drive 2,100 visitors to your site! Making things even more compelling, each of these 2,100 visitors is actually pre-qualified, ie they visited your site because they did a search on your type of product/service and then clicked on your advert.

This concept contrasts sharply to a mail shot being sent to the masses or an expensive advert placed in a magazine in the hope that it will catch the readers' eye.

With these figures, you could ask, why don't I shift all my marketing budgets to search marketing? Any marketer knows they need an integrated set of marketing messages delivered across various types of media. However, what this highlights is that if search marketing is not part of your marketing mix – some serious questions need to be asked!

Growing companies without the marketing muscle and budgets of the larger corporates and brand names need to get creative with their marketing spend. Traditional advertising in magazines, on radio and using mail shots is unbelievably expensive, which is why more and more marketing budgets are being transferred from traditional to online marketing and search engine advertising.

## ROI scenarios

Marketers love search marketing because results are so easy to track. For example, you can measure how many people see your ads, how many people click to your site and, most important, how many of these people convert to a sale or sales leads from an online form.

Because the whole sales process is so easy to track, you can allocate your budgets into areas or search phrases that are delivering conversions rather than just traffic. Here are examples:

**Pay Per Click**

| | | | |
|---|---|---|---|
| Spend: | £2,000 | Est Cost Per Click: | 20p |
| Visitors: | 10,000 | Conversion Rate: | 2 per cent |
| Conversions: | 200 | Sales Conversion Rate: | 20 per cent |
| Sales: | 40 | Sales Revenue: | £20,000 |

**Profit £18,000**

This example assumes that your website converts 3 per cent of its visitors to sales leads via an online form or phone call, and that your sales team converts 20 per cent of these leads to sales at an average sales value of £500.

## Search Engine Optimization (SEO)

Returns from investing in SEO are more difficult to calculate because the traffic is not pay per click based. Also, investing money in SEO today will bring ongoing rewards in the longer time, whereas a magazine advert or mail shot has a one-time effect.

The same principles still follow, however. For example, if SEO were to deliver an extra 5,000 visits per month over the next four years, then this would be 240,000 visitors from natural search listings. You can then calculate your site's conversion rate ratios and sales values in the same way as in the above example.

The difference is that rather than paying per click, you would need to employ an internal SEO professional or external agency to manage your SEO campaign – which represents a fixed cost.

Potential returns from an SEO campaign depend on several factors, including your products or services, your industry sector, size of market and size of geographical target market. For example, a software company selling globally would naturally have much greater potential ROI than an office cleaning business that only operates within a small local town.

In conclusion, if you have a limited budget, deciding whether to invest in SEO is a case of calculating how much sales revenue you are getting from traditional marketing. If you can estimate how much sales revenue is generated from spending £15,000 on mail shots, then this helps in deciding whether investing the same amount in SEO is feasible or not.

## Key success factors

### Conversions

If you are spending money driving traffic to your website, then make sure that your website is geared up to convert the traffic, otherwise it is counter-productive. The fundamental to good website conversion is making sure your site gives visitors a good reason to engage with you.

Implementing clear, enticing calls to action can have a huge impact on the leads and sales generated from your website. When was the last time you visited every page of your website to see whether each page has a call to action that encourages the user to engage with you?

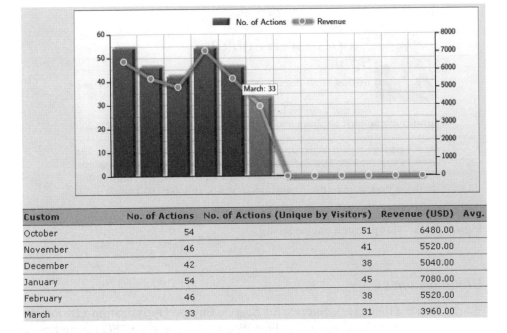

| Custom | No. of Actions | No. of Actions (Unique by Visitors) | Revenue (USD) | Avg. |
| --- | --- | --- | --- | --- |
| October | 54 | 51 | 6480.00 | |
| November | 46 | 41 | 5520.00 | |
| December | 42 | 38 | 5040.00 | |
| January | 54 | 45 | 7080.00 | |
| February | 46 | 38 | 5520.00 | |
| March | 33 | 31 | 3960.00 | |

**Figure 4.4.2**  Report showing number of website conversions per month

Good conversion enhancement methods are white papers and free reports, as these give your visitors something of real value.

## Reporting

As with any marketing campaign, you need visibility on feedback on results. We use www.clickmetrix.net for all our client campaigns because it offers the best reporting features for a very low price, from £12 per month. An example report is shown in Figure 4.4.2.

Good reporting should tell you which search phrases and which traffic sources are giving you traffic that converts on your site. Traffic is of no value unless it converts to a sales or lead, and knowing which phrases are converting tells you where to focus your budgets.

## Ethical practices

Anyone implementing SEO should follow best practices and the guidelines provided by the search engines. There is an SEO technique known as spamming, which has given SEO a bad name in some quarters, because this can result in your site being completely dropped from search engine listings. Before employing any SEO agency, make sure you are 100 per cent clear on their approach before signing a contract. There are lots of methods classed as spam by the search engines; if you are unsure read the article 'Stop Search Engine Spam 'available at http://www.clickthrough-marketing. com/resources/articles.php; see Figure 4.4.3.

Home » Articles » Stop Search Engine Spam

☆ Add to Favourites

## Stop Search Engine Spam

**Author:** Phil Robinson, Search Engine Positioning Expert

**Review your web site to ensure that you are not spamming search engines and risking your site being banned.**

Most people know that spamming search engines is bad. There are many variations on the definition of search engine spam. Simply put, it the process of trying to mislead a search engine spider into thinking that a web site is relevant or more relevant to search

**Figure 4.4.3** 'Stop search engine spam'

## Useful resources

White Papers (18 Pages). Successful Search Engine Optimization (28 Pages). Successful Pay Per Click Marketing. Free Website Assessments: SEO Health Check; Positioning Report. Available from www.clickthrough-marketing.com

Phil Robinson is an experienced online marketing consultant and founder of ClickThrough Marketing, a UK-based search engine marketing agency.

ClickThrough offers proven best practice search marketing services to help businesses reach new customers within the online marketplace.

Prior to founding ClickThrough, Phil worked in several management positions for IT and internet companies, responsible for driving online marketing strategies.

For more information, visit www.clickthrough-marketing.com.

# Events

*Why hold an event in preference to other marketing activities? asks Gill Troop, Managing Director of Cactus*

Unless you are a professional event organizer, you will probably not have considered holding an event, and almost certainly not as part of your marketing strategy. Your imagination may not have stretched further than the office Christmas party and even then the organization will have been left to the MD's PA and the girl from accounts.

Events are a method of communication and should be viewed and approached in much the same way as other methods – advertising, websites, brochures, meetings, direct mail and so on. The rules used to plan and assess these forms of communication also apply to the staging of an event, no matter how large or small. The event may be a fairly formal affair – a press conference for example – or something more light-hearted such as a summer party for favoured clients. Both types require the same level of planning and commitment.

## Objectives

Before rushing out and hiring a hall or an event organizer, ask yourself, why? What do you hope to achieve? How will you measure it? Why would an event work better than a newsletter? How would an event work with other planned marketing activities? Your objective will determine the type of event to be held and the required budget.

## Types of events

There is any number of occasions where an event would be appropriate. For a product launch for example – a live demonstration and the opportunity to answer questions (and take orders) on the spot can never be achieved through direct mail (although you might use direct mail to promote the launch and trawl for attendees).

A press conference – where information is time sensitive and required to be disseminated to a select audience – a live event is likely to garner greater coverage than an e-mail; a seminar discussing a new piece of legislation imparts information to your clients/prospective clients whilst showcasing you as the company with your finger on the pulse. There are others too – corporate hospitality, for example, should never be underestimated. Whilst generally understood to be a large bar bill and not much more, a successful event of this nature will engender warm feelings towards your company. And then there are road shows, internal staff events such as team building days, the AGM, shareholders' meetings and so on.

## Events: the benefits

An event is intensely personal; although you may have 300 invited guests, each one of those guests should have been 'captured' by your own staff and as such it becomes a one-to-one communication. This is important for new and growing companies where relationships are still being built. It is also cost-effective in terms of time and money – think about having to arrange 300 individual meetings.

Events also give a sense of participation and therefore immediacy. A client that has been to see your latest widget (and used it) is more likely to place an order than one who has seen it on a flat piece of mail.

There is virtually no wastage. Very few events have (or should have) an open door policy. Whilst you may not wish to tie down potential attendees to a definite yes/no, you should know who has been invited and have a good idea of who will turn up. You are also therefore able to control the size of your audience.

There is no clutter. You are not competing for a share of voice in a magazine with several of your competitors. You have a direct line of communication to an invited audience who will receive only one message.

Above all, the live event offers the opportunity to present your company. It allows an audience to understand your culture and values by the way in which you interact with them. A company that comes across as extremely professional in the way in which it conducts itself will win business from competitors who may charge less for a similar product or service.

## Budget

How much will it cost? As with all things, this depends on the event. Clearly there are differences in costs associated with running a seminar for 20 people in your board room and staging your version of Party in the Park. Assess your objectives before choosing the type of event. Once you have decided on the type of event (or events, if a series), think about how many people will be involved. There will be a level of refreshment required and the budget will dictate whether you serve a cup of tea and a biscuit or bring out the Bolly. Or will it? If the Bolly is the right route to go, then that has to be built into the budget.

Never skimp on the parts of the event that directly interplay with the attendees. Foul wine may be cheap but will cost you more in the long run, no matter what size the event. Seating for 30 when 100 turn up and many are left standing at the back of the room, unable to see, will leave a lasting impression – the wrong one. A summer party in the middle of the countryside may sound classy but if you are not prepared to arrange (and pay for) transport back to town, change the venue. The ideal way to set the budget is to plan out the event that you want without going over the top but including everything as if money were no object. Then work backwards and look at alternatives if you can't afford the original. It doesn't have to be Bolly anyway.

## In-house or agency?

Whether you use an event organizer or handle the project in-house will depend on a number of criteria – level of expertise and experience, budget, time. If you run so many events that you have a dedicated in-house team then you may still benefit from delegating some of the organization to a specialist supplier. Production, for example, which incorporates AV and staging, can be a nightmare if you haven't experienced it before. Whilst organizing an event is largely a case of using common sense and being aware of the logistical aspects, specialist suppliers are often required – large format printers for banners, suppliers of logo-printed napkins, delegate packs, portaloos. Many of the specialist suppliers work directly with the client but it can sometimes make life easier to have an agency oversee all of these, if you have the budget to cover their fees. If you have not held an event before, it is as well to seek advice. Most event organizers and specialist suppliers, realizing that there is huge competition in this market, should be willing to discuss and advise *before* you have to make a commitment.

## Checklist

At the risk of stating the obvious, it's always advisable to create a checklist at the start of planning an event. 'Who's got the key?' is an embarrassing question when you have 20 clients outside on the pavement. There are many elements in the organization of an event, some not so obvious. Here are just a few:

- ∎ *Insurance* – make sure you are covered for all eventualities – guests falling off the stage, signs falling on heads, bad weather if it's outdoors, someone helping themselves to your laptop.
- ∎ *Venue* – make sure it suits your event – if it doesn't, go somewhere else. Remember to read the cancellation policy very carefully and check what the price includes.
- ∎ *Travel and accommodation* – depends on how big your event is and how many need this but usually worthwhile handing to a specialist travel company.
- ∎ *Marketing* – don't forget to send out the invitations and publicize the event. Try to be a little more creative than just sending an e-mail – a clever teaser is likely to trawl more attendees, unless your event is a shareholders' meeting, which may require a little more gravitas.

- *Content* – set deadlines for your contributors well in advance to give yourself a fighting chance. There will always be one who writes his speech at the pre-event warm up in the pub the night before.
- *Branding* – contrary to popular belief, items such as overprinted napkins, conference banners, delegate bags and menus are not left overnight by the Logo Fairies. Some items can take three to four weeks to produce, so give your suppliers as long a lead time as possible, otherwise you may be disappointed. The good ones will always try to meet your brief, so if one supplier tells you it can't be done in time, try another one.
- *Sponsors* – share the cost of your event by getting non-competing companies to put in cash in return for their logo on show. A canapé company should give you a discount on your cocktail nibbles if you advertise (discreetly) the fact that they have supplied them.

## Measuring success

As with all marketing activity, there should be a post-event assessment. Refer to your objectives. If the event was designed to sell product, how much was sold? How many leads were generated? How many letters of thanks from clients were received (yes, people still send them when they have been impressed)? How much press coverage was created?

Above all, make sure that leads are followed up. Too many companies put a lot of effort into staging an event, fail to follow up contacts made and then declare the whole thing a waste of time.

For further details, visit www.cactusevents.com.

# Organizing a conference

*Organizing a conference is a high-pressure activity, not recommended for those of a nervous disposition. Yet, well done, it can be tremendously exciting and rewarding, says Tony Rogers of the British Association of Conference Destinations*

Conferences are at the forefront of modern corporate communications, whether this is for internal communications (sales meetings, training seminars, board retreats, annual general meetings, for example) or as a vehicle for communicating with key client groups (product launches, technical conferences, corporate entertainment). 'Conference' is a generic term to describe a diverse mix of communications events.

Corporate conferences are now more intensive, business-related events than was the case during the 1980s and 1990s. Return on investment (ROI) is one of the buzz phrases across the industry, emphasizing the need to measure the effectiveness of all investments and activities, including those investments made in a company's workforce.

Surprisingly though, despite the high profile that conferences enjoy and the messages they convey about a company, relatively few conference organizers have received any formal training. For those expecting to find themselves in the hot seat as an organizer or meeting planner, this chapter sets out some essential guidelines.

## Planning for your conference

Clearly, there are different factors to take into account when planning a conference for 500 as opposed to a meeting for 20, but the essential components are the same. The checklist below sets out those ingredients that remain common regardless of the size and nature of the event.

# THE ONE SHOW

## 21-23 February 2006, Earls Court, London

International Confex attracts more event and conference organisers than any other UK events show; if you organise conferences, meetings and events, Confex is the place you need to be.

- ◆ Corporate hospitality and entertainment
- ◆ Overseas venues, destinations and incentive travel
- ◆ Exhibition and conference support services
- ◆ UK venues, destinations and incentive travel

**INTERNATIONAL**
**CONFEX**

For more information call now on:
Tel: 0207 921 8177  www.international-confex.com

**THE UK'S BIGGEST EVENT FOR PEOPLE ORGANISING EVENTS WORLDWIDE**

## Location and communications

There is a well known saying within the conference industry that organizers base the choice of venues for their events on three main criteria: location, location and location! It is indeed true that location always figures largely in the selection process.

We are fortunate in that the UK is justifiably one of the leading conference locations in the world because it can offer, in a relatively small area, tremendous diversity of scenery, a very high quality of facilities and technical support, and an almost infinite variety of ideas for social programmes and incentive events.

## Venue choice

Having decided on the general location of the event, the next step is to draw up a shortlist of potential venues. There may be a very wide choice, including: purpose-built conference centres, civic halls, hotels, universities, management training centres, or one of the many unusual venues now increasingly popular (stately homes, castles, sporting venues, tourist attractions, even a lighthouse or two!) Often the size and requirements of the event will help to whittle down the shortlist, but questions such as the following can help:

- Is the event residential and, if so, is it important for all delegates to sleep under the same roof? Could they be accommodated in different hotels and transported to the venue? Will delegates all require single bedrooms, or is there the likelihood that some double or twin rooms will be needed?
- Are delegates expecting a venue with its own leisure facilities?
- Does the event require a country-retreat atmosphere with few external distractions? What are the options for social activities nearby (if the conference programme permits time for these)?
- Within the venue, is there the correct combination of rooms available for plenary sessions, syndicate groups, catering, possibly an accompanying exhibition?
- What style of seating will be needed (boardroom, theatre-style, classroom, hollow-square, herringbone, U-shape are just some of the options)?
- Is there good access for disabled delegates, or for bringing in display material?
- Is a stage necessary, and where can this be erected in the room?
- Does the main meeting room have pillars obstructing delegates' view?
- Is there natural light and, if not, does this matter? Will the room blackout satisfactorily? How noisy is the heating and air conditioning system?
- Does the venue have a dedicated conference coordinator who can assist with the detailed planning and arrangements?
- Are there other venue staff with whom you will be working and, if so, when will you be able to meet them? At what stage will the sales manager – usually the organizer's initial point of contact – pass on the booking details to colleagues, who then become the main points of reference?
- Are there in-house technical staff to operate audiovisual equipment? If so, is there an additional charge for using their services? If there are no such staff on site, what arrangements does the venue have with independent audiovisual companies, and

what do they charge? What audiovisual equipment is needed during the event? (Normally this can be decided quite close to the event, unless the requirements are very specialized.)

Cardinal rule: *never book a venue without visiting it first – a site inspection is a must.*

## Delegates, dates and budgets

It is unlikely that precise delegate numbers will be known from the outset but calculations should be as accurate as possible. Will delegates be attending on their own or will partners attend with them (for some or all of the time)?

If the event is to be held mid-week, rates charged are likely to be higher than at a weekend. Significant reductions can be achieved by holding the event at least partially over a weekend because hotel occupancy levels are generally lower. Most venues publish delegate rates as packages for both a day event and a residential event. It is also possible to ask for room hire rates and catering rates separately, and sometimes these may be cheaper than the integrated package. It is certainly worth remembering that the published rates are *always negotiable!*

---

### Sources of help and advice

Organizing a conference is a high-pressure activity, not recommended for those of a nervous disposition. Yet, well done, it can be tremendously exciting and rewarding. Help and advice are available.

One such source of assistance is the British Association of Conference Destinations, BACD. All of the major British conference destinations are members of BACD, representing almost 3,000 conference venues throughout the British Isles, from Inverness to Jersey.

BACD members are an ideal starting point when beginning to plan a conference, because they each have a dedicated team able to offer a range of free and impartial information and advisory services. Such services are likely to include some, if not all, of the following: advice and assistance in locating a suitable venue (whether for 10 or 10,000 delegates), arranging familiarization or inspection visits, booking hotel or other accommodation for residential events, providing conference packs for delegates, helping to organize social programmes and pre- or post-conference tours, arranging transport, laying on civic receptions, advising on local service providers, etc.

Through its national network of member destinations BACD can assist conference organizers by offering a free one-stop venue location service: BACD Venue Location Service, freephone: 0500 140 100, or online at: www.bacd.org.uk.

Further details on BACD and its members' services and other information on the conference industry are available from British Association of Conference Destinations, 6th Floor, Charles House, 148–149 Great Charles Street, Birmingham B3 3HT, tel: 0121 212 1400; website: www.bacd.org.uk.

A second source of information is International Confex. Confex is *the* organizers' show and is held annually in February at Earls Court, London. It offers everything needed by UK and international meeting planners with some 1,200 exhibiting companies from over 70 countries. International Confex is the place to source all the new ideas you need to ensure your events are up to the minute, professional and effective. International Confex is more than an exhibition – the Confex Conference runs alongside and provides a valuable educational platform for visitors and includes presentations and case studies from agencies, corporate companies and associations. For more information please go to www.international-confex.com.

# Licensing

*Robert Sales of Swindell & Pearson suggests that growing companies should include licensing in their strategic thinking, as a potential way of increasing revenue and obtaining revenue from new areas*

When licensing, a company licenses one or more of its rights to a third party to use those rights as agreed in the licence, and the third party pays for the privilege of working these rights.

## Free beer?

It may sound too good to be true, but effective licensing can come close to approaching this ideal. In licensing, a company can seek rewards by allowing somebody else to work its rights, in places and in ways that the company presently cannot or does not work these rights itself.

A good licence arrangement may provide a steady income stream for a company, for little effort on its part.

## Why license?

Aside from obtaining 'free beer', there may be one or more markets out there that a company is unable to supply. This may be because the company is too busy, may not have appropriate expertise, or doesn't have sufficient capacity to supply a particular market. Alternatively, it may be a market that the company cannot supply satisfactorily without significant investment in arranging distribution, local partners and the like. A licensee may already be established in this market, and may readily be able to add the company's products, services or other rights to its existing business in this market.

Another scenario is that the rights are in a field in which the company does not have sufficient knowledge and/or reputation. It may be possible that the company's rights are applicable in a field in which the company has no track record or experience.

It may be that a company cannot, or is not ready to, enter a particular geographical market. Accordingly, rights in that market could be licensed to a company established in that area, which may be a local partner.

## What can be licensed?

The usual rights to be licensed are intellectual property rights such as patents, designs, copyright, trade marks or know-how. In view of this care must be taken when seeking to obtain these rights. Strategic thinking is necessary in deciding which types of protection to seek, how broad the protection should be, and geographically where to seek protection.

For instance, if a company knows it can only service the UK market, it may seek for a licensee for the US market, and therefore protection should be sought in both the UK and United States.

# Particular rights that might be licensed

### Patents – let's share the great idea

Patents can be granted for a wide range of inventions, as long as the basic criteria of novelty and inventive step relative to previous arrangements are met. If licensing is a possibility, broader protection may be sought than would otherwise be the case, to provide protection for areas which may not be of direct interest to the company, but where licensing may take place.

Ron Hickman became a multi-millionaire by licensing the Workmate® to Black & Decker®. Mr Hickman struggled for many years in achieving this success, and when necessary brought legal proceedings against various infringers of his patent rights.

Most patent licensing is not so dramatic. Possible licensing scenarios include a start-up UK firm making electronic testing equipment. The new testing product has proved very successful and the firm is hard pressed to meet demand in the UK and EU, let alone elsewhere. In view of this it has licensed a US company to make and sell the product in the United States. This provides profits from a market it cannot fulfil itself.

A West Country manufacturer of traffic cones has developed a new moulding process which helps to provide a stable base for its cones. This moulding process has a wide range of potential applications. It has already signed a licensing deal with a Northern Ireland firm which makes garden furniture, and negotiations are about to start with a Scottish manufacturer of children's toys, with a view to using the moulding process on its products. Again, this provides profits from a market it cannot fulfil itself.

### Designs – a grand design?

There are many instances of the licensing of designs. For instance, men's suits and pottery dinner sets bearing designs by Jeff Banks are available in our high streets.

A wallpaper manufacturer may turn to licensing its very successful designs for use on other products such as bed linen or general furnishings, for use as coordinated items, or stand alone ranges. In both cases, profits are being obtained from markets for which the licensor does not have manufacturing experience.

## Copyright – how far can it be spread?

Again there are many instances of copyright being licensed. For example, the copyright in characters in films, television series and cartoons are widely licensed on diverse products such as yogurts, T-shirts, board games, footballs and bed linen. The income from such licensing deals can significantly supplement the income from the original film or other work, without the film company needing to establish itself in these other markets.

## Trade marks – exploit the brand

A company's brand can be its most valued asset. The brand may be what attracts customers, and may provide a guarantee of quality, durability, value, exclusiveness, or reliability.

The goodwill in a brand can be taken into new areas by licensing. For example, the well known and respected brand JCB®, originally known for agricultural and earth-moving equipment, has been taken by licensing into the field of power tools, lawnmowers and elsewhere, to provide the same message of quality to purchasers of these products.

An example of potential licensing would be when a company purchases the assets including the main trade mark of a well known brand in the baby care field. This mark has been used for over 100 years by this UK family firm which has now fallen on hard times, due in no small part to competition from the Far East. The purchaser of the assets now intends to make only a small number of high quality premium products under the brand. This is where its expertise lies. This company also intends licensing the trade mark on other products, though, still in the baby care field, but which will be made and sold by a foreign company, bearing the well known UK brand. Strict provisions have been put in place to ensure that the quality of the foreign made products will be appropriate to this esteemed UK brand. Thus, the licensor gains profits from markets which are outside its own expertise, by careful choice and control of a licensee.

## Know-how – tell others how to

Know-how covers trade secrets such as recipes, process steps and conditions, and the like. As the only protection for know-how is confidentiality, care must always be exercised to retain this confidentiality. Once a secret has been lost it can never be regained.

An example of licensing here is the recipe for a particular biscuit. The recipe is licensed for manufacture abroad, and particularly for sale to the expatriate market in the United States, who wish to purchase this special typically British biscuit. Strict provisions are provided in the licence to maintain the secrecy of the recipe. The British manufacturer is able to gain profits from the expatriate market without setting up overseas.

# What you should be looking for in a licence

## Licence basis – should you put all your eggs in one basket?

Licences can be exclusive, sole or non-exclusive, and can be restricted to particular subject matter and/or geographical areas. An exclusive licence only allows the licensee to work the rights as defined in the licence, and precludes even the owner of these rights from using such rights as defined in the licence. A sole licence is similar to an exclusive licence, except that the rights owner also retains the rights to use their rights. A non-exclusive licence further permits the rights holder to work the rights and also license other parties under it.

## Licence scope – what can they do?

It is important that this is accurately defined and tied in with the relevant IP rights. Many products will be covered by a number of IP rights, and these should generally all be covered in the licence. The licence should define precisely what acts can be carried out under the licence, where these acts can be carried out, and by whom.

## Consideration – what's in it for us?

Most commonly the consideration is a royalty, which may be a fixed percentage of a figure. Alternatively, fixed royalty figures can be provided, which can be index linked and can avoid some of the complexities of percentage royalties.

Royalty rates can vary considerably. Five per cent of the selling price of a mechanical item may be a reasonable royalty. With products such as pharmaceuticals where there is a very long lead time usually incorporating significant R&D, testing and approval, there may be a royalty rate of 70 per cent of the selling price.

When negotiating a royalty figure it is always worth bearing in mind that 2 per cent of many sales is usually more than 20 per cent of a very small number of sales. Therefore any royalties should aim to be realistic for both parties so as to enable significant sales to take place whilst providing an appropriate income for the rights owner. A sliding scale royalty may be agreed such that if significant sales take place, a lower royalty rate per item may be payable.

To encourage a licensee to be proactive, and particularly with exclusive licences, a minimum annual royalty may be appropriate. It is also common practice for a signing-on fee to be payable, perhaps to reflect the costs incurred to date in obtaining appropriate IP protection.

## Other provisions – nuts and bolts

A number of other provisions should be considered and covered in a licence. These provisions may include defining what will happen if an infringement takes place, if

IP rights are not granted or are revoked, and whether a public indication or marking should be given to indicate that the licensee is working under a licence.

Licensing can also have implications under competition law, so good legal advice is important.

## Summary – don't miss out on a potential bonus

Licensing can bring in extra revenue, especially from markets which a company may not be able to serve itself. To be able to successfully license, it is necessary to have in place appropriate IP rights, covering what could be licensed and where.

Therefore strategic thinking is required at the outset to decide how and where there is potential for any innovation, and whether one or more third parties may be required to fully develop and realize the potential of the innovation.

Robert Sales is a Partner in Swindell & Pearson, UK and European Chartered Patent and Trade Mark Attorneys. Robert acts for a diverse range of clients from the aerospace industry to yogurt manufacturers, in relation to their varied IP interests. He obtains patent, trade mark and design protection for his clients around the world, as well as advising on potential infringement of such rights. He also advises his clients on the rights held by their competitors and others, helps to evaluate those rights, and advises on how to avoid infringing such rights and if appropriate how to attack those rights. Further information is available from rsales@patents.co.uk.

# The value of franchising

*Like all winning formulas, franchising is open to abuse, says Johanna Roughley at the British Franchise Association*

Fast food chains like McDonald's and Domino's Pizza are two of the first names that spring to mind when thinking of franchising. Both businesses have become very successful by using business format franchising to expand, but one look at the British Franchise Association's (BFA) membership shows the franchise industry is as diverse as the imagination of the person whose idea it was to franchise their business in the first place. BFA members cover all aspects of franchising, from high street hairdressing and organic vegetable distribution to children's music education and landscape gardening.

The 2005 NatWest/BFA franchise survey reveals that franchising – currently a £9.1 billion industry in the UK – continues to expand, both in popularity and economic terms. UK franchisors and franchisees are optimistic for the future, with 88 per cent of franchisees reporting profitability in the 2005 survey. A total of 718 franchise systems have been identified, with an estimated 327,000 people employed in franchising across 13 different industry sectors.

Given these statistics, franchising is an attractive option for those wanting to start their own business, but who would prefer the back up of a well known brand. BFA Director General Brian Smart said franchising worked because the franchisee operated under an established brand and used a proven business system.

'Franchising covers a very wide range of industries, and is strong in both business-to-consumer and business-to-business markets. Perhaps this is one of the greatest appeals of franchising – it is able to satisfy varying levels of business aspirations.

'When buying a franchise you are investing in a business that has a proven record of success – franchisees are recruited to replicate a business's methodology, continue its success and help it grow.'

Mr Smart added that the BFA only accepted as members those franchisors who invested in good franchising. 'The BFA is a standards-based organization whose job it is to identify and recognize good franchisors. Franchisors can only be members of the BFA if they are good franchisors, that's the whole point.

'Franchising, like every business method, can be abused. We turn away from the franchise exhibitions we support three out of four applicant companies. Two come back having changed their franchise agreement or the disclosures they make to prospective franchisees – so we make a difference out there, in front of the public, where it counts.'

Here are some reasons to choose franchising over starting your business from scratch:

- Franchising provides a variety of businesses you can buy into and has something for everyone.
- Franchised businesses range from multi-million pound operations to part-time businesses run from the spare bedroom, so there is something for every budget.
- Franchising has been proven to be one of the safest ways of starting a new business compared to other business start-ups. In the 2004 BFA/NatWest franchise survey, 95 per cent of franchisees reported profitability.
- Franchising is a means of starting and running your own business with a very high success rate, provided you choose a good franchise in the first place.
- A good franchise will offer you a proven business format with initial and continuing support. Franchisors often have field support staff to help franchisees.
- Your business will operate under an already-established brand that has been developed and proven in the marketplace, and the franchisor continues to research market demands so you don't have to.
- Franchising gives you the opportunity to build a profitable business that can be resold, if you choose to.
- You don't have to come up with the business idea – someone already has and tested it so you don't have to make any expensive mistakes. You should receive a comprehensive operations manual and training programme as part of the franchise agreement.
- The franchisor has a marketing, sales and advertising strategy to promote the franchise network so you benefit from an holistic approach.
- As part of a franchise you benefit from network buying power so your costs are lower, plus you have greater access to franchising because banks look favourably on the franchise sector.

While franchising is a successful industry, Mr Smart warned people thinking of buying into a franchise to research the franchisor and the market well before signing on the dotted line. 'At the end of the day, you as the potential franchisee must be prepared to be realistic. The secret is to err on the side of caution and do your homework.

'Researching a personal business investment deserves dedicated time. Just because a franchise business is up and running does not mean that the same amount of research is not required.'

The British Franchise Association is a voluntary self-regulating body, set up in 1977 from within the franchising industry itself. Accredited BFA members have proved they are an established business and that they offer a fair and ethical franchising opportunity. More than 280 accredited franchise brands proudly display their BFA membership and, as part of this membership, are reaccredited on a regular basis against the BFA's Code of Ethics.

The BFA works to increase awareness about good business practice within franchising. All members must adhere to its code of practice, which helps assure individuals buying into a BFA-accredited franchise business that they are dealing with an established company offering a fair and ethical franchise opportunity.

In addition, BFA membership is a benchmark of quality providing public recognition for franchisors. This quality standard not only adds to the franchisor's brand but to the value of each and every franchisee within the BFA-accredited franchise network.

For further details, contact The British Franchise Association, Thames View, Newtown Road, Henley-on-Thames, Oxon RG9 1HG, tel: 01491 578050; website: www.british-franchise.org.uk.

# High-level telemarketing

*Your organization is almost certainly already using the phone for generating new business in one form or another, says Niall Habba, Managing Director of the Telemarketing Company. The pity is that it is probably not seeing much return for its efforts and may even be unknowingly breaking the law*

Of all the marketing channels available to businesses, outbound telemarketing is generally seen as the most intrusive. To the person in the street, it means little more than family dinners interrupted by scripted calls from pushy agents offering cheap phone calls or double glazing. Years of bad practice by a small number of companies have badly damaged consumers' acceptance of cold calls. However, the reality is that 'spray and pray' scripted cold calling of consumers is just one small subset of telemarketing. In fact, the term describes a huge range of distinct activities, from consumer to B2B and from brand building customer care calls to appointment setting and sales lead generation.

Despite its poor image, some types of telemarketing are still amongst the most cost-effective ways of building a new business pipeline. In the case of outbound B2B telemarketing in particular, conducted without scripts and with well trained callers, it remains a highly effective route to market. A well run campaign should see your sales teams provided with a steady flow of appointments and sales leads to follow up. A low cost team of expert callers, working a well chosen database of prospects, should act to multiply the performance of an existing sales team.

Scripted calling has become less and less effective in recent years. Prospects are becoming highly resistant to scripted calls and it is getting harder to retain callers who are happy to work off a script for seven hours a day. Unscripted calling allows agents and prospects to engage in a proper two-way dialogue and feels more natural to both parties. Due to the calibre of caller required to hold a productive unscripted dialogue, the costs of this method may be fairly high, but the return on investment should be dramatic and it offers several advantages over other forms of direct marketing, like immediate, actionable feedback and the ability to combine market research with building a continual feed of sales leads and appointments. Contrary to what you might think, well executed unscripted telemarketing can even ensure that calls to prospects which don't yield an immediate result will present your company's brand in a positive light, building in long-term value.

Almost every firm in the country currently uses telemarketing in one form or another to find new business. Use of the phone is an integral part of any new business effort. However, because the work is generally carried out in an unstructured manner, by staff with a range of responsibilities, it's not generally thought of as 'telemarketing'. Few businesses apply much thought to it and as a result the activity receives little focus and often generates a very poor return.

Even when a firm has some form of explicit telemarketing strategy in place, there are two typical scenarios: either an expensive field sales team are forced to grudgingly cold call for a few hours a week, or someone relatively junior and untrained is allocated the role of drumming up new business on the phone. Neither situation is really satisfactory. Highly paid salespeople generally see cold calling as a necessary evil at best and are hugely expensive on an hourly basis – they really belong out in the field, closing deals face to face. If they are good salespeople they will be able to build their own sales pipeline on the phone, but it's usually a hugely inefficient way of doing so. In the second scenario, the lone telemarketer will often also be involved in general marketing support and may end up spending more time doing administration jobs than chasing up new prospects. Often it's hard to recruit and keep people for this kind of role, and after five or six weak performers have drifted in and out of the job many firms lose faith in the whole notion.

## What's the alternative?

Any business selling to business customers that can articulate its USPs and knows which market it wants to address should be able to use outbound telemarketing to good effect. The biggest decision to make is whether you wish to outsource the activity to an agency or to carry it out in-house. The in-house approach has a great deal of appeal, principally in the areas of cost and control. To many organizations, the idea of using an outside agency can be daunting. At first sight, the costs appear high compared to employing a few junior members of staff. More fundamentally, many businesses are reluctant to outsource their first point of contact to a third party. However, both of these fears are worth further scrutiny. There are also several other key considerations to take into account.

### Costs

The true costs of telemarketing are not restricted to the salary costs of the agents. There is management of the campaign and the calling team, staff recruitment and training, desk space, systems and equipment, phone charges and legal compliance costs. Many of these are excluded when comparing the 'outsourced' and 'in-house' approaches, but they all contribute to the overall expense of the exercise. It is often the case that an agency, with economies of scale, can offer a lower overall cost, even before performance considerations are factored in. However, with larger teams, the right environment and constant levels of activity, it is possible to work more cost-effectively in-house.

## Control

One of the biggest fears when outsourcing to an agency is losing control of telephone contact with new prospects. Businesses that have spent years building their brands are understandably reluctant to give an unknown third party access to their pool of future clients. However, any decent agency will be able to demonstrate that they are able to protect, and improve, a brand's image as a result of their work. First, look at how the company presents itself – any company that doesn't strike you as professional in presenting itself is unlikely to present you to your prospects as you'd like. Further evidence should come in the form of sample calls, the list of organizations they work for, and testimonials and references from current clients. Membership of trade bodies such as the Direct Marketing Association or CCA are also important guarantees of professionalism.

There is also a perception that there is more control of the conduct of the campaign when a team is in-house than when they are at an agency many miles away, or possibly even in a different country. Technology has rocketed ahead with solutions to this problem, primarily through the means of digital call recording, improved IT systems and the web. Views will always differ on this subject, but if an agency is able to provide call recordings to you by e-mail or direct link and gives you free access to performance statistics and to the call centre itself, control is arguably as good as when you're running an in-house team.

## Management

You or someone in your organization may have the relevant experience and the time to implement an in-house telemarketing campaign successfully. For those who don't, trying to manage a team and their performance can be a great challenge. An external agency can manage both the people and the campaign for you and leave you to concentrate on other things. It can ensure team and individual performance matches pre-agreed SLAs. It should also continually optimize the campaign through team coaching and managing the prospect data and calling patterns.

## Scale

One of the biggest challenges when setting up an in-house telemarketing operation is one of scale. Often, the requirement is for a very small team – maybe one or two callers. Sometimes requirements fluctuate wildly from nothing at all in quiet periods to large teams of agents to follow up a mailing, for instance. Trying to manage an internal team in either case can be a real headache. Small teams sometimes lack the dynamics and competitive edge of larger operations and changes in levels of activity can be costly or impossible to accommodate. In either instance, an agency can deal with the problems of coaching and motivation and of swings in demand.

### Legal compliance

The legal constraints around telemarketing have been tightened in recent years. New rules have been introduced with penalties for non-compliance and they have wide-reaching consequences. For instance, it is a little appreciated fact that any business that uses the telephone to approach new customers must not call phone numbers registered with the Telephone Preference Service (TPS). This applies just as much to the lone salesman making a few prospecting calls to a full blown telemarketing company running hundreds of agents. Failure to comply carries a £5,000 fine. There are two registries, one for consumers, which contains several million phone numbers, and one for businesses with several hundred thousand. The rules and penalties are the same for both. There are various solutions, from regular scanning and suppression of your prospect database to screening services provided by your telephone carrier. Alternatively, an agency should ensure compliance with both TPS and the full spectrum of data protection legislation.

### Systems

Call centres have a specialized infrastructure focused completely on delivering optimal performance. Entry costs have been high, so digital call recording, specialized CRM platforms and highly developed individual monitoring have been the preserve of large scale operations. Recently, technology has moved on and there are now several web and network-based 'call centre' solutions available that are much more affordable. It's worth considering, though, that training and expertise are still required to get the most out of them.

## What next?

Whether you choose an in-house or outsourced solution to your telemarketing needs, the key is to do *something*. Your organization is almost certainly already using the phone for generating new business in one form or another. The pity is that it is probably not seeing much return for its efforts and may even be unknowingly breaking the law.

With the right approach or the right outsourced partner, unscripted outbound telemarketing is still a great tool for unlocking sales opportunities. Used well, a solid new business pipeline and a productive dialogue with your prospects and customers are within reach.

Niall Habba is Managing Director of the Telemarketing Company, the UK's leading privately owned business-to-business agency. Established in 1990 and specializing in unscripted calling, the firm offers outsourced database cleaning, market research, appointment setting and sales lead generation. Further details can be found on www.ttmc.co.uk.

# People and performance

# It's Time to Look
# at the Bigger Picture

Ortus specialise in the provision of Interim Managers and
Human Resource professionals across all industry sectors, nationwide.
For more information please contact Alexander Raubitschek

33 Sloane Street, London SW1X 9NR
Telephone: 020 7556 2980,
Facsimile: 020 7245 6711
Email: info@ortusinterim.com
www.ortusinterim.com

A member of
The EMR Group
of companies

# High performance

*In sport, and business, there are four rules for peak performance, says Ali Gill of Getfeedback*

Getting the right people in the right jobs and giving them the tools they need to perform to the very best of their ability is not a job 'for the boys', it's the holy grail of business success. Even in the very best run organizations (small or large) up to a quarter of the employee population will be actively thinking of leaving or just *spinning along*, either under- or over-challenged but definitely not fully engaged and contributing to their max. This isn't an issue of goodwill on the part of the individuals concerned; it's the result of insufficient application of the rules of high performance, ie how to get the best from people.

No business is too small to start applying the rules of high performance. Think of a small business as a sports team. Even the smallest sports team will clearly define the job it wants each player to do, will systematically review the performance of each player and the whole team after each game, and will celebrate success. In business it's the same: a job needs to be designed, performance needs constant review and the story of the business needs to be written.

## High performance rules

### 1. Carefully design the job that you want a person to do

There are a number of characteristics that make a job great to do. A great job includes meaningful work, responsibility for outcomes and knowledge of results. If you design a job with these three elements, your employees will be twice as likely to be motivated, satisfied and productive. 'Meaningful work' means providing the opportunity for the individual to use a variety of skills and apply them to tasks that are important to the success of the business, ie if the tasks aren't completed successfully the consequences will be obvious. 'Responsibility' means that there is sufficient autonomy such that an individual can see where his or her responsibility starts and ends. 'Knowledge of results' means that there must be a mechanism for individuals to get feedback about the results of what they do and how they do it, so that they can work out how to do it better and differently next time round.

## 2. Get the right people in to the right jobs

In sport as in life, it is important to play to your strengths. It is easy to imagine that sports men and women are super-competent, but in reality they vary as much as any other person. Some are plagued with lack of self-confidence which keeps them practising and practising, others will take on anyone at anything and never seem to doubt their ability. In sports teams colleagues quickly work out what the strengths and limitations of each person are. In training, individuals work to eradicate limitations; in play, the team pulls together to maximize the strengths of each individual. What matters is that every single person is an individual with important assets and is treated as such.

Knowing a person well means knowing what they can do (their capability and competence), and what they are willing to do (what motivates them). Motivation is a key concern for businesses today. When you read someone's high octane CV it's all too easy to conclude that a person 'can do' anything. Even when scored against competencies in assessment centre exercises, individuals seem to have the 'can do' to do a number of things well. But their performance in the real-life work situation will ultimately depend on not just their competence but also the extent to which they are motivated to perform in that particular role. Selecting people on this basis of 'just competence' is a one-way street, ie what the individual can bring to the job (the 'can do' factor), but this will have no bearing on whether the job is going to suit the individual. Assessing intrinsic motivation makes selecting people for a job a two-way exchange by taking into account the extent to which the individual will thrive in the role (the 'will do' factor), and it consequently often proves to be a more powerful indicator of overall success.

A motivational style profile will tell you straight whether an individual needs structure, prefers to work alone, likes taking on seemingly impossible tasks or is ultimately motivated by achieving things through others. Profiling the job for its motivational attributes tells you which one of these is important. Let's face it, with the best will in the world only a certain number of people make great change agents, great CEOs or great people managers, and if you want people to succeed in their roles, it's important not to recruit a Ferrari when an off-roader is required!

## 3. Tell it straight

One of the biggest contributors to employee performance is straightforward, accurate and fair, detailed feedback. A study of high performing organizations conducted by the Corporate Leadership Council in 2002 concluded that informal feedback from a knowledgeable source is the single biggest performance lever available to an organization. In the same way that individuals leave sports teams because of their coach, individuals leave businesses because of their manager. Estimates conclude that over a third of employees leave for another job because their manager didn't give them sufficiently challenging feedback. Employees who receive regular, fair and accurate, detailed feedback are more likely to invest more in trying to do their job better and differently.

Feedback must take two forms: first, managers must help employees find tangible solutions to specific work challenges. If your salesperson can't decide how to price a deal, he or she will need tangible support, there and then, otherwise he or she can't deliver on his or her promise. Providing solutions or direction on how to resolve issues is a fundamental part of a manager's role.

Secondly, managers must provide voluntary, detailed, immediate and positive feedback about performance to employees. There isn't a right time and feedback can't wait until a performance review: it must be given regularly and voluntarily. For an athlete, a part of the daily regime is feedback for the purposes of improvement. Feedback comes from colleagues and coaches alike. It's not structured and formal, but informal, regular, detailed and focused on improving performance: 'Your concentration was poor in that last session which is ruining the passing sequence. Think back to the last session, you were really focused on the phases of the sequence, the feeling, the timing and the routine. I want you to apply that again, zone in on the timing then you will be more focused and it will help the rest of the team.'

In sport every detail counts; in business it does too. Genuine, focused feedback on agreed outcomes makes the difference in how quickly people improve performance and in how much effort they will put in to doing things better. There are few people who don't want to improve. Without feedback, employees don't have the tools they need to perform.

## 4. Make success and failure memorable

When training for the Olympic Gold, success along the way often gets missed, yet strangely, when you stand on the podium the medal is nothing without all the memories of what got you there. Like any good story, the final success is more memorable if getting there has been something of a quest. Remember Steve Redgrave at the Sydney Olympics 2004 and the story of his five gold medals: the 'shoot me if I get in a boat again episode'; the 'years of suffering episode' when against all odds he overcame diabetes and colitis; the 'transformational coach episode' winning with an 18-year-old school boy, Matthew Pinsent on board. Business is like this too, a series of unique episodes.

Each business needs to write its own story. If you want the story of your business to bind employees together, your story needs to be colourful and engaging. To write the quest you must help people to make successes and failures memorable. Clive Woodward, England Rugby Team Manager for the 2003 World Cup was infamous for sending the boys out for a beer when the team failed. Whatever your methods, inclusion and good humour are important for encouraging people to tell their stories and make both success and failure a memorable part of the story.

## Apply the four rules for success

However exciting your product, motivated people will not give their best unless you apply these four simple rules:

1. Design jobs that are meaningful.
2. Recruit the right people in to the right roles.
3. Give people the tools they need to perform.
4. Encourage all employees to write the story of the business.

You do the maths: what would it mean if 25 per cent of your employees were just 10 per cent more engaged and productive 100 per cent of the time?

Getfeedback believes that 'talent' is the single biggest issue facing organizations and is working with some of the world's most forward-thinking organizations to help them make best use of their talent to measurably improve business performance. Clients include B&Q, Cadbury Trebor Bassett, BAA Terminal 5, Energis, HSBC, Vauxhall, AstraZeneca and Nissan.

Through combining robust web-based technology and consultancy services, Getfeedback always seeks to develop the talent solution that will have the greatest impact on a client in the shortest time possible. If there isn't an existing solution then Getfeedback, strong believers in practical innovation, will invent it, making best use of existing technology to rapidly deliver on what the organization needs most.

The company's co-founding directors are Ali Gill and Steve Bicknell. Contact: Ali Gill, tel: 0870 011 6300; e-mail: ali.gill@getfeedback.net or visit www.getfeedback.net.

# Just-in-time talent

*John Thomas of the Professional Contractors Group on harnessing freelance talent for growth and competitiveness*

Over 99 per cent of companies in the UK employ less than 250 people and account for 55 per cent of non-government employment. Officially classified as small to medium-sized enterprises (SMEs), one of the many challenges these companies face is having the right resources, at the right time, to support their business growth. SMEs are often reliant on the performance of a few key individuals who typically have to adopt multiple roles.

A growing trend towards freelancing and flexible working could help SMEs to overcome this potential barrier to growth. Professor Richard Scase, from the University of Kent at Canterbury, has predicted that 40 per cent of the UK's workforce will be freelance by 2010.

The global economy is restructuring and in its wake changing the entire way in which businesses and labour markets operate. New business models are based on interworking between organizations and individuals. Freelance, interim and fixed-term assignments have become a white-collar phenomenon. Accessing key resources is more important to the success of a business than owning them; if that is true of ICT and physical infrastructure, it is even truer of human capital.

Tomorrow's winning businesses will be those that have built up a bank of first-class freelancers and trusted advisers, and that have great networks that they can use to leverage value and ideas into their businesses. They will have developed freelance relationships of real quality and trust, so that their freelance contractors and consultants will be advocates for their businesses when they are not working with them.

John Knell of the Intelligence Agency says, 'Just-in-time talent allows organizations to be agile and competitive. Making the best of freelance talent requires a change in

mindset, moving the emphasis from ownership to access. Any company that ignores freelancers will be turning its back on a segment of the labour market that is rich in talent, ideas and value.

'The network economy is creating the reputation economy,' he says. 'Freelancers live or die by their reputations – on the quality of their last piece of work, on their networks, on their ability to make things happen quickly and effectively.'

Freelance consultants and contractors are not looking for employers to whom they can belong, but networks in which they can thrive. Equipped with sought-after knowledge and networks, they are the expert pollen of the new economy, moving quickly between projects and assignments, transferring ideas, skills and positive attitudes. Jon Leach, Head of Integration at Chime Communications plc, describes them as 'media age mercenaries' who are 'educated, teched-up and confident in their ability to sell their services and move flexibly from project to project'.

Freelancing used to be the only option available to those who could not find permanent employment. Self-employment has now become the status of choice, the preferred way of working, for the very best talent in all sectors. SMEs, which need to be adaptable to changes in demand, can help maintain their competitive advantage by using freelance talent.

As Emma Brierley, chief executive at Xchangeteam says, 'Organizations need access to talent rather than infrastructure. They want to be able to tailor expertise to suit their requirements and pay for performance rather than tenure.'

## The benefits of using freelancers

- *Staffing flexibility.* Manage requirement uncertainty and take advantage of rapid, low-cost hiring and/or obligation-free downsizing.
- *Access to high calibre professionals.* Expert consultants are notoriously difficult to find and often harder to afford. Most are committed to project-based work where they can use their skills and experience.
- *Knowledge transfer and best practice.* Freelancers bring knowledge and best practice into your organization for the benefit of your permanent staff. Their experience is often enriched and enhanced by working for several clients.
- *Meeting project deadlines.* Freelancers usually have the experience, knowledge and expertise to be able to contribute and add value from the outset. Just as important, they are free to focus solely on the task in hand.
- *Cost-effective deployment.* Independent freelancers provide a genuine low-cost solution, without costly overheads to support or the burden of employment costs and responsibilities. Freelancers are project-focused, so that one pays only for the time it takes, or for performance of the agreed task or project
- *Value for money.* Freelancers generally charge hourly or daily rates based upon their skills, experience and expertise. As well as benefiting from minimal recruitment costs – or even none at all – their clients typically need not worry about statutory expenses such as employers' National Insurance Contributions (NICs), voluntary benefits such as pension contributions and training costs, or additional perks and benefits.

## Tax and employment status

New tax rules came into force in April 2000 that potentially affect freelance contractors and consultants who offer their personal services through a company. The IR35 rules mean that in certain circumstances a freelance contractor or consultant may be viewed as a 'disguised employee' by the Inland Revenue and taxed accordingly.

So what does this mean for SMEs wanting to hire freelancers? First and foremost, it is essential to have a *contract for services* with the freelance business, not a *contract of service* or employment contract. This contract should include the following elements:

- A substitution clause allowing the work to be performed by another person provided by the freelance business; there will usually be terms relating to right of veto, suitable qualifications and so forth.
- A clause specifying that there is no 'mutuality of obligation' between the parties; in other words, there is no 'obligation, on the one hand, to work and, on the other, to remunerate'.
- A clause stating that the freelance personnel will not be subject to supervision, direction or control as to the manner in which they render the agreed services; freelancers are professionals who will use their own initiative as to the manner in which the services are delivered.

The good news is that the Professional Contractors Group (PCG) – the not-for-profit trade association representing freelancers in the UK – provides its members with draft contracts that have been vetted by experts in employment status, tax and commercial law.

The benefit to an SME client entering into such an agreement is that it removes all potential ambiguity about the employment status of the freelance contractor, eliminating any possibility of employment rights being claimed – holiday and sickness pay, redundancy and so forth. The termination clauses in these contracts typically allow the client to end the agreement with little or no notice.

## Raising the quality bar

More and more public and private sector organizations in the UK and in Europe are insisting that their suppliers have UKAS-accredited ISO 9001 certification. Less than four months after PCG introduced its groundbreaking Quality Systems (QS) scheme for small freelance businesses, Transsol Ltd was named as the first member business to receive ISO 9001:2000 certification under the scheme.

Transsol, which specializes in engineering, safety and risk management in the railway environment, passed its external ISO 9001 audit at the end of February. Managing Director Stuart Mealing says, 'I believe that this will mark a major change to Transsol's fortunes; it will now be indistinguishable from the larger consultancies, with whom it competes, in the eyes of end clients. Our pursuit of ISO 9001 has been very well received by our clients, and we are now able to bid for contracts from which we were previously barred.'

PCG's UKAS-accredited scheme has been developed and delivered in partnership with BVQi, the independent certification body of Bureau Veritas, and Qualsys. Vic Bowen of BVQi says, 'This new system of certification is perfect for the freelance sector. It establishes an even playing field in terms of quality business processes and will open up a wide range of new business opportunities for freelancers that previously would have been unattainable.'

PCG's chairman, Dr Simon Juden, believes that the scheme will enable freelancers to demonstrate credibility and quality to all markets. 'In times when offshoring is rightly perceived as a threat to those competing on price,' he says, 'PCG (QS) enables freelancers to compete on value, and enhance their value add to end clients and to UK plc.'

## Freelancers making their mark

The freelance community harbours some of the brightest and best talent in the UK.

Dr Mike Unwalla has been appointed Principal UK Expert for software documentation by the British Standards Institution (BSI). His business, TechScribe, helps software companies to provide clear user documentation for their products. Announcing the appointment, President of the Institute of Scientific and Technical Communicators, Gavin Ireland, said, 'Good user documentation can save industry millions of pounds. We nominated Mike for the important role because of his proven commitment to the Technical Communication profession.'

Leigh Mount is a subsea construction engineer who has been freelancing since 1977 and travels all over the world for clients in the oil and gas industry. A recent project in the Gulf of Mexico involved laying rigid steel pipelines in 7,600 feet of water, and at one stage of the operation a load of 700 tons on the winch, equivalent to a car park full of Minis. Eleven world records were set during the project. Leigh says, 'As a freelancer, you live or die by your reputation, and are only as good as your last job. I see myself as a true consultant, retained by my main client for my industry knowledge and experience.'

Melanie Francis has been freelancing for nine years. Her company, Melf Computing, specializes in developing Microsoft Office templates and reporting solutions, and has completed projects for Sainsbury's, Merrill Lynch and a diverse range of creative, consulting, research and manufacturing businesses. One of its clients, Snapshots International, publishes over 1,700 reports covering 35 industries within 25 countries. Research director Barbara Bigos said that the automated report writing macro produced by Melf had saved time and ensured consistency and greater accuracy in their reports, allowing them to dedicate more production time to the research process, resulting in high quality products for their clients.

Colin Butcher, technical director of XDelta, is an expert on high availability and safety critical infrastructure projects and vice-chairman of the HP User Group. He was chosen as one of four finalists in the BCS IT Professional 2003 awards, in recognition of work done with Hewlett-Packard and OpenVMS Engineering. Judges said that he had helped customer organizations to simplify and understand their main technical areas in relation to business needs, actively encouraging knowledge transfer and acting as a mentor to the different parties involved in the development and implementation of IT systems.

The Professional Contractors Group (PCG) was formed in May 1999 to protect and promote the interests of the freelance community. PCG's aim is to work for proper recognition of independent freelancers as a genuine and valuable sector of the economy, generating wealth and employment, providing industry with a flexible workforce. A not-for-profit organization, PCG represents over 12,000 freelance businesses that pay an annual membership subscription. For further information, see http://www.pcg.org.uk.

Having worked with PCG for over two years, most recently as chief operations officer with responsibility for member services and operations, John Thomas was appointed chief executive officer at the beginning of 2005. In a career spanning nearly 30 years, 21 of which were at various divisions of ICL, John has undertaken a range of project management and programme director roles and projects, mostly in the IT sector. His activities have encompassed operational management, both in-house and outsourced, service level management, the development of strategic alliances, board-level troubleshooting and sales and programme management. He moved into contracting five years ago.

# The frontiers of management

*It can be hard for managers to imagine how quickly change is accelerating, says Roy Paget, British Academy of Advanced Training*

The global interchange of design, knowledge and communication created by the world wide web is producing a rate of change which, in its cumulative effect, is far outstretching the human brain's capacity to cope. The net effect of this is that performance cannot be measured by past or present standards, but must be measured by a concept of performance future. In other words, many of us realize that we could be doing so much more if only we could assimilate the flows of incoming knowledge.

So how can individual managers and organizations cope with this techno-problem, for I believe it is this ability to cope that is at the very frontier of management? Manage this problem and any organization will rocket off into a new future powered by this constant power of change. Those who fail to manage it will find it harder and harder to stay in the race, never going forward and eventually sliding back inevitably into collapse. Here are some outward and visible signs of this problem:

■ no detailed process for handling change;
■ little or no effective stress management;
■ relaxation and stress are not included as a vital part of everyone's training;
■ organizational performance in terms of performance future is low;
■ no real strategy for resolving conflict caused by change;

- poor negotiation skills to convince people to buy into change;
- little or no training in brain compatible communication and learning skills;
- few self-managed teams are set up and working effectively;
- no understanding of the effects of emotional intelligence.

## Why management must study the process of change

The rate of change is accelerating to such a degree that our imagination is not sufficiently trained to keep up with it, therefore it is essential that organizations train all employees in the process of change and how to manage the process in their lives.

Many leaders have little or no training in the process. Most organizations rise or fall based on how well they manage the introduction of change and the control of uninvited changes in their environment.

Leaders must fully understand the change process to move their organizations successfully through the turmoil of today's economic environment and into the future. Many corporations faced with a lack of, or diminishing, resources find that this exerts increasing pressure on their leadership to proactively respond to planned and unplanned changes. A primary role of the future success of an organization is senior management's ability to assimilate change, then formulate and articulate a clear vision, accompanied by implementation of strategic goals and objectives.

A rogue element has been introduced to the challenge of change management: in addition to facing more and faster changes, leaders are often confronted with too many new choices. Their skills for handling more and faster changes do not serve them well when dealing with unprecedented changes.

Lacking training or knowledge, the great majority of leaders come to rely on instinct and experience, rather than a full understanding of the change process. Some out of fear of change resist the inevitable transformation of their organization. This tends to put the organization at risk when facing unanticipated as well as planned change. The key difference here is between people being change managers or change resisters.

Change is the primary cause of personal and organizational stress. There is a direct relation between the amount of change in an organization and physiological changes in the people who work there. The more changes introduced into a shorter period of time, the more stress people and the organization as whole experience. Organizational stressors which surface during a major change process have been found to cause health conditions in people, and negatively affect perceived work effectiveness.

## Lessons to be learnt

From observation of the change processes in a number of organizations, lessons in positive change management have emerged. To be a change manager, not a change resister, successful leaders commit to being perpetual learners. They learn the ways of their organizations and continue to explore new ideas.

## Work with the group

Senior managers have to work with what they have at hand, which requires careful study of the history of the group, and gives many clues to members' behaviour. What has formed them in the past? How have they evolved and matured? A clear under-standing of 'what drives the group' must be achieved, before a leader can introduce new elements. Ignorance of or purposely ignoring the natural order of groups is likely to cause a change strategy to fail.

## Confront fear of change

Asking people to make significant behavioural changes is the most frightening request one can make of them. Stress levels in organizations and people are directly linked to the level of change experienced. Underestimating their fear response and potential resistance is the most consistent mistake made by leaders when introducing change.

## Consider the group's perspective

When attempting to gain a group's support for needed change, the greatest leverage lies in discovering what self-interest they have in maintaining the status quo and what self-interest they have in making changes. A leader must walk in their shoes and appeal to their self-interest, if it supports the overall organizational plan and does not create new problems. If senior management approaches the group or organization from the members' perspectives and understands what they have to lose, they will be able to design interventions that don't immediately trigger individual defence mechanisms.

## Build trust

If the doors to change are not open, then interventions must concentrate on team-building, trust-building, and open and honest communication, prior to the introduction of change. If the senior manager can lower the work group's fear levels, he or she can open the doors to change. If the doors to change are open, or even partially open, then the strategy should concentrate on methodologies that will keep them open. Authentic participation in the change process, with many opportunities to raise issues of concern, will help keep a group open to the possibility of significant change.

## Avoid manipulating the workgroup

The worst change strategy is for a leader to pretend to listen to the work group and con-sider their concerns, having already decided what is appropriate in advance. This type of approach will backfire, because people will quickly perceive that they are being manipulated and conclude that the process is dishonest.

Another strategy that leads to failure is to only involve employees in negative changes. If the leadership of an organization jealously guards the decision-making prerogatives during good times, it can't expect a very positive reaction when it turns around and says: 'We have to cut 20 per cent of the workforce and we want you to help us decide who should go!' Employees will get involved in these types of 'invited' change processes out of self-preservation, but this approach does not build the foundation of trust needed for productive future change.

## Be willing to compromise

If senior management focuses on predetermined outcomes and displays unwillingness to compromise, the possibility of work group support is minimized. Involved employees will suggest changes that greatly improve the original plan, because the people most heavily affected by a plan will correct its obvious defects. Employees are much more likely to support a new set of ideas that they have had a key role in shaping. When a senior manager approaches the group or organization from the members' perspective, he or she will be able to design interventions that don't immediately trigger defence mechanisms.

## Allow group ownership

Ownership of the proposal for change is vital to a successful change process. If the ideas are generated by the leader, then the leader should construct a process that allows the group members to take and make the ideas their own.

## Actions vs words

People trust their leaders' actions, not their words. If words and actions are consistent, then a manager's credibility will be high. The staff will take their cues from the behaviour of senior staff members, despite all declarations of intent. Senior managers must follow up on the change process. Most employees quickly 'burn out' on changes that are announced on a regular basis, but are not consistently reinforced over a period of time. One well-researched change process that is properly implemented with employee support is worth more than numerous new programmes that are poorly prepared and presented in the same time period. The energy that senior management puts into new projects quickly becomes derided and employees may give the impression that they are 'on-board' with the new set of ideas, but privately complain about the 'latest waste of effort'.

## Reward new behaviours early

A senior manager cannot wait for examples of completely changed behaviour to surface before rewarding the new behaviour. Managers spend much more time catching employees doing something wrong than recognizing what employees do right! Reinforce any significant movement in the right direction.

## Financial rewards rarely reinforce behavioural change

A false assumption held by many leaders is that the only effective way to reward or motivate their staff is by financial rewards. Most financial rewards are given on a yearly basis and have little impact on daily behaviour.

### Manage the myths and realities

During each stage of this process, senior management needs to manage the myths and realities of the organization. Most managers believe that what they know and believe are the facts and therefore attention should be paid to their beliefs. They behave as if most other sources of information are irrelevant. Employees on the other hand will pay equal or greater attention to myths, rather than organizational realities. Rumours that flow rapidly through an organization gain greater validity in employees' eyes as they are retold by greater numbers of people. Leaders must understand that rumours become realities if they are believed and acted upon.

### Integrity – the most important variable

The most critical variable in the change process is a leader's personal integrity. Do the work group have good reason to trust the leader? Do the leader's actions and words match? Are they sensitive to the group's needs? Do they treat group members as they would like to be treated? Does the leader communicate with the work group in an open and honest manner?

## Summary

The successful change manager is one who is committed to being a perpetual learner. Myths, realities,and historical cultures need to be acknowledged and managed toward a new set of priorities and values. Leaders who are change managers address and reduce the fear of change that naturally exists in the work group. They build trust and confidence rather than attempting to manipulate the work group.

This is emotional intelligence in action.

Roy J Paget is a neuro-psychologist and a leading authority on brain-based and right-brain learning techniques. He is deeply committed to making a positive, significant, lasting difference in the way people learn and has devoted his life's work to raising the human potential and personal effectiveness of senior executives and their staff. His unique approach to consultancy and people development has assisted companies from both the UK and abroad to dramatically increase their business.

Since gaining his PhD in right-brain thinking, Roy has become a highly respected author, lecturer, TV and radio personality both nationally and internationally and features regularly on BBC local radio. In his clinical work, he has successfully treated hundreds of people in their personal quest for harmonious and balanced lives.

Roy is also the founder of the British Academy of Advanced Training, a company dedicated to empowering people and organizations towards achieving greater success and increasing their performance capabilities.

Contact details: The British Academy of Advanced Training Limited (BAAT Ltd), 22 Pebble Mill Road, Edgbaston, Birmingham B5 7SA, tel: 0121 471 1451; fax: 0121-415-5388; e-mail: enquiries@baatltd.com; website: www.baatltd.com.

# Tomorrow's leaders

*Grow your own talent, says Carl Gilleard, chief executive of the AGR, by recruiting from the 170,000 graduates who enter the workforce every year*

Very few businesses, large or small, local or global, do not employ graduates these days. Why is this? And what is it that differentiates graduates from the rest of the labour market?

The answer to the first question is straightforward – they form the largest fresh talent pool. In round figures there are 300,000 first degree graduates a year emerging from universities in the UK. Take away those who go overseas, those who continue in higher education and those taking a gap year, and there are still something like 170,000 entering the UK labour market. Frankly, it's hard to ignore them!

Moving on to the question of what differentiates graduates, there are several compelling reasons for recruiting and developing them:

- Undertake at least three years' higher education during which they will gain detailed knowledge and understanding of a discipline. As important, they will learn how to manage their learning and that's an essential requirement in the fast changing world of work. Reflect on how many new skills you have had to acquire in the past five years. The chances are that in the next five years you will learn even more – that's the world that graduates are moving into.
- Employers rarely recruit on the basis of a degree alone. Increasingly they recruit against a set of competencies required to do the job. It would be wrong to assume that fresh graduates lack the competencies that businesses require. Studying and participating in extracurricular activities both help to develop valuable skills in students. And let's not forget that it is a rare student indeed who has not accumulated

# THE CASE FOR MEMBERSHIP

**The AGR is the definitive source of authoritative advice and support for any organisation that is a recruiter of graduates.**

There are many compelling reasons why employers should join the association, but chief amongst them are...

**Members gain access to:**
*Expertise and Education*

- By participating in training and development programmes

- By networking and sharing experiences with other recruiters

- By joining one of our industry wide sector focus groups (We also operate focus groups in Scotland and Northern Ireland)

- By attending seminars and conferences to learn of the latest in best practice

- By making use of AGR's information and advice line and online discussion forum

**Keep up to date with:**
*News and Information*

- Through regular surveys of graduate salaries, vacancies and trends

- Through access to the cutting-edge research including 'Adding Value Beyond Measure' which investigates the added value that graduates bring to organisations.

- Through our magazine 'Graduate Recruiter'

- Through our information-rich website (www.agr.org.uk)

- Through member news alerts

**Recruiting graduates is an important and expensive commitment and for a very small investment you can help ensure you do it well. AGR also represents your views, giving you a voice with the people and organisations that influence and are affected by graduate recruitment.**

**In a nutshell,** AGR is the Authority on Graduate Recruitment – the resource to turn to for leading-edge thinking, for definitive data and for best-in-class advice, training and support.

**To open the case,** contact **Mark Davies** at AGR on **01926 623236** or email **mark@agr.org.uk**
AGR, The Innovation Centre, Warwick Technology Park, Gallows Hill, Warwick. CV34 6UW

the collective voice of graduate recruiters

bags of work experience by the time he or she graduates. They earn and learn at one and the same time.

■ Being at university, often away from home, aids emotional as well as intellectual development. That extra maturity should help graduates be clear about what they want to achieve and how to go about it.

■ Forget the notion of 'dumbing down'. Even though the expansion of higher education has resulted in a wider range of abilities among the student intake, if employers want to identify and attract 'top talent' to ensure that they maintain their competitive edge, then it is to universities that they must turn.

■ Most graduates are at the starting gate as far as careers are concerned. They are open to new ideas and approaches, eager to learn and prove themselves. They fit the 'grow your own' model to a tee.

■ Many organizations want their workforce, for sound business reasons, to be representative of the communities they serve. The current crop of UK graduates is the most diverse ever.

So how do employers go about ensuring they get their share of the graduate talent pool?

With more graduates year on year, the challenge is to identify and compete for those you really want to attract to your business. Graduate attraction is the cornerstone to any recruitment campaign. Ask yourself:

■ Why do you want to recruit graduates?
■ What do you want them to do?
■ How are you going to train them to do it?

Put another way, what do you expect from graduates and what can they expect from you in return? Utilizing your market brand is important although easier for some businesses to exploit than others – especially those new to graduate recruitment.

Targeting the right graduates is the next challenge. If possible adopt an integrated marketing approach, incorporating written materials, media advertising, website content and other activities such as on-campus presentations and careers fairs. You don't necessarily have to spend vast amounts of money. AGR member organizations, even those that recruit hundreds of graduates each year, look for ways of reducing unit costs. It's not a big splash you are after but a campaign that gets the right messages across to the right types of candidates making the best use of resources including online technology and face-to-face contacts.

The next step is selecting the 'best fit' candidates from the application pool. Some employers receive large numbers of applications and narrowing the field down to manageable proportions can be quite a challenge. Screening criteria have to be lawful and fair. As well as having regard for existing employment legislation, take note of the impending age discrimination Bill which, from October 2006, will outlaw selection criteria based on dates of birth.

Increasing use is made of telephone screening, online testing and self-deselection exercises to help candidates decide whether or not a vacancy is right for them before making a formal application. Whatever tools are used, try to ensure that there is enough flexibility to avoid missing out on the unpolished diamond.

There are plenty of external providers to turn to if the circumstances fit. Outsourcing the process is an option if you don't have the expertise in house or if you are looking to reduce costs. Greater use of technology is another option, but a balance has to be stuck between price and quality. Never forget that today's candidate may be tomorrow's customer. A bad application process could cost businesses dearly in the long run.

Beyond screening, employers who are recruiting more than one or two graduates often use assessment centres to help make the final selection. Perhaps the best assessment tool is work experience where both the business and the individual get the opportunity of an 'employment trial'. There are a range of such arrangements, from summer internships to year-long sandwich placements, not forgetting the part-time student employee. Too few employers target this pool. The beauty of work experience is that all types of business, large and small, can arrange *quality* placements. I stress quality because the one downside of offering work experience is that if the experience is bad, it causes more harm than good.

So, is it worth the effort to recruit graduates? Well, the 600 plus businesses that form the membership of AGR clearly think so. But don't just take our word for it! In 2004, we commissioned Dr Anthony Hesketh, of the Management School at the University of Lancaster, to undertake research into the added value that graduates, and in particular structured graduate programmes bring to organizations.

*Adding Value beyond Measure* demonstrated a raft of advantages in employing and developing graduates, all of which benefit the bottom line:

■ The capacity to articulate innovations and the ability to cope with the changes that this brings. Graduates *can* see the wood for the trees!
■ Developing faster than other employees and adding value more quickly. They hit the road running and demonstrate leadership qualities at a faster rate.
■ The skills to articulate ideas into the cut and thrust of working life, despite their limited experience.
■ Stimulating change in a fast moving world – not just accommodating it.
■ Not looking at things and thinking, 'That's too difficult' but coming up with a solution and being innovative because they want to make their mark.

Hesketh's research suggests that graduates contribute a massive £1 billion of added value to the UK economy each year. But before you all rush out and grab the first graduates to emerge from your local university, remember to ask yourself the questions contained in the early part of this chapter.

Then you have to consider how you nurture and develop the talent you have brought to your organization. Whatever the size of your business it is important to have a strategy designed to develop talent. Ideally, set up a development programme. Here are a few lines of advice to take on board if you are starting from scratch:

■ Learn from best practice both within your own sector and elsewhere (AGR is a sharing network that does just that).

■ Establish what you hope to get out of the programme (including a clearly defined business case).
■ Gain buy-in from the business, from the Board down.
■ Ensure you have an induction programme in place.
■ Create an environment where the graduates can learn and grow.
■ Encourage employees to take responsibility for their own learning.
■ Establish a support network (consider mentoring).
■ Consult experts in learning development (externally or internally).
■ Keep things fresh by refining your training to the changing needs of the business.
■ Monitor and evaluate the graduates' development.

This last point, of course, is crucial to justifying the effort and expense of recruiting and developing graduates. Start by measuring their contribution to the business in terms of profit by assessing the delivery of projects and meeting agreed targets. Then measure their learning and development and rate of progress through the programme. This will in turn give an indication of the graduate's future potential.

AGR is party to a new tool that has been developed by the University of Lancaster Management School. Called the 'Graduate Score Card', it is designed to help organizations monitor both costs and returns and make informed decisions about future investment and strategy. This is done through a variety of means including benchmarking measurement against other businesses.

Graduate recruitment is not a cheap option but it's a vital one for any business that believes that the contribution of their human capital is a major driver to business success. Building your own talent pipeline is going to have a much healthier impact on your bottom line than being at the mercy of the experienced hire market.

Ultimately, the choice lies between growing your own or buying in experience. As one employer put it in the research report, do you do a Chelsea or do you have your own academy?

Further details from the AGR (The Association of Graduate Recruiters), The Innovation Centre, Warwick Technology Park, Warwick CV34 6UW, tel: 01926 623236; website: www.agr.org.uk.

*Adding Value beyond Measure* can be purchased directly from AGR.

# Executive search for smaller businesses

*Alex Steele of A Steele Associates has ten ways of finding the best candidates in executive searches*

There are a number of services available in the recruitment market and by far the most common is contingency, ie agencies supplying CVs and only being paid a fee if an individual is hired – the fee is contingent on a hiring being made. Agencies will maintain a database of candidates and/or will advertise your requirement in a composite ad in either the trade or national press. Depending on the strength of relationship with the agency, this method is low risk financially but could potentially be time-consuming in people-hours spent wading through inappropriate CVs. If the agency is not au fait with your business you may have no control or guarantee that candidates sourced will be screened or, in extreme cases, interviewed. Some businesses might enter into a 'preferred supplier' relationship in which they commit to giving that supplier all their requirements but at a reduced hiring fee. It is important in those circumstances to ensure that the best candidates are not being supplied elsewhere at a better rate.

At the other end of the spectrum there is executive search which, contrary to the general view, is not solely the province of large businesses with equally large budgets. It can be tailored to suit the needs of any business that wishes to benefit from a bespoke and dedicated recruitment service. Smaller businesses can be deterred from considering executive search services by the misconception that a retained search is an expensive alternative to the success-based contingency process. While it is true that the overall fee for search services can be higher than those charged in the contingency market you, the smaller business decision-maker, may well take the view that the extra cost is justified in terms of ROI by the bespoke and manageable service that you will receive in return.

Having made the decision to invest in the services of a search consultancy you might wish to brief a number of firms and ask them to pitch. Firms can be selected on the basis of reputation, particularly if they are specialist in any given market, by word of mouth, or by reference to trade directories. There are a number of risk management and comfort criteria that should be met before signing on the dotted line. The following are the key issues:

1. Insist on meeting all the people likely to be involved in the conduct of the assignment, ie not only the consultant who would lead the assignment but anyone likely to be representing the business in the marketplace. *Would you be inspired to join your business if you met these people?*
2. Feel confident that these individuals would add value to the process by projecting a professional image through their understanding of the business, its products, its management ethos and its potential. *Do they have a feel for your business? Do they share the passion? Can they sell it?*
3. Feel comfortable that you could work with the lead consultant and that you are prepared to be guided by him or her and able to accept constructive comment on how the assignment should proceed. He or she may tell you that the company needs to project itself differently at interview stage, or that the impression that candidates are gaining from the interview process is not as originally planned and needs to be altered. However, you must also feel comfortable that the lead consultant is similarly mature and reasonable enough to act upon any constructive comment that you may feel it necessary to make. *Be flexible and open to new ideas, but you are buying their expertise, so make it work for you.*
4. Ensure that all candidates, particularly those who are unsuccessful, will be treated professionally and courteously so that they retain a positive view of your business to take back to the marketplace. *The recruitment process, particularly search, is a PR/marketing opportunity, so take full advantage.*
5. Ensure that regular, at least weekly, updates on progress/timeline will be available throughout the assignment. *Be aware of your responsibility to process candidates at an appropriate rate, as well as the need for candidates to be presented for consideration within the timelines agreed.*
6. Read the terms of business thoroughly and be absolutely clear on those terms that relate to when retainers and stage payments would be payable and what criteria would have to be met in order that those payments are due. Generally speaking, retainers would be payable at commencement of the assignment, ie your signing of the agreement/contact. Shortlist fees, where appropriate, would be payable upon your acceptance of the shortlist. Shortlist definitions may vary but are usually either upon your acceptance of the proposed shortlist or your completion of the shortlist interviews. Completion fees are payable upon completion of the assignment, ie written offer, acceptance of and confirmation of start date. However, in the case of long lead times, ie extended notice periods and/or covenants leading to 'gardening

leave' periods, there may be some flexibility. *Read the terms of business and the proposal document carefully and query any issues that are not clear.*

7. Most search businesses will have reasonable clauses to protect their commercial exposure during an assignment, so again you must be clear on what is expected of you and what is deemed reasonable by either party. Those clauses are usually included to cover costs should an assignment not reach completion which, for the search firm, is not only a financial issue but potentially one of reputation. *Therefore it is imperative to ensure that both parties agree specific and reasonable terms that cover such an eventuality.*

8. Ensure that an agreement is reached to cover the way forward in the, albeit unlikely, event that the successful candidate leaves your employ in the short term, typically six or twelve months. *Each case would be judged by you and your search firm on its merits. The strength of your ongoing relationship and the mutual trust that you develop would be key in reaching a workable agreement.*

9. Understand in advance what your likely expenses exposure would be. In most circumstances a search firm would seek recompense for candidate expenses incurred during the course of the assignment and would normally cover reasonable travel/accommodation expenses within the UK. If the search criteria included overseas candidates then clearly the travel expenses would be higher. *Make sure you fully understand your exposure prior to signing any agreement.*

10. *The relationship between you and your search service provider should be a mutually beneficial business partnership with both parties concerned solely with hiring the best candidate available and enhancing your reputation and standing in your marketplace.*

# Work–life balance in smaller companies

*It's common sense. Work–life balance is good news for smaller companies, says Margaret Adams of The Adams Consultancy*

When businessmen and women hear the term 'work–life balance' it is often in the context of the latest court ruling which seems to hamper businesses' abilities to work profitably, or when new legislation appears to bring more regulation, more red tape and more bureaucracy to every business.

And yet, smaller businesses – if they but knew it – are often the leading lights in implementing the work–life balance agenda. This is good news, because the work–life balance agenda is one of the best business improvement tools available to anyone running a business today. Unfortunately, many small businesses are unaware of their successes in the work–life balance arena and hence struggle to capitalize on their achievements.

It's important to remember that work-life balance means different things to different people. Forget trying to pin down a definition which satisfies everyone: you won't find one. Think instead of the benefits that using the work–life balance agenda can bring to your business. This is not a difficult task. There are lots of them:

■ Your staff are more productive and generate more profits.
■ You hold on to the people you want to keep.
■ Your staff are better motivated and more content at work.
■ Your staff are healthier and take less time off sick.

People running businesses also need to be aware that the work–life balance agenda itself is a movable feast. The focus shifts regularly. In 2005 the key issues are:

■ employee health and well-being;
■ strategies for reducing work-related stress;
■ reconciling flexible working with business needs.

The area gaining a lot of publicity at present is *employee health and well-being.*

So, the key question is: how does work–life balance help businesses?

The answer focuses on the concept of balance and the fact that what goes on in one component of a person's life is likely to have an impact on the others. When things go wrong at work those issues also affect the person's life outside work. Likewise issues affecting people's personal lives, such as the serious illness of a loved one, or the need to take on long-term caring responsibilities, affect people's work. Problems at work or in a person's life outside work lead to the work–life balance being upset.

Employers can have a huge impact on their employees' health and well-being by ensuring that work and the work environment are not sources of health problems for their staff. With billions lost each year to the UK economy because of employee absence due to ill-health, making even a small dent in this problem is worth the effort.

Small businesses have ready-made advantages over larger concerns. In small businesses owner-managers are likely to be closer to the workforce – literally – and see people very regularly, often every day. They are likely to see the links between poor working conditions, chronic and debilitating ailments such as back problems and poor personal productivity, or the links between badly designed working arrangements including computer systems and the frustration and loss of motivation these cause their staff. When they are presented with such problems, those running small businesses are likely to take action quickly to improve matters.

However, well-being is not just about preventing illness and infirmity and removing the causes of such problems from the workplace. There is scope for employers to promote health and well-being actively as health, according to the World Health Organization, is not just about the absence of illness but is also about physical, mental and social well-being.

With this is mind, employers may seek to enhance their employees' well-being by banning smoking on their premises or by providing fruit in staff eating areas. They may provide healthy living guides and seminars. They may encourage people to walk between sites or to local appointments wherever practicable. They may insist that people take a proper break at lunch time. They may provide health club membership as an employee benefit, something that is seen as an enviable 'perk', especially by younger workers.

Going hand-in-hand with the promotion of employee health and well-being is the task of reducing work-related stress, that is 'the adverse reactions people have to excessive pressure or other types of demand placed on them'.[1] This process begins with occupational health and safety but moves quickly to broader well-being issues.

Many guides to stress reduction emphasize that the amount of control people have over the way they do their jobs is important in reducing work-related stress. People working in small businesses – including the people who founded them – often have extensive personal autonomy about how they do their jobs and the pace at which they work. Many people choose to work in small businesses to achieve these benefits. They are also important factors in creating sound work–life balance. Little wonder then that people in small businesses are often happier at work than people working in larger organizations and being happy at work goes a long way towards helping people to achieve sound work–life balance.

However, it's impossible to write about work–life balance without mentioning flexible working and to note that small businesses have been quick to adopt flexible working arrangements. Many small businesses recognize that the ways in which work is organized are catching up the demands of the marketplace for 24/7 and 365 days a year availability of products and services. Such demands do not sit well with a Monday to Friday, 9 to 5 working week.

Small businesses have also been quick to realize that people at work value varied working patterns. It's not just people with caring responsibilities who wish to work flexibly. People approaching retirement may wish to work in a different way from how they worked in their 30s and 40s. Some people just want to change the balance in their lives and have more leisure and less work. Flexible working can accommodate all of these options to help people to achieve the work–life balance which is right for them whilst allowing them to contribute to their employing organization's success.

In short, flexible working arrangements are the means by which the changing needs of the marketplace and people's changing expectations about work itself are reconciled, especially in small businesses. Flexible working strategies used today include variations in hours and patterns of working, for example part-time and reduced hours working, job-sharing, responsibility and career breaks, compressed working hours and self-rostering arrangements. They also include varying the locations at which people work, for example, home working and mobile working.

*Therefore, with or without government intervention, flexible working has arrived and small businesses know it.*

So if work–life balance is all about common sense, and many small businesses have embraced the work–life balance agenda without realizing it, where's the problem?

The challenge for small businesses is to avoid losing their common sense approach to work–life balance as they grow. What works well when a business is small is often lost when that business expands. If small businesses do not recognize the value of their common sense approaches to work–life balance, they are even more likely to be swept away as growth drives them forward.

So all in all it's worth keeping track of your common sense work–life balance successes because they are almost certainly making a measurable contribution to your business's success. Common sense and business sense lead to the same conclusions on this occasion. Work–life balance is good for people at work and good news for business.

## Note

1. *An Example of a Stress Policy*, Health and Safety Executive, www.hse.gov.uk

The Adams Consultancy helps businesses to manage staff more productively, to remove barriers to business success through effective people management and to enhance people's work–life balance as part of their business growth strategy.

Margaret Adams is a fellow of the Chartered Institute of Personnel and Development (CIPD) and the author *of The Work–Life Balance Trainer's Manual* (Gower, 2003, www.gowerpub.com). She is a consultant and trainer who has written articles on work–life balance and related themes for a range of journals including *People Management* and the *Times Educational Supplement.* She can be contacted at: mail@TheAdamsConsultancy.co.uk

# Keeping on the right side of the law

*When employment law is developing so rapidly, any mistakes can be particularly costly for growing companies, says Mike Bird, Product Leader, Employment Practices Liability Insurance at Royal & SunAlliance*

Companies of all sizes face a constantly shifting legal and regulatory landscape in relation to employment practices. Even large organizations with well-resourced HR departments and access to sophisticated legal advice can find it challenging to keep track of all their changing duties and obligations. But failure to comply with the relevant legal provisions can have a particularly significant impact on smaller companies – hurting both cash flow and, potentially, reputation. Consequently this is one area no growing business can afford to ignore.

We live in an increasingly litigious society, and all the recent publicity surrounding payouts made to individuals alleging unfair dismissal or discrimination has encouraged a growing number of employees to pursue claims through the Employment Tribunals Service. A total of 197,365 claims were brought during 2003–2004 across all jurisdictions, compared with 172,322 the previous year. The average award for cases involving unfair dismissal was £7,275 in 2004, and on 1 February 2005 the compensatory award limit was increased from £55,000 to £56,800. In cases involving discrimination there is no upper compensation limit, with a growing number of claims now resulting in six-figure awards. These figures do not include the legal costs incurred by companies in defending themselves.

The most recent change on the legal landscape came with the implementation from 1 October 2004 of the Employment Act 2002 (Dispute Resolution) Regulations

2004 dealing with dismissal, disciplinary action and grievances in the workplace. This is an area to which businesses of all sizes should pay close attention to protect themselves both from awards, should an employment tribunal find against them (or the courts on appeal), and from additional financial penalties now imposed for failure to adhere to the prescribed procedures (see below).

Employers already have a statutory obligation to provide employees with a written statement outlining their terms and conditions of employment such as their salary, job title and details of the employer's provisions for handling disciplinary matters and responding to employee grievances. Good practice also dictates that an employer should take steps to ensure that staff are fully aware of procedures relevant to their employment (eg, by setting them out in an accessible employee handbook or company intranet site).

The new regulations mean that employers must now comply with the minimum procedures for resolving grievances, disciplinary action and dismissals. Under the regulations, the procedures are incorporated into the terms and conditions of employment for all employees.

From the employer's point of view, the devil is very much in the detail where the new regulations are concerned. It is well worth paying punctilious attention to the prescribed procedures. Failure to comply with an applicable procedure will render a dismissal automatically unfair even where the employer's actions appear reasonable in all other respects. It is for the employer to prove that it has complied with the procedure. So, it may be worth looking in detail here at what employers must do to comply with the new regulations.

The regulations introduce separate statutory procedures for handling disciplinary issues and dismissals and for resolving employee grievances. Both procedures are intended to resolve as many disputes as possible prior to the stage at which they would be taken before a tribunal.

The standard disciplinary procedure involves a three-step process. Once you, as an employer, have decided that disciplinary action may be required against a member of staff you are required to set out the reasons for that belief in writing and present these to the employee concerned.

Step two involves a face-to-face meeting with the employee. The employer should explain why disciplinary action is thought to be necessary and allow the employee a right of reply. The employee is entitled to be accompanied at the meeting by a certified trade union official or a work colleague. Following this meeting, you as the employer should advise the employee of your decision and inform them of their right to appeal should they be unwilling to accept it.

In practice it may very well be that an employee will decline the opportunity to attend such a meeting but the important thing is that they should be invited. Their failure to accept or attend a proposed meeting may well count against them. Your failure to offer a meeting will almost certainly be construed as a breach of procedure, making it far harder to defend any subsequent claim and leaving you open to additional punitive awards for non-compliance.

Step three in the process – if the employee disputes the outcome – is an appeal meeting. Where possible, this meeting should be attended by a more senior employer representative than at the first. Again the employer must afterwards inform the employee of their decision and the reasons for it.

The standard grievance procedure requires employees to put any grievances in writing. Again the employer should invite the employee to a meeting to discuss the grievance. That meeting should be held in reasonable time and a right of appeal must be made available. Under this procedure, the employee must also wait at least 28 days before taking their grievance to a tribunal. This requirement should help employers to resolve grievances internally.

Employers should resist the temptation to circumvent the statutory procedures. In so far as it is possible to generalize, the two key disciplines to observe are, first, keeping full and detailed records at every stage in the process – setting out the evidence and the rationale to support all decisions you make – and, secondly, at all times to act in a reasonable fashion.

Ignoring these procedures will have serious consequences for the employer. When dealing with employees with one year or more of continuous employment, failure to comply will automatically render their subsequent dismissal unfair. Breach of procedure by the employer also triggers a mandatory minimum basic award of four weeks' pay awarded to the employee and any compensatory award made will be augmented by between 10 and 50 per cent. However, where the *employee* has not complied with process, the award will be *reduced* by the same factor.

The new procedures should focus an employer's mind when terminating any contract of employment because they are an additional obstacle in an already complicated area.

Employment law has developed rapidly over a short period of time and continues to do so. All of this strongly underlines the case for taking these issues very seriously indeed as an employer. The best approach will always be to act prudently, calmly and with the benefit of appropriate professional advice. It is important to understand what is expected of you as an employer in terms of procedures – and to adhere meticulously to the relevant guidelines. At the very least, this will ensure you face disaffected employees across a level playing field.

As a last line of defence, it is also worth bearing in mind that Employment Practices Liability (EPL) insurance exists to provide cover against both the costs of defending any of the claims discussed above (as well as other litigation relating to employment practices) and any awards made. The legal cover provided by EPL insurance is triggered the moment a claim is notified – providing the assurance of proper advice, support and representation. With the increasing extent and volume of litigation being brought by current and former members of staff against their employers, taking out EPL cover may well be an appropriate precaution for growing businesses in the UK.

Royal & SunAlliance is one of the world's leading multinational general insurance groups focusing on all major classes of general insurance. Royal & SunAlliance currently transacts business in some 130 countries looking after 20 million customers, and employs around 28,000 people worldwide.

# Cash flow and working capital

# Improving cash flow

*The management of cash in a business, in particular the working capital cycle, is the most critical area of any business' management, even for successful enterprises, says Mark Standish, a corporate finance partner at Mazars*

It is a sad fact of life that businesses go bust when they run out of cash. Nevertheless, even profitable businesses can go bust.

We measure the success of a business by its profitability, so the concept of a successful business going under defies logic. Once you understand how this can happen, the importance of cash management becomes startlingly clear.

A business runs into trouble when there is insufficient cash to meet payments as they fall due. This is, ironically, one of the key tests of whether a business is considered to be a 'going concern'. The symptoms are familiar: terms to suppliers are stretched; rent payments are delayed; deferred terms on tax payments are sought; the bank is asked to extend credit lines; even payments to staff may be affected.

Whilst these symptoms are usually associated with a failing business, they can also affect profit-making businesses. Sales are used as a measure of profit, but receipts generate cash. Sales can actually create demands on cash (eg paying the workforce, raw material suppliers and VAT charges). Until invoices are paid, the business can have a cash shortfall, and if creditors remain unpaid for too long, the business will be brought down.

We will now consider in more detail the sources of and demands on cash, and provide some tips to help manage these.

## What are the sources of cash?

### Trading receipts

Trading receipts are the mainstay of a business cash flow. Sales of products and services, correctly delivered, invoiced and collected will provide the underlying income stream of the business.

In spite of the importance of trading receipts, it is an area of the business that is often neglected. Invoices are issued late or incorrectly, statements are not sent in a timely fashion, and too much credit is extended to the wrong debtors.

### Sale of assets

In many businesses, asset sales form an important part of the cash flow cycle; typically those with vehicle fleets, such as coach companies, hauliers or companies with a large sales force. When the vehicles are replaced, usually on some form of finance arrangement, the residual values may exceed any outstanding finance, and also the book value of the assets. This creates both a cash flow boost, and also an enhancement to the profit figures. Printing and engineering machines may also produce this effect where they have strong residual value.

However, selling assets to meet a short-term cash problem is simply buying time; the underlying cause must be addressed.

### Equity

This is the cash invested by the shareholders at the outset, and from time to time fresh funds are injected by way of equity. It is committed money that can only be realized on sale or restructure, and in small companies this figure is usually quite modest. Often funds are injected when new shareholders or investors join the company.

### Loans

Loans are a flexible way of introducing cash to a business. Shareholders or directors can assist cash flow, without tying up equity.

Banks and finance companies also provide loans to a business, although these generally are for asset purchases or to finance the growth of the business. It is very difficult to raise loans from financial institutions if the business is in difficulty.

However, loans usually have strict repayment terms which incur penalties in default, so if the underlying business is not generating cash then loans are also only a short-term solution.

## What are the demands on cash?

### Overheads

Overheads are the fixed costs of business: they include premises, utilities, admin, wages and a host of other general items that do not vary with sales. Close scrutiny of these costs usually enables savings to be made. The key to success is flexibility and a quick response to underlying trading conditions. However, remember to build overhead costs slowly and carefully, because they cannot be shed so quickly.

## Fixed asset purchases

These should be reviewed critically at the outset. Will new plant improve productivity and thus reduce cost of sales? Will changing the car reduce servicing and running costs? Will the new premises improve capacity? Many businesses struggle after major capital purchases.

## Tax

Tax should not be overlooked. Businesses in trouble tend to use VAT collected for 'more pressing' needs, but this is a very short-term solution, and soon the payment of VAT will itself become a 'pressing' need. The timing of many taxes is also a challenge, being payable in arrears for a period of success. If the fruits of that success have not been set aside, the bill may arrive when there is no cash available.

## Dividends

As a tax-efficient method of taking remuneration, dividends are very popular. It is tempting to take dividends after a successful trading period, but they should be balanced against the trading needs of the business and the competing demands for cash. Again, a recurring theme among failed businesses is the over-extraction of cash in good times, leaving too little in the pot should trading become difficult.

## Working capital

This is perhaps the most important area, and the least understood. The issue is discussed in more detail below.

## Some tips to improve cash flow

- Invoice promptly and regularly, send interim invoices for long jobs.
- Consider factoring or invoice discounting.
- Sell redundant assets when the price is good, not when you need the money.
- Don't give away equity to employees – sell it or exchange in lieu of cash bonus.
- Take loans out when the business is prospering and negotiate best terms.
- Build flexibility into the fixed cost base, eg shorter leases, outsourcing, dual supply.
- Buy fixed assets on finance to preserve cash; negotiate best terms.
- Review and plan tax management twice yearly with your adviser.
- Declare but don't pay dividends – this will preserve the tax benefit, but aid cash flow.

## What impacts on working capital?

There are only three key variables: debtors, stock and creditors.

### Debtors

Control and management of debtors is critical to good cash management. Debtor days can be influenced by effective invoicing, monitoring and collection. Remember also to set payment terms with customers that *your* business can afford, and be prepared to walk away from sales if necessary.

Non-payment is a hazard of business life, but can be mitigated with good management strategies:

- don't extend significant credit (if any) to new customers who are not known to you;
- set appropriate credit limits and monitor closely;
- consider insuring the debts.

### Stock

Stock absorbs huge amounts of cash in many businesses – overstocking is not a sensible business strategy. Whilst debtors can be used to raise finance, stock invariably cannot, so it should be treated more cautiously:

- look for 'just in time' suppliers where possible;
- be ruthless with obsolescence: promote it, discount it or, if necessary, scrap it;
- carefully balance discounts received with the cash flow benefits of extended terms;
- be creative with suppliers, negotiate terms – sale or return, commission sales, etc.

### Creditors

Creditors are a key source of finance for any business, but they must not be abused, or the consequences may be severe:

- synchronize order dates to maximize credit period;
- review purchasing regularly;
- review overhead suppliers and service providers as well as raw material suppliers.

## How to finance working capital

### Debtor finance

Businesses can use the collateral of book debts to raise finance. It is a popular funding source, available from a large number of banks and finance houses, keeping the market competitive.

*Factoring* is a method whereby the debts are assigned to a finance house, which takes over the management of the debt collection function. It is appropriate for smaller businesses, and can assist a credit control function. It is notified to the customers of the business.

*Invoice discounting (ID)* is similar, in that funds are advanced against book debts, but ID is more 'light touch' in terms of the management of the facility, and does not substitute for any of the credit control function in the business. It may also be confidential (CID), where the customers are not aware that their debts have been assigned. It is suitable for larger or more sophisticated businesses.

In both cases, credit insurance is often available, and many providers also lend against export sales. Many of these facilities are linked to turnover, so as the business grows, so does the level of available facility. This is very useful for a growing business.

## Stock finance

Stock finance is often combined with debtor finance, as stock is not regarded as good security. There are exceptions in certain industries, for example the motor trade, and some commodity businesses. Trade finance and discounted bills are also useful tools to help importers finance stock purchases, but often require an order from a customer to complete the financing chain.

Bank overdrafts are used to finance all forms of working capital requirement, but they are an unsophisticated tool that can be withdrawn on demand, usually at the worst time for a business.

In summary, the management of cash in a business, in particular the working capital cycle, is the most critical area of any business management. Remember, businesses go bust through lack of cash, not necessarily lack of profit.

Mark Standish is a partner in the Corporate Finance team at Mazars, the accounting and business advisory firm. Before joining Mazars, Mark spent more than 25 years in corporate banking and structured finance. He has managed the financial affairs of hundreds of SME clients, through success and recovery, with a focus on good cash management.

Mazars acts for some of the fastest-growing entrepreneurial companies in the UK, offering a complete range of accountancy and business advisory services, including audit and assurance, tax advisory and compliance, corporate recovery and insolvency, consulting, forensic and investigations, corporate finance and financial services for private individuals.

Tel: 01908 664466; e-mail: mark.standish@mazars.co.uk; website: www.mazars.co.uk.

# Make more profit

*Your company could – and should – be more profitable, but there's a bullet that you have to bite, says Martyn Swan, Managing Director, Profitbuilder International Limited*

Hands up everyone who would like to increase their profits...

There are *only* three things you *can* do to increase profits:

1. You can increase your volume.
2. You can cut your costs.
3. You can improve your price.

## Which is the best lever to pull?

Well, that depends on your current position, but let's make some assumptions. Pulling one lever often has an effect on another, but we'll keep them separate for the moment. Let's assume our sales revenue is 100, our variable cost of sales is 50 and our overheads/fixed costs 40. We're currently making 10 per cent net profit. Look at what happens when we pull each of the profit levers in turn.

### 1. Volume

If we increase volume by 10 per cent, our sales go to 110. Our variable cost of sales would also increase by 10 per cent to 55, but let's assume that we can squeeze the extra volume out of our existing overheads of 40. Our profit is now 15 (up by 50 per cent).

A 10 per cent increase in sales gets us a 50 per cent profit increase. If 10 points on our top line gets us 50 points on our bottom line, 1 point would get us 5. The gearing factor is 1:5.

## 2. Costs

Say we cut our overheads from 40 to 35 (a reduction of 12.5 per cent). Our sales revenue and variable costs remain the same, but our profit goes to 15.

So a 12.5 per cent reduction of our fixed costs gives us a 50 per cent increase on our profit; if 12.5 gets us 50, then 1 gets us 4. The gearing factor is 1:4.

## 3. Price

Finally, what happens if we improve our price by 5 per cent (I don't mind if we do this by charging more or reducing our discounts or other give-aways; hence the word 'improve' rather than increase). Our sales volume stays at 100 but our revenue goes to 105. Our costs don't change – it doesn't cost any more to produce an invoice for £105 than one for £100. Our profit is now 15.

A 5 per cent improvement on our price has given us 50 per cent on our profits. If 5 gets us 50, 1 gets a 10 – a gearing factor of 1:10. Table 6.2.1 shows this in a tabular form.

**Table 6.2.1**  The gearing factor

|  |  | Increase volume by 10 per cent | Reduce fixed costs by 12.5 per cent | Improve price by 5 per cent |
|---|---|---|---|---|
| Sales volume | 100 | 110 | 100 | 105 |
| Variable costs | 50 | 55 | 50 | 50 |
| Overheads | 40 | 40 | 35 | 40 |
| Net profit | 10 | 15 | 15 | 15 |
| Profit increase |  | 50% | 50% | 50% |
| Gearing factor |  | 1:5 | 1:4 | 1:10 |

So all three actions have individually produced a 50 per cent increase in profits. Three different ways of achieving the same result. But which was the strongest of the three factors? Have a look at the gearing factors: 1:5 for volume, 1:4 for costs but a massive 1:10 for price.

The first – and most important – message in all the work we do: there is absolutely nothing that you can do that has as magical effect on your bottom line as getting a price increase through – or stop giving it away in the first place.

*OK, so price is the strongest lever. But hefty price rises are a thing of the past, aren't they?* This next bit will surprise you.

Let's go back to our cost and profit model that we used above. And this time, instead of pulling each of the levers independently, let's look at the effect if we work all three simultaneously. But I'm not going for unrealistic sales increases, or slashing and burning costs, or racking up prices to scare off customers. What happens if we just get a very small increase in each factor? As I said, this bit will surprise you.

Suppose we increase our sales volume by just 1 per cent then this is what happens. Our variable costs increase in line by 1 per cent to 50.5 but our overheads will stay the same. We won't need to open another site or take on new people just to handle a volume increase of 1 per cent.

So our net profit rises from 10 to 10.5 per cent, as shown in Table 6.2.2.

**Table 6.2.2**    The effect of increasing sales volume

|                | | *Inc vol by 1 per cent* |
| -------------- | --- | --- |
| Sales volume   | 100 | 101 |
| Variable costs | 50  | 50.5 |
| Overheads      | 40  | 40 |
| Net profit     | 10% | 10.5% |

Next stage, take our new numbers and cut the costs by just 1 per cent. The total costs in this example are 50.5 variable plus 40 fixed, total 90.5. In round figures, a 1 per cent reduction would equate to 0.9, giving us a new total cost figure of 89.6.

Deduct this from our new sales revenue of 101 we achieved in the previous step and we find we are now making profits of 11.4 per cent, shown in Table 6.2.3.

**Table 6.2.3**    The effect of cutting costs

|                |      |      | *Cut costs by 1 per cent* |
| -------------- | ---- | ---- | ---- |
| Sales volume   | 101  |      | 101 |
| Variable costs | 50.5 |      |      |
|                |      | 90.5 | 89.6 |
| Overheads      | 40   |      |      |
| Net profit     |      | 10.5% | 11.4% |

And finally, let's improve the price, again by just 1 per cent. We can do that by increasing all our prices by 1 per cent or by reducing our average discount from 25 per cent to 24 per cent, it doesn't matter which way. All that matters is that we achieve a small 1 per cent price improvement.

Our sales volume stays at 101 but our revenue goes to 102. Our costs stay the same (it doesn't cost any more to produce slightly higher invoices) at 89.6, which gives us a new net profit of 12.4 per cent, as shown in Table 6.2.4.

**Table 6.2.4** The effect of improving the price

|  |  | Improve price by 1 per cent |
| --- | --- | --- |
| Sales volume | 101 | 102 |
| Variable costs | 50 | |
| | 90.5 | 89.6 |
| Overheads | 40 | |
| Net profit | 11.4 | 12.4% |

So where has all that got us? Let's compare where we started to where finished; see Table 6.2.5.

**Table 6.2.5** Comparison

|  | Start | Finish |
| --- | --- | --- |
| Sales volume | 100 | 102 |
| Variable costs | 50 | |
| | | 89.6 |
| Overheads | 40 | |
| Net profit | 10% | 12.4% |

Our net profit has risen from 10 per cent to 12.4 per cent, an increase of 24 per cent! And we achieved this by actually not doing very much:

■ We did *not* go on unrealistic sales drives.
■ We did *not* have to take an axe to the costs, slashing and burning, firing people left right and centre and all that other unpleasant stuff.
■ And we did *not* frighten the life out of the customers by whacking up the prices.

All we did was very gently but firmly concentrate on getting a very small increase in volume, a very small reduction in costs, and a very small improvement in prices.

But, I hear you say, these are only the results with the figures you chose, our numbers are different. And yes, you're numbers are different. But the result will be the same. I challenge you: run the 1 per cent improvement on your numbers and I'll guarantee that you'll get significant results, quite possibly considerably more than 24 per cent profit improvement!

You'll be amazed at how much more profitable you could be *without* having to make major changes in your operation – but with one (small) proviso. If you are currently making net profits of more than 10 per cent, then to get really significant improvements you need to make changes not by just 1 per cent but by 2 per cent. Sorry about that, but that's the price you pay for being more profitable than other companies; the more successful you are the higher your target! Ain't life a bitch?!

And once you've run the numbers for your company, have a look at each change individually.

First, which change, looked at individually, had the *biggest* effect on your profits? In virtually every case it will be price. And which change, looked at in isolation, was the *least* effective? You'll find it was volume.

So, three profit points to sum up:

1. Of the only three things you can do to increase profits, improving your price is usually *by far* the most effective.
2. Using volume increase as a means of increasing profits is usually the *least* effective way.
3. You will improve your profits *significantly* if you instigate a programme to just improve each of the three profit levers slightly – no need to go overboard (unless you want to!)

## *One final point*

If you want to be more profitable then one way is to work a lot harder by selling more (if you can find the extra volume in today's markets) or if you prefer you can fire lots of people or otherwise reduce your costs, and yes, both these ways will work. But if you are serious – really serious – about wanting to be more profitable, to get the best lasting results you're going to have to bite the price bullet.

As we have seen, price is the most effective way of increasing profits but it is usually the hardest to achieve (isn't that always the case – the things that are the best for you in this world are always the hardest to achieve!) The real trick in all of this is to improve your price without losing volume. And that can certainly be done, but it usually is rather more subtle than simply raising all your prices.

So don't give up if it doesn't work at first. Keep going, you'll find a way. Nobody said it was meant to be easy; the potential rewards are too high! Of course, if you would like some help you only have to ask!

Some of the areas where we help our clients are:

■ Where do you have some pricing power – which of your products have the ability to sustain a small price improvement?
■ Which markets, which applications, would support small improvements?
■ Which customers are more likely to accept small price improvements than others?
■ Where in the organization are prices leaking – and therefore profits?
■ How to get discounts back under control – and how to reduce them?
■ How to get better value-added pricing, and stop giving stuff away for free to customers who want low prices as well as all the bells and whistles?
■ How to squeeze better prices from existing customers – quite often without them even noticing?

■ How to identify those products where prices are too low (and probably have been for years)?

■ And last on this list but far from last in possibilities, where does the *real* responsibility for profits lie in your organization (clue: almost certainly *not* with the boss) and how to get these people on your side in the drive for increased profits. Without them, you're sunk. You won't make it. With them, you'll thrive and go on to bigger and better profits!

Martyn Swan is Managing Director of Profitbuilder International Ltd and is happy to talk through these numbers with you. To contact him, tel: +44 1273 208225; e-mail: martyn@profitbuilderint.com or see www.profitbuilderint.com.

# Complete control

(As enjoyed by 37% of UK companies with 50 to 500 employees*)

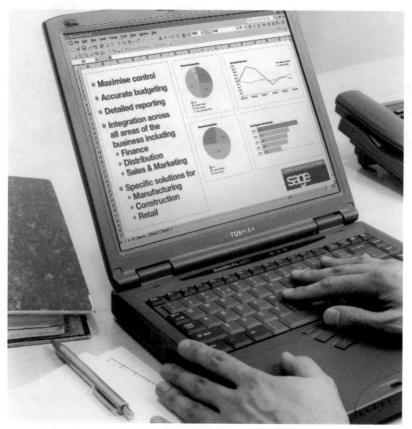

For further information on Sage business management solutions, visit **www.sage.co.uk/ThinkBig**, call **0845 111 9988** or send your details to us using the reply slip provided.

## If you thought Sage was only for smaller companies, think again.

We are the UK's leading provider of business management software solutions to large companies with 50-500 employees*.

We have more than 20 years' experience and some of the UK's best-known businesses on our books. So we know what growing and large companies need-software that maps to complex business processes and solutions that integrate all areas of the business from finance, sales and marketing to industry-specific operations.

We offer scalable software solutions to support your business today and in the future.

*source: TNS Business Software Survey 2004

POWER TO RUN YOUR BUSINESS

sage

# Managing financial complexity

*Growth is a catalyst for change in business management systems, says David Pinches of Sage*

## So what is growth, anyway?

As a headline statement, a business might announce, 'Last year we experienced 10 per cent year on year sales growth.' But behind that apparently successful announcement there is inevitably a much bigger story. So, just what does this statement really mean in terms of the day-to-day running of the company?

The usual interpretation is that the business is simply selling more of its products or services. But to whom? Perhaps it is selling more of the same to existing customers. Or maybe it has invested in developing new products and services to address new markets and for cross-selling to existing customers. What is certain is that the sales growth will impact on every part of the business. As a business grows it becomes more complex and therefore must ensure that its financial and operational controls grow to protect profitability and cash flow.

## Anatomy of a small business

In the early years of a business's life, most if not all the processes and procedures are in the heads of a small team of people. Invariably, the person at the top knows every detail of what's going on. The important task of 'doing the books' is fulfilled either by an employee or, quite often, by the firm's accountant.

This is a dynamic and flexible team, well-equipped to drive sales and able to provide an enthusiastic, high quality of service to a growing number of customers. Most likely, the business is servicing a niche in the market originally identified by the founder as being the opportunity for starting the business in the first place.

However, when sales are driven at the expense of all the other business processes, real risks to the business will arise.

## Risky business

So this is the point when things can start to get tricky. Increasing sales but maintaining service levels with the same number of staff becomes more difficult. Furthermore, there may be more suppliers, a need for larger premises, further investment in vehicles and plant and machinery and a myriad of other things to consider. And it's not just a matter of recruiting more staff. They have to be the right people and able to understand the processes, assuming they have been defined in the first place!

More employees, suppliers and investment in infrastructure also increase the need to not only trade profitably but to bring in those profits fast enough to pay the bills.

It is reported that around 50 per cent of small businesses are still trading after their first three years. In most cases, the ones that didn't succeed didn't plan to fail, they just failed to plan. And the reasons given for failure may be numerous but, in the final analysis, there is really only one – the business simply ran out of cash.

So, whatever the size of the business, sound cash flow forecasting and management is the key. Again, there are many elements to consider but careful control of profit margins combined with first class collection of customer accounts are top priorities.

In an ideal world all customer accounts, regardless of size, are of equal importance. At the start of this process is risk assessment. After all, it's pointless taking orders from customers who can't, or won't, pay. At the other end, a large number of small uncollected debts can damage cash flow just as much as one large overdue account. And then there's the balance between prompt payment and maintaining good customer relationships to manage.

But there are other things to consider in planning growth. The business may well have found a great niche but someone else will want to exploit it eventually. It's a competitive marketplace so, unless the business can just keep increasing its prices, standing still is definitely not an option.

Clearly the solution is to look for new products and services, to sell to new and existing markets, with the aim of increasing profits and maintaining cash flow and enabling further investment in the areas of the business that need it.

True, running a successful business isn't easy. However, there must be solutions to support budding and established entrepreneurs manage these multiple challenges or, indeed, no business would succeed. And there are. Based on the fact that *everything* a business does has a financial impact, then the underlying answer lies in the efficiency of the accounting systems.

# The answers are already there

Most businesses with more than five employees, or even less, have already seen the benefits of running a computerized accounts system just to keep the books in order. However, within that basic accounting information lies the real potential to create a truly powerful and proactive business management system. Clearly, then, the next step is to unlock that potential.

Bookkeeping alone is no longer sufficient, although the accountant's role is still vital in maintaining the raw data. What is important is to be able to use that data to make sound business decisions day by day as well as shape future strategies and vision.

So, let's consider these issues and how high quality business management software can make a significant contribution.

As new staff join the business, tasks should become better defined to avoid duplication and to maximize individuals' skill-sets. In this very much role-based environment, it is imperative that the software system is powerful and flexible enough to map to the ever evolving business processes as well as individuals' needs from the system.

# Credits and debits where they're due

Two key areas where high quality accounting and management information software systems can make a real difference are customers and suppliers. Both represent a constant and real opportunity to maximize profit and cash generation. A proper understanding of customers' ability to pay, payment performance, sales queries, buying patterns and margins is invaluable to any business. After all, customers who are dealt with professionally will stay loyal to suppliers they trust, sometimes even when the price is not quite right.

It is logical then that the converse applies too. Suppliers will deal on more favourable terms with customers they can trust to manage properly the processes of ordering, receipt and payment for the goods and services provided. And minimizing the risk of over/under-ordering further benefits cash, the bottom line and customer relationships.

# Getting the full picture

But the issue is a lot wider than just customers and suppliers. Accurate and timely information has always been the life blood of every organization's decision-making process. However, the pace of the marketplace and its increasingly global nature mean that it's no longer viable to wait until after the year end to see a financial photograph of the business.

Today, the full picture must be available immediately to enable proactive and effective corporate management of any function from a stationery order to the five-year plan.

Of course, all businesses possess the data they need but the only way to fully unlock its potential is by implementing good business management software systems.

## Making the right choices

Five years on from Y2K, many businesses are looking to upgrade their accounting software again. This is an opportunity not to be missed to ensure that their systems match their current business model – and to build in room for further growth.

During the last 20 years or so there has been massive growth in the availability of 'off-the-shelf' packaged software solutions to help manage every aspect of the business. These provide a more cost-effective option than the constant redevelopment of in-house systems. In recent years there has been a considerable, and welcome, consolidation in the packaged software market and only the best software suppliers have survived.

Some of the packages are very much for general use, such as accounting for example, whilst others are highly specialized. It is therefore highly important that the general use packages are capable of integrating effectively with specialized solutions.

But this is not the only consideration. Right up front, the business must assess its own current and future information needs as accurately as possible before it seeks out the software to match them. The next step is to test those needs against the potential solutions available and make sure they fit as tightly as possible.

Arguably, this is of particular importance right now as, five years into the new millennium, many organizations are looking to change or upgrade their management information systems.

So, other questions need to be asked. For example, the systems selected may seem fine but will the supplier be around in the long term to support and develop them? What software and internal/external support reputation does the supplier have? Are the systems widely used, making it easy when staff changes occur, and easily referenceable? Are they developed with future technology advances in mind?

Together, top class management and business software all but ensure market leadership, either now or some time in the future, through the right choices being made at the right time.

As a wise businessman once said, 'Turnover is vanity, profit is sanity and cash flow an absolute necessity!'

David Pinches is currently Director of the Accounts and ERP market unit within Sage. David has a wealth of experience in the business software industry, both in the UK and internationally, most recently with roles as General Manager, Marketing Director and Head of Strategy.

Sage is the world's leading supplier of business management software, offering solutions for all sizes of business from start-ups to large corporate organizations. The only technology company in the FTSE 100, Sage is head-quartered in the North East of England.

# Managing liquidity for growth

*Anna Koritz and Catherine Adair-Faulkner of The Royal Bank of Scotland discuss how to manage liquidity to support business growth and why it is a matter of corporate life and death. They also draw on their extensive international experience and extend the discussion to the important and interesting aspects of managing international liquidity*

## Liquidity matters

Adequate liquidity reserves are an imperative for corporate investment, growth and innovation. A company's liquid assets allow the company to honour its commitments to creditors – both lenders and suppliers. This is the stretch component of the balance sheet that allows a company to invest in an idea, an asset or raw materials, add value and stay operational until payment is received in return for the value that has been delivered. The entrepreneur who fails to actively manage liquidity will not be able to grow or even sustain his or her business.

## How much liquidity is needed

Each company should be encouraged to create and implement a treasury policy, agreed by the Board of Directors, which includes all relevant risk limits and key target ratios. This has always been an integral part of good treasury management but has never been more paramount than in the wake of Sarbanes-Oxley compliance requirements. One of the measures that should be clearly defined is the minimum level of liquidity to be retained at any time.

The appropriate size of the liquidity reserve will need to be assessed for each individual company as a function of, for example, the volatility of cash flow, seasonality of business, strength of the balance sheet and the risk aversion of shareholders. The minimum liquidity level is sometimes expressed as a percentage of the annual turnover and sometimes as a multiple of the average monthly cash disbursement. Certain companies prefer to keep liquidity reserves proportionate to a certain percentage of the loans due to expire over the next six months.

## Defining liquidity

Generally, liquid assets are considered to be those assets which can be accessed on demand, without penalty cost, and used to execute payments. Cash on instant access accounts and committed credit lines definitely form part of that category. To that is usually added 'assets which can be sold in a liquid market', or 'marketable assets'. Most money market instruments that are traded in a market with narrow spreads belong to that category. This generally applies to government-issued securities, but sometimes also to corporate debt issues.

## Don't forget the basics

When growing a business it is important to put in place sound and effective cash management processes and behaviours right from the start. By ensuring all cash is collected from customers as early as possible and that favourable supplier payment terms are obtained, significant liquidity can be released from the company's balance sheet rather than externally funded. This will also have a directly positive impact on the company's profitability.

## Forecasting liquidity

One of the most important functions of the corporate treasury is liquidity forecasting. In a crisis situation, the quality of a company's short-term liquidity forecast may determine the survival of the business. Forecasting liquidity matters!

## Short-term liquidity management

Short-term liquidity forecasting is performed in order to manage the short-term liquidity fluctuations in an optimal manner and to ensure that sufficient liquidity reserves are always available.

Depending on the company's specific needs, short-term liquidity management usually includes a monthly forecast one year ahead and a daily rolling forecast for the next two to four weeks. The monthly planning aims to capture any seasonality of liquidity levels. The classic example is the reduction in ice cream sales in the winter season, but also, for example, a service company may have lower invoicing during the holiday season, but salaries and suppliers still need to be paid on time. A degree of seasonality is present in most business activities and will affect liquidity requirements.

For efficiency in cash flow forecasting, use the 80/20 rule. It is the significant cash movements that will materially impact the company's liquidity. This means that in a larger group with many subsidiaries and centrally managed liquidity, the minor subsidiaries can often be excluded from the regular liquidity forecasting activities, unless they are in a particularly sensitive stage from a liquidity point of view. Likewise, the day-to-day forecast can generally be focused on the significant cash flow items – customer receipts, payroll, large supplier payments, tax, etc. Given that there will always be an element of uncertainty, particularly as regards the timing of customer receipts, focusing on the larger items will generally get you close enough to enable efficient liquidity management. This is entirely practical and realistic. However, as with most management information, a liquidity forecast needs to be actively managed, updated and monitored in order for it to add lasting value.

To allow for an element of imprecision in the forecast without incurring cost to the company, it is important to ensure your bank provides you with the appropriate bank accounts in the relevant currencies to ensure you have adequate return on funds held on bank accounts and that credit lines allow for reasonable cost of credit when required without incurring unnecessary overdraft rates. Your bank relationship manager will be able to help you establish the right solutions.

The main sources of cash flow to be captured in the liquidity forecast are shown in Table 6.4.1.

**Table 6.4.1**   The main sources of cash flow

| Cash flow | | Possible to forecast |
|---|---|---|
| Receipts | + Customer receipts | Partly |
| | + Refunds | Partly |
| Payments | – Salaries | Yes |
| | – Supplier payments | Yes |
| | – Tax | Yes |
| | – Interest | Yes |
| | – Amortization | Yes |
| | – Dividends | Yes |
| | – Other | Partly |
| Financial | + Expiring investments | Yes |
| | – Expiring loans | Yes |
| | + Existing loans | Yes |
| | – Existing investments | Yes |
| **Today's surplus or deficit** | | Mostly |

The table illustrates that, in fact, most payments are possible to forecast, at least in the short term, but it is generally more difficult to forecast receipts. How well you are able to forecast receipts depends largely on whether the business relies on a small number of customers paying large invoices infrequently, or predominantly relies on large numbers of small payments.

## Long-term liquidity management

The purpose of the long-term liquidity forecast is to provide management with information for long-term decision making regarding liquidity reserves, capital structure of the balance sheet as well as investment and acquisition decisions.

Long-term liquidity planning is normally performed three to five years forward. The main difference between short-term and long-term liquidity planning is that when planning with a longer horizon, a larger number of uncertain parameters need to be considered, such as price changes, demand fluctuations and salary increases as well as macro-economic parameters such as interest rates and inflation. It goes without saying that the further out the cash flow stretches in terms of the time horizon, the more susceptible to unpredictable influences it becomes. This must not act as a deterrent, but should be a consideration.

Performing long-term liquidity planning makes it necessary to make assumptions about the future. Therefore, this activity is best performed using a simulation model where it is easy to make changes to the assumptions and simulate different scenarios.

The long-term liquidity forecast contains the same elements as the short-term liquidity forecast, but when simulating long-term liquidity it is usually easier to utilize traditional cash flow analysis, starting with the balance sheet and the profit and loss statements, as illustrated in the example in Table 6.4.2.

## Cash pooling

As the business grows, the need will most likely arise to hold several different bank accounts for different purposes or for different group entities in different locations, including overseas. As a rule, an enhanced interest rate will be paid on a larger balance. It is also safe to assume there will always be a spread between debit and credit interest rates. Therefore, the growing company will benefit from establishing a group account solution where the bank effectively treats the net cash balance of the company as one balance and allows off-set of positive and negative balances for calculating interest. This is known as 'cash pooling', 'cash netting' or 'balance set-off'.

A good solution also offers 'shadow administration' to enable the company to effectively allocate to each bank account the interest due on the balance contributed to the pool from that account. This is typically referred to as 'interest apportionment' or 'interest allocation'. Your bank will be able to advise you on which solution is most appropriate for your needs at each stage of growth.

A proactive treasurer will look to actively manage surplus funds. Any surplus can be extracted from the cash pool and invested in higher yield instruments. However,

**Table 6.4.2**   Cash flow analysis

| Cash flow analysis | | Percentage of revenue |
|---|---|---|
| Sales | 1,000 | 100 |
| Cost of goods sold | 600 | 60 |
| **Gross profit** | **400** | **40** |
| Salaries | −100 | 10 |
| Operational costs | −75 | 7.5 |
| Other costs | −25 | 2.5 |
| **Profit before depreciation** | **200** | **20** |
| − tax | | −54 |
| ± accounts receivable | | 50 |
| ± accounts payable | | 25 |
| ± stock | | −20 |
| **Operative cashflow** | **201** | |
| ± debts | | 50 |
| ± financial profit | | −5 |
| ± dividends | | −10 |
| − investments | | −400 |
| **Funding requirement** | **−164** | |

some cash pool solutions will offer an equivalently enhanced interest on the net pool surplus. This is often an attractive and practical solution for the growing company.

# Managing international liquidity

## Matching cash flows in foreign currencies

As the business expands internationally, it may be beneficial to open foreign currency bank accounts for the most frequently traded currencies, instead of converting currency at each transaction. You can then use your receipts to make payments in the same currency. Apart from reducing the number of currency conversions, this also eliminates the foreign exchange risk for the part of the cash flow which is perfectly matched, ie those receipts which are immediately used for payments in the same currency. This is basic hedging. The more centralized the account structure, the higher the matching opportunity will be. Thus, pooling bank accounts will also bring this additional benefit.

## Timing differences managed with swaps

If there are timing differences between receipts and payments, these can be managed with the help of currency swaps. If a foreign currency is received today and the same currency will be needed in a month's time, an alternative to keeping the currency on account for a month may be to convert it to the base currency at spot rate today and simultaneously buy it back with a forward value at a fixed price agreed today. This is called 'transacting a swap' and is often used to complement or as an alternative to the more complex cross-currency pooling solutions. Your bank will once again advise you here.

## Bank accounts abroad

Opening bank accounts abroad becomes attractive as the number of overseas transactions becomes substantial. This may be as a result of increased export sales, substantial supplier payments abroad, or perhaps the establishment of overseas operations. Most relationship banks, and certainly The Royal Bank of Scotland, will be able to introduce a UK business to one of their cash management partner banks overseas. When choosing a banking partner overseas it is worthwhile considering immediately how those accounts can best be managed from the UK and ensure there is an efficient automated solution in place for reporting balances and initiating overseas payments over the main relationship bank's electronic channel.

## Pooling internationally

The same principles apply to cash pooling across borders as to domestic cash pooling. The method we recommend for cross-border pooling is called 'zero' or 'target balancing', also known as 'cash concentration'. This involves transferring all positive balances into master accounts in the UK and simultaneously topping up any negative balances overseas to a zero or customer chosen target balance. Depending on how significant the company's overseas balances are, this can be achieved manually or automatically, on a daily basis, weekly or even less frequently if preferred. Of course, when multiple jurisdictions are involved, it is important to ensure the tax and legal framework is favourable and that no adverse tax effects arise.

Cross-border pooling solutions have traditionally involved opening accounts with a branch of the same bank in each relevant country. This is no longer the case. Extensive partner bank networks now offer automated solutions for cross-border cash management whilst allowing companies to retain their local in-country and often strong banking relationships. In addition to facilitating cross-border pooling, these indigenous banks are often major players in their home market offering a full range of local services and solutions. A partner bank structure can also offer a 'fast-track' implementation, especially where customers have established existing accounts with partner banks. A 'win-win' for liquidity management indeed!

Anna Koritz is Head of International Cash Management Products and Catherine Adair-Faulkner is Director of International Cash Management Sales at The Royal Bank of Scotland. Both have many years' experience of assisting and advising companies on liquidity matters. Anna is the author of European Cash Management – A guide to best practice, published by John Wiley & Co in 1999, and Catherine is both Chairman of the education board and examiner for the ACT's International Cash Management Certificate.

For further information, visit: www.rbs.co.uk. The Royal Bank of Scotland plc, registered in Scotland, no 90312, registered office: 36 St Andrew Square, Edinburgh EH2 2YB.

# Make this your toughest decision of the day.

Graydon UK offers a number of recognised specialist services in commercial credit risk management, credit reports and credit application processing. These services enable you to manage your commercial risk and maximise business opportunities, by providing instant access to over 60 million credit reports covering businesses in more than 130 countries. Each of our packages provides specialist information in different areas of credit control, yet they all deliver the same single positive outcome - complete peace of mind and confidence in your workplace. So the tough decisions you make on a day-to-day basis should get much, much, easier. For further info call Graydon on 020 8515 1410 or visit www.graydon.co.uk

Minding your business. **GRAYDON**

# Slow payments

*Avoid pressure on cash flow and run a credit check, says Martin Williams, Managing Director of Graydon. It is cheaper than you think*

For growing companies, the priority is usually chasing sales and driving up revenues. Credit management is rarely given much consideration when a major new order is won. Instead, the reaction is one of gratitude, excitement and relief. But it is worth pausing for a moment and asking about payment terms, explaining why in servicing the order it is important for invoices to be settled strictly on time. Forgetting to spell this out at the beginning is a sure way to start to put pressure on cash flow.

Take the instance of a new graphic design agency that won an order to produce some packaging for a leading retailer. Because it was going to account for 75 per cent of sales, the agency took on two extra people. Within two months, one had to be made redundant, because the retailer was not sticking to its credit terms. It would have been better for the design agency to find out where it stood at the beginning and avoid taking on fixed costs. By taking on a contractor or a freelance, it could have avoided putting its growth into reverse.

It is a common problem for smaller companies working with corporates. They should always ask themselves whether they have the infrastructure to handle the order, as well as being aware of the dangers of putting all their eggs in one basket and relying too heavily on one major customer.

The cost of running a credit check has fallen significantly in the last 20 years. A report that would once have cost £35 can now be bought online for under £10. Most of the 4 million companies in the UK are covered. Yet only 40,000 to 50,000 regularly check the credit histories of their customers. The rest are happy to win the business and ignore potential trouble with their cash flow until it hits them.

Most growing companies cannot afford a full-time credit manager to chase their bills, so here are 10 ways to improve cash collection:

1. Ensure your company has got a signed contract with the customer that clearly states your payment terms.
2. Buy a credit report from a recognized credit reference agency, especially one that collects trade payment information on how large companies pay their bills, eg Experian, Graydon and Dun & Bradstreet. Too many small businesses still rely on historical balance sheet information obtained from Companies House when making their initial credit assessment on new accounts, or worse still, take up the two trade references provided by the prospect on their credit application form. All companies are probably able to ensure that at least two of their suppliers are paid promptly each month!
3. As part of their internal control procedures, large companies often require signed purchase orders before paying invoices. Ask the manager/department placing the order whether they need to raise an internal purchase order and, if so, whether they have done so covering the value of the order. Ask for a copy of the purchase order. Note, however, that some large companies require invoices from suppliers to quote the purchase order number before they are paid.
4. Remove excuses for delayed payment. After dispatching goods, ensure that your customer has received them and that there are no problems with quantity or quality. Effective management of queries, before and after they occur, can make a huge difference to your cash flow position.
5. Send statements to your client at different times of the month to when you send your invoices. Sometimes this tactic can provoke questions, particularly when original invoices have been lost, not received, or mislaid.
6. Confirm with your client when your bill is expected to be paid, remembering to ask whether they have specific cheque run dates. Many large companies have two cheque runs a month.
7. If payment is delayed, chase your money by telephone rather than letter – some experts in this field say that the telephone method can be 80 per cent more effective! Another tip – if you are phoning a large company and can't get through to the extension number you have been given in the accounts department, try phoning the number right next to it, ie if the last four digits of the number are 3476, phone 3475. You're bound to be somewhere close to the person or department you want.
8. Maximize your leverage. Try to establish how valuable the product you're selling is to your client. It may be a vital component in a manufacturing process, especially if it has been developed to the client's own specifications.
9. Keep abreast of news that may affect the creditworthiness of your key clients. Put their names on a low-cost monitoring service with a credit reference agency. There is nothing worse than being the last to know when something has happened to one of your key customers; and lastly...
10. Try to establish a personal rapport with one or two people in your client's Accounts department. The personal touch never fails!

The message could not be clearer. If SMEs follow this advice, they will find that cash flow difficulties will ease. This course of action will be far better than doing nothing about slow payments from large organizations (apparently, half of small businesses continue to suffer slow payments in silence for fear of losing 'valuable accounts'), or do the extreme opposite – close the account. One thing is certain. Large companies are not going to change their payment habits overnight. It is time for SMEs to take positive action for themselves.

For more information contact:

Graydon UK Limited – www.graydon.co.uk
Dun & Bradstreet – http://dbuk.dnb.com
Experian – http://www.experian.co.uk
Federation of Small Businesses – http://www.fsb.org.uk
The Better Payment Practice Group – http://www.payontime.co.uk

Martin Williams has spent the last 30 years in the Credit Information Industry. For the first nine years he held a number of management positions with Dun & Bradstreet UK, but was transferred in 1984 to Dun & Bradstreet Europe, as part of a high level team employed to help Dun & Bradstreet companies in Europe to computerize their operations. In 1987, Martin moved to Graydon, which is now one of the top five players in the UK. Since 1989, Martin has been a Board Director of Graydon UK and became Managing Director in 2001. Martin is currently the President of Eurogate, a network of European Credit Information Agencies, of which Graydon is a part. He has also been a member of the Institute of Credit Management in the UK since 1991, and is also a regular presenter and speaker at credit management forums in the UK.

Graydon UK is one of the leading database information providers specializing in credit risk management. The company helps clients reduce the uncertainty of commercial risk by providing a high quality package of credit scoring, credit rating and credit risk management services. Graydon provides access to credit information and reports on more than 68 million companies in more than 130 countries worldwide. The Graydon group is owned by Atradius, Coface and Euler Hermes, three of Europe's leading credit insurance organizations. For additional information, visit www.graydon.co.uk.

# Managing tax online

*Tax is faster online according to HM Revenue & Customs*

If you're busy running a growing business, filling in forms and working out your taxes may not seem to be the best use of your limited time. But it's got to be done. HM Revenue & Customs appreciates this and has been working to provide you with services that aim to be efficient and customer friendly and make handling your taxes easier.

## What are the benefits for me?

HM Revenue & Customs' Online Services are a quick and convenient way for you to deal with a whole range of tax-related issues, whether they are for your own personal tax affairs or your business. Benefits of our online services include the following.

### Speed

No one likes spending time sending and receiving forms, let alone filling them in. That's why HM Revenue & Customs' Online Service is such an attractive and quick option. The service provides you with instant acknowledgements when you send forms and file returns online.

### Convenience

You can put the calculator away. If there are calculations to be made, our online service will do it for you. In addition, the service is available day or night so you can use it whenever it is convenient for you.

# Online Services
## from HM Revenue & Customs

**Leaders in the field of UK government online transactions, we provide a range of secure and easy to use online services for:**
- Individuals and employees
- Employers
- Businesses and corporations
- Agents and tax practitioners
- Software developers

**Whatever your business, our customer-focused services enable you to interact with us at your convenience.**

www.hmrc.gov.uk

 HM Revenue & Customs

## Security

HM Revenue & Customs has taken measures to ensure that sending information and using our online services are safe and secure. Registration for online services is a straightforward process that involves a number of safeguards designed to protect your privacy – much like the process you would go through to open a bank account. We constantly monitor the services for any potential security breaches. Security measures that we have implemented are: 1) access is by User ID/Password; and 2) all information that you send and receive is transmitted through a 128-bit Secure Socket Layer connection (SSL).

HM Revenue & Customs is a responsible data user and is subject to the provisions of the Data Protection Act.

## Efficient

Our Online Services are more reliable and more efficient than using paper. Not only do they free up storage space, they also cut down on post and administration. And because data passes between computers without manual intervention, there is less chance of information being misinterpreted. So, it can actually help you run your business more efficiently and may even save you money.

# What services are available?

The following is an alphabetical list showing the range of online services we offer:

- Agents – visit the 'practitioner zone' on our website.
- Child Benefit Online.
- Construction Industry Scheme Online – Electronic Data Interchange (EDI).
- Corporation Tax Online.
- Electronic payment service.
- PAYE Online for Employers – Electronic Data Interchange (EDI).
- PAYE Online for Employers – internet.
- Self Assessment Online – Electronic Lodgement Service (ELS).
- Self Assessment Online – internet.
- Self Assessment Online for Partnerships and Trusts.
- Software Developers – visit the 'practitioner zone' on our website.
- Stamp Taxes Online.
- Tax Credits Online.

Here's more about the services that may be useful to you.

## Corporation Tax Online

Having all the information you need at hand is critical for any business. This service is a quick and convenient way for businesses and corporations to:

- file company tax returns (CT600), which include accounts and computations, over the internet;
- view liabilities and payments for each accounting period and any interest or penalties that have been charged;
- set up and manage other users and assistants from within the organization allowing them to use the service on your behalf.

## PAYE Online for Employers

Our PAYE Online for Employers service is the simplest, quickest and most convenient way to:

- send and receive a range of in-year forms;
- file end of year returns;
- receive statutory notices (tax codes, etc) and reminders;
- set up and manage other users and assistants from within the organization so that they can use the online services on your behalf.

Your employees benefit too: online transmission means employees can get the right tax code faster. And pension and benefit records are updated at the end of the tax year much quicker if sent online.

## Self Assessment Online

Tax doesn't have to be taxing! This service lets customers:

- complete and file tax returns;
- view the latest copy of a Statement of Account;
- view payments/credits and how these have been allocated;
- view liabilities by tax year including interest, penalties, surcharges and repayments;
- view and change addresses and contact details;
- ask tax-related personal questions;
- opt to receive notifications and reminders by e-mail or text message.

# How do new users register?

Registration is a straightforward five step process. Simply log on to HM Revenue & Customs' website at www.hmrc.gov.uk, choose a service from the 'do it online' section and then select 'Register' from the 'I am a new user' section. The five steps are described below.

## Step 1. About you

Enter your full name, then enter your e-mail address (optional).

## Step 2. Create password

Create a password you can remember, as you will need this every time you access our Online Services.

## Step 3. Enter details

We then ask you for some facts to ensure your personal details are secure. What we ask will vary depending on the services you are registering for.

## Step 4. Accept terms and conditions

You will need to read the Terms and Conditions and select 'Accept' before you continue.

## Step 5. Note User ID

A User ID will now be displayed. Please make a note of this. You will need to use it, together with your password, every time you access our Online Services.

Once you have registered, the following items will be posted to you by the Government Gateway within seven days: a) written confirmation of your User ID with a handy keep safe card; and b) an Activation PIN for each service you have chosen.

The reason we send you the Activation PIN by post rather than by e-mail is to ensure additional security. Please use the Activation PIN within 28 days or it will expire.

To get started and find out more information about all HM Revenue & Customs Online Services and future developments, visit www.hmrc.gov.uk.

# Maximising tax reliefs in a growing business

## Introduction

The economic challenges faced by growing businesses today inevitably direct the attention of their owners and directors towards improving free cash flow as well as profitability. Tax reliefs available to shareholders, and to the business itself, can at one level provide fertile ground for improving post-tax returns, but at another equally important level can assist the entrepreneurs that own them to raise finance, and help the company to retain key staff and improve free cash flow.

After reading this chapter you should be able to identify the tax opportunities that exist and plan whether and how your company can utilise them.

## Shareholder reliefs

### Enterprise Investment Scheme (EIS) Relief

External shareholder reliefs can be invaluable when raising equity finance. One of the most important is Enterprise Investment Scheme Relief (EIS).

If the company is a trading company and its activities qualify under the legislation, an individual can receive 20% income tax relief on investment of up to £200,000 per year and capital gains can be rolled over against the cost of the shares, deferring £80,000 of capital gains tax per year for higher rate tax payers. Where income tax relief is claimed, capital gains on sale of shares in an EIS qualifying company are tax free.

There are various restrictions on shareholders and the companies themselves in the three years following the fund raising, although most trading companies, with some notable exceptions such as farming and property development companies, will qualify.

Similar tax relief is also available to corporate investors through the corporate venturing scheme.

### Loans to shareholders in unquoted trading companies

In certain circumstances, shareholders can also benefit from interest relief on loans taken out to acquire ordinary shares in unquoted trading companies. This can be a valuable relief to employee and non-employee shareholders.

### Spin outs from research institutions

Where academic research is developed into a commercially viable proposition, shares in the 'spin out' company set up to exploit the intellectual property can be acquired by researchers in a tax advantageous way. The researcher will need to be employed by the research institution or the spin out company engaged in the research, and acquire shares by virtue of his employment. The benefit of these provisions is that the value of the intellectual property is disregarded when calculating any benefit taxable on the employee researcher. The combination of this and other provisions should result in no, or minimal, income tax being paid on acquisition of the shares and only capital gains tax being paid on the disposal.

## Losses on unquoted company shares

Further relief is available where an unquoted trading company's shares become worthless. In that situation the capital loss on shares subscribed for (rather than purchased) can be set against an individual's income and not just their capital gains. The relief must be claimed in writing.

# Operational

## Capital allowances

Capital expenditure will often qualify for tax relief.

Capital allowances spread tax relief over a long period. If expenditure does not qualify for immediate tax relief as a repair then relief can be available on the capital cost under one of the following provisions:-

- Plant and machinery capital allowances, where relief is given on a reducing balance basis at an annual rate of 25% or 6% for long life assets. For small or medium sized enterprises, accelerated first year allowances at a rate of 40% are available on most expenditure and some energy saving plant and equipment qualifies for 100% relief in the year of acquisition.

- Industrial building allowances, where relief is given at an annual rate of 4% on cost whilst the building remains in industrial use. Relief is also available on office space and other non-industrial space in an industrial building providing its cost accounts for no more than 25% of the cost of the building as a whole.

When renovating or fitting out premises and especially with a new build, it can be advantageous to ask the Quantity Surveyor to identify and schedule the cost of new plant and machinery so that the more favourable plant and machinery allowances can be claimed on that expenditure rather than industrial buildings allowances or no allowances at all.

## Research and Development Special Tax Relief

Small and medium sized companies engaged in research and development that spend at least £10,000 on such expenditure in a 12 month period can qualify for research and development tax relief. Qualifying expenditure includes staff costs, consumables and external contractors.

Relief can be given as a deduction, giving 150% relief for the costs against income. However, the Treasury has acknowledged that many research and development companies will not face an immediate corporation tax bill and so allow relief at 24% of the actual expenditure up to the maximum of the PAYE and NI paid in the period.

There is helpful guidance to the definition of research and development in accounting standards and DTI guidelines.

## Employee and director rewards
### Share plans

One of the most tax efficient methods of rewarding employees is through an Inland Revenue approved share plan.

The most important of these for growing businesses is probably Enterprise Management Incentive share options (EMI).

EMI options are tax favourable arrangements that facilitate an award to employees of options over shares worth, at the time the options are granted, up to £100,000. The company has to meet certain criteria. The maximum limit on the value of all options issued under this scheme is £3 million and this scheme is only available to companies with net assets of less than £30 million.

There is no income tax on grant of the options.

Neither is there a tax charge on exercise, providing the exercise price is at least equal to the value of the shares at the date the options were granted.

The principal advantage for employees however is that on a later disposal of the shares, capital gains tax taper relief starts to run with effect from the date the options were acquired, not when they were exercised and converted into shares, allowing employees to benefit from a 10% tax rate, providing the options and shares have been held (in combination) for two years.

Other schemes also exist and might be considered. Another type of plan – a company share option plan – can be used to grant options of up to £30,000 in value per option holder to selected option holders.

Save as you earn (SAYE) plans facilitate share purchases from savings and share incentive plans exist which can be used to award shares to employees. These awards may be augmented by the award of additional ("free") shares and shares acquired out of an employee's pre-tax salary.

### Salary sacrifice and pension planning

Employee salary sacrifice and corresponding company contributions to an employee's pension scheme can be a very tax efficient method of rewarding employees. Neither tax nor National Insurance (employer's or employee's) is payable on the contributions.

## Benefits

Other benefits such as mobile phones, relocation expenses, work related training, free breakfast for cyclists, certain medical treatment and some accommodation costs can also be tax efficient and might be considered by a growing business.

A company should seek a dispensation from the Inland Revenue obviating it from the requirement (and cost) of reporting business related expenses on employees' P11ds. Dispensations are most commonly given for travel and subsistence expenses although the Inland Revenue must be assured that all expenses are formally approved and compliance matters are being dealt with appropriately.

Jon Sutton is a partner in Dixon Wilson. His clients include family controlled businesses and their owners and growing unquoted companies. He has worked extensively with these companies and their owners on business plans, fundraising, corporate structuring, employee remuneration and share options, tax credit claims and EIS structured investments. He has advised on purchase, including MBO, through to sale and tax efficient exit.

Dixon Wilson is based in London. The firm offers a partner led, personal service to its clients.

Contact details:

Jon Sutton

Dixon Wilson

Rotherwick House

3 Thomas More Street

London E1W 1YX

jonsutton@dixonwilson.co.uk

Tel: 020 7680 8100

Fax: 020 7680 8101

HYPERLINK "www.dixonwilson.com"www.dixonwilson.com

# Property and locations

# BUCKINGHAMSHIRE: THE FIVE STAR COUNTY
## The Place of Choice

Buckinghamshire, the Five Star County – the Place of Choice – is full of opportunity. A slender county, 40 miles long, sweeping from the Thames to the west of London and halfway to Birmingham in the north. It is a mixture of woodlands, parklands and agricultural valleys, is prosperous and successful with an exciting mix of cultures, heritage and diverse communities.

The picturesque and historic market towns of Buckingham, Princes Risborough, Old Amersham and Beaconsfield add to its character and contrast with Aylesbury, the administrative centre of the County and High Wycombe both main centres of economic activity. It is home to a population of nearly half a million and is set to grow still further, Aylesbury Vale and Milton Keynes have been identified in the Sustainable Communities Plan as areas of growth. All these features combine to create a strong economic, social and environmental foundation on which to build a successful future.

Buckinghamshire's economy is presently worth around £5.6b and is one of the top ten business locations in Europe. It is home to many international companies such as GE Healthcare, Citrix, Pinewood and Shepperton Studios, Johnson and Johnson, McCormick, Martin Baker Aircraft, Ercol and Goodrich Power Systems, all having chosen to locate in the County because of its natural environment, education, quality housing, diverse workforce and access to motorways, airports, railways and low unemployment.

Situated in the centre of the Oxford to Cambridge (O2C) Arc a region of high technology growth, Buckinghamshire is set to take the advantages the growth will bring to its economy and attract the high value-added companies. Silverstone, the home of British motor sport, Stoke Mandeville Hospital with its world renowned Spinal Injuries Unit and Pinewood, the world famous centre for film-making are all world leaders in their own field.

The County is extremely proud of its high educational attainment through its grammar and upper schools and Buckinghamshire can boast the only private university in the country, the University of Buckingham, which majors on entrepreneurship and providing business solutions for growing companies.

There never has been a better time to invest in Buckinghamshire – make it your 'Place of Choice'.

*For further information please contact:*
Development Services
Room 813
Buckinghamshire County Council
County Hall
Walton Street, Aylesbury
Bucks HP20 1UY

Tel: 01296 382157
Fax: 01296-382060
Email: env-edt@buckscc.gov.uk
Website: www.buckscc.gov.uk

# Prospects for commercial property

*The future is bright for commercial property, says Richard Yorke at Experian Business Strategies*

## Why is commercial property important?

The commercial property sector accounts for a large slice of the UK economy. The British Property Federation (BPF) estimates that the sector employs 1.1 million people, contributes £40 billion to the Exchequer in taxes and accounts for 6 per cent of GDP (more than twice the size of the oil industry, for example).

### Commercial property at a glance

- The commercial property sector accounts for 6 per cent of UK GDP.
- Total returns of 18.3 per cent in 2004, with retail leading the way.
- All-property rents set to rise by 2.1 per cent in 2005.
- Total returns expected to grow by 10 per cent in 2005.
- Average annual rental growth of 2.6 per cent between 2005 and 2008.
- Growth in total returns of 8–9 per cent between 2005 and 2008, with industrial property the strongest performer.
- Central London the best-performing office market over the medium to long term.
- Strongest out-turns for retail rents expected in historic towns.
- Greater London and the South East set for best rental growth in the industrial sector over the next four years.

Commercial property is also an important investment asset. The BPF and Investment Property Databank (IPD) estimate that pension and insurance funds invest about 8 per cent (£85 billion) of their assets in commercial property. Many observers expect this to increase markedly over the next few years, acknowledging the advantages of commercial property as an asset. Knight Frank suggests that net investment totalled £2.3 billion in 2004, the highest level since the 1970s.

Moreover, bank lending to property rose to £115 billion at the end of 2004, a 16 per cent increase on the year before. In addition, the anticipated introduction of Property Investment Funds (PIFs) and tax-efficient property vehicles will increase consumer choice and investment flows into property.

## How has commercial property performed?

The wall of money coming into commercial property reflects the fact that it has been the best-performing asset class over the last 10 years, averaging total returns of over 11 per cent. IPD reports that total returns shot up to 18.3 per cent last year, and thereby significantly outperformed equities (returns of 12.8 per cent) and gilts (just 6.8 per cent).

Within property, at the *retail*, *industrial* and *office* markets level, the most impressive returns were seen in the retail sector, averaging 20.5 per cent in 2004. In contrast to previous years, standard shop units (+21 per cent) performed better than shopping centres (+18 per cent), although both trailed retail warehouses (+22 per cent).

The strong growth in retail returns reflects strong investor demand and a shortage of available properties, as well as rising rents, which grew by 4.0 per cent last year. By property segment, retail warehouses (+6.5 per cent) and shopping centres (+3.7 per cent) saw the strongest growth in rents in 2004. This reflects a combination of strong occupier demand (in the face of strong retail sales) and restricted supply (exasperated in part by restrictions on out-of-town development).

Industrials have put in a similarly strong performance in recent years, reflecting robust demand (especially from the warehouse and distribution sector, which has benefited from the strength of retail) and lack of availability. The King Sturge Industrial Floorspace Survey reports falling availability across Britain, and a slowdown in new construction. Overall, returns increased by 16.8 per cent in 2004 (rents increased by 1.1 per cent).

The office market has been more subdued. Offices registered returns of 15.2 per cent last year, after a poor out-turn in 2003, while rental growth has been negative for a number of years due to a lack of occupier demand and high vacancy rates. The downturn in the tech sector and the slowdown in financial and business services have meant that London and the South East (especially the Thames Valley) have generally been worst hit. However, rents stabilized towards the end of last year, anticipating stronger occupier demand and falling availability.

In contrast, regional centres have performed better, being more sheltered from the international economy and less dependent on the types of sectors that have faltered.

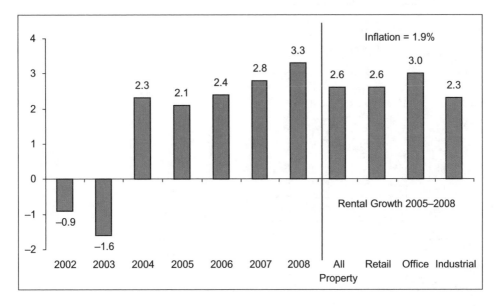

**Figure 7.1.1**   UK property – availability and returns

In addition, the public sector has been expanding, and with it the demand for occupational space. Consequently, cities such as Bristol, Leeds and Birmingham have enjoyed continuing demand, which has been frustrated by a lack of suitable space. In response, new additional space, some of it speculative, is coming on stream.

## What is the outlook for commercial property?

A modest increase in rents is in prospect this year, as the economic recovery is consolidated and demand remains healthy. All-property rents are forecast to rise by 2.1 per cent, a slight dip on last year's 2.3 per cent expansion. Going forward, a sustained acceleration in all-property rental growth is forecast. Annual rates of increase are projected to average 2.6 per cent between 2005 and 2008.

In terms of total returns, we expect a solid performance in excess of 10 per cent in 2005. This is down on last year's record, but still five times the rate of inflation and likely to be better than equities or gilts. In the longer term, we expect returns to remain healthy at between 8 and 9 per cent, again ahead of equities and gilts.

Looking at the three property sectors in more detail, the office market is set to experience a revival in rents this year (+1.7 per cent). Although the supply overhang has become less severe in London and the South East, the strongest rental increases are seen in the North of England and Northern Ireland. Total office returns of just over 10 per cent are forecast for 2005.

The office sector outlook is expected to continue to improve steadily, as employment creation is maintained and excess supply is taken up. From 2006, average rental growth of 3 per cent is projected to outperform both the retail sector and the industrial sector, while total returns match those for industrials by the end of the forecast.

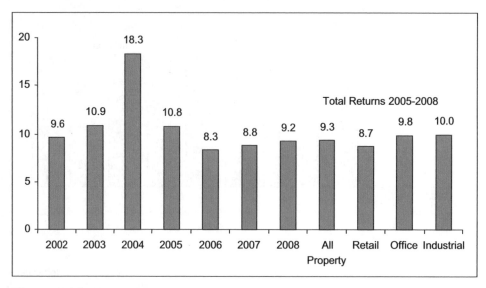

**Figure 7.1.2**   UK property market – total return forecasts (annual percentage change)

Conversely, retail is expected to slow after several years of strong returns and buoyant rental growth. Retail sales have slowed dramatically in recent months and this is likely to feed into reduced demand for retail space. This year returns are set to edge back to 10.7 per cent and, while rental growth remains stronger than in other sectors, it decelerates from 2.4 per cent to 1.9 per cent. Over the medium and longer term, retail is likely to slip behind both offices and industrials in terms of total returns.

Industrial property is set to be the strongest performer for total returns over the medium and longer term. Although total returns are less buoyant from 2005, the market holds up well against other sectors. Returns are estimated to average 10 per cent over the next four years, compared with 9.8 per cent in the office sector and 8.7 per cent in retail. Steadily improving rental growth reinforces these figures.

## Where are the hotspots?

We expect office markets in London and the South East to recover, reflecting growing demand from the tech and financial and business services sectors. In Central London, the West End, South Bank and Docklands are registering marked increases in take-up. We expect this recovery to be maintained, and Central London to be the best-performing office market in the UK, over the medium and long term.

Offices elsewhere in the UK have been more resilient to the economic downturn. Rental growth is set to accelerate over the period 2005–08, averaging 3.3 per cent year-on-year. Centres in the East Midlands (Nottingham and Leicester) and the North West (Manchester) are expected to lead office rental growth, continuing to benefit from buoyant local economies, healthy investment flows and strong demographics. Indeed, stronger take-up and lower levels of availability may mean that new developments will be in short supply, creating further development opportunities.

In office markets, both income and economics have a large influence on returns: many of the strongest centres combine strong local economics with above-average income return. Centres in the East of England and the East Midlands, such as Norwich and Leicester, are expected to post the strongest returns.

Retail centres are less reliant on local economics, with location regarded as a more important driver of performance. Many of the strongest out-turns for rents are expected in the UK's historic towns (Bath and Harrogate, for example), which attract a large number of tourists. Among the major cities, Manchester is expected to be one of the strongest performers over the next four years.

Successful industrial markets are to be found where manufacturing activity recovers most robustly. The towns that offer the best rental growth over the next four years tend to be in Greater London and the South East.

Richard Yorke heads Experian Business Strategies' Property Business and is responsible for property-centric analysis. The Property Business undertakes around £5 million-worth of consultancy and sales each year. Richard has nearly 10 years' experience working in economics and property for investors, developers, agents and planners. He is a member of the Society of Business Economists, Society of Property Researchers and Investment Property Forum. For further information e-mail: richard.yorke@uk.experian.com; tel: 0207 355 8212.

Experian is a global leader in providing information solutions to organizations and consumers. Its Business Strategies Division provides an unrivalled understanding of individuals, markets and economies in the UK and around the world. We have an international team of over 300 researchers, analysts and consultants, generating insight and advice on a wide range of marketing, public policy and business issues.

# Abertawe Swansea

*creu'r llwyfan ar gyfer busnes*    *setting the scene for business*

| Am gefnogaeth ragweithiol gyda: | For proactive assistance with: |
|---|---|
| Hwyluso datblygu | ● Development facilitation |
| Cyflwyno safleoedd datblygu strategol | ● Delivering strategic development sites |
| Cychwyn busnes | ● Business start-up |
| Cynlluniau adfywio canol y ddinas ac ardaloedd | ● City centre and area regeneration schemes |
| Ariannu allanol | ● External funding |
| Gwybodaeth economaidd | ● Economic intelligence |
| Datblygu cynaliadwy | ● Sustainable development |

Contact our economic and strategic development division:

Cysylltwch â'n tîm datblygu economaidd ar is-adran:

☎: +44 (0) 1792 636978

**www.swansea.gov.uk**

CITY AND COUNTY OF SWANSEA • DINAS A SIR ABERTAWE

# SWANSEA – *for quality business, for quality life*

With more than £1 billion of investment expected over the next few years, it is hardly surprising that Swansea feels it stands on the threshold of a new era.

A string of developments throughout the city is making it not only a destination for businesses and visitors but also a place where the people of Swansea can be proud to live and work.

Swansea is an exciting and thriving modern city full of potential for the investor and developer. **SA1 Swansea Waterfront** is an ambitious new development currently being delivered by the Welsh Development Agency. At least £200million of private and public sector funding is expected to be invested into this exciting waterfront regeneration project for the East Side of the city. The overall design of the project allows for imaginative mix of land uses and incorporates a requirement for urban design of the highest standards so as to create a vibrant and attractive environment for workers, residents and visitors. An extensive programme of work is currently underway with progress being made on residential and office schemes and work expected to start soon on a major hotel, a new church, a private hospital and a comprehensive leisure and entertainment complex.

If a strategic location is the key to your business success, **Swansea Vale** can offer an ideal setting close to the motorway and a favourable climate for business growth. More than £25million has already been invested in roads, services and landscaping and the development now boasts an extremely attractive business environment of infrastructure and prepared sites.

Formerly home to the Felindre steelworks and situated adjacent to the M4 (with direct motorway access), the **Felindre Strategic Employment Site** has been in the world spotlight during the past two years as a service area for the Wales Rally GB. This location provides a significant development opportunity for business and high-tech industries.

A recent study cited Swansea as one of the best places to live in the UK and anyone wishing to improve their **quality of life** will be attracted to this modern, cosmopolitan and very friendly city. The environment of the city and surrounding area is unique. With first class amenities and Britain's first designated Area of Outstanding Natural Beauty, it offers some of the best sandy beaches and scenic countryside in the UK.

Swansea is now home to Wales' **National Waterfront Museum**. A £30million project, it will open to public in summer of this year and tell the story of Wales' maritime and industrial heritage. It will be a prime attraction with an anticipated 250,000 visitors per year.

The £11 million **Wales National Pool**, which opened last year, will be the venue for international swimming competitions over the next 10 years and the centrepiece of a new £3 million Sports Village.

As from this summer, a new **20,000 seater Stadium** will become the venue for Swansea's football and rugby clubs, providing an exciting and modern location for the city's teams and fans.

Work is nearing completion on the redevelopment of a major city centre site – **Salubrious Place** – including a 116 –bed hotel, a range of cafés, restaurants and bars as well as a public multi-storey car park, which will complement Swansea's well-established and dynamic leisure and café quarter in Wind Street. Work has already commenced on a second phase, which will accommodate a multi-screen cinema complex, a casino and residential.

These are only a few of a number of exciting developments, which are bringing substantial economic benefits to the area as well attracting further investment interest. Other recently approved projects include a 29 storey residential tower block within the Maritime Quarter, a championship golf course with associated executive housing. Within the City Centre, work is progressing on the design of a major new bus interchange and the redevelopment of a key retail area.

**For further information please contact the Regeneration Department,
City and County of Swansea on +44 (0)1792 636 978.**

# The Isle of Man

**Your Business Here** – The Isle of Man is the ideal place for developing businesses. It offers a world class telecommunications infrastructure, a competitive operating environment and a low rate of corporation tax. Combine these real commercial benefits with easy access to Government and an enviable quality of life and the Isle of Man remains an attractive location to set up and grow a business.

**Trade** – Although part of the British Isles the Isle of Man is not part of the UK or the EU. However, trade policies agreed with the UK and the EU encourage export to these jurisdictions. Geographically, the island is well positioned for trade and business travel.

**Grow** – The Isle of Man has maintained its AAA rating from both Standard & Poor's and Moody's with the release of the most recent national income figures for 2004. The per capita GDP ratio is up 4% on the UK. Annual growth is 6.3% in real terms with the UK estimated at less than 2.7% growth and the EU experiencing 2.5% growth for the same period. Growth of 12% in the e-business, retail and high tech manufacturing sectors demonstrates the importance of these sectors to the local economy.

The reasons for this impressive growth and economic performance can be attributed to the policies of the Isle of Man Government delivered by Treasury and the Department of Trade & Industry (DTI). The main function of the DTI is to encourage further economic diversification through increased foreign investment in the Island.

**Compete** – The DTI offers a package of grants and incentives which help to encourage local businesses to grow, develop and remain competitive on a global scale. The DTI continues to educate and train local workers to provide businesses with a highly skilled, IT literate workforce. The DTI offers advice and assistance to decision makers who are considering the Isle of Man as the ideal location for their business.

**Low Tax** – In addition to the assistance available from DTI, the Isle of Man is a low tax jurisdiction. There are real benefits available to individuals and businesses to be had by residing in a low tax offshore jurisdiction. Treasury continues to develop a low taxation environment with 0% corporation tax being implemented in 2006. This combined with 0% Capital Gains tax and easy access to the UK stock market provides a very attractive operating environment.

**Communicate** – The Isle of Man has a telecommunications network with secure resilient high bandwidth connections which will meet the needs of any ICT or e-Business. Local network operators, ISPs and software development companies continue to lead the world in telecommunications. IT and e-Business comprise a significant proportion of the local economy and contribute to the continued successful economic performance of the Island.

**Contact –**

Visit our website:

**www.gov.im/dti**

For more information please contact the Department of Trade & Industry's Economic Development Group directly:

Economic Development Group
**Development Manager**
**Hamilton House**
**Peel Road**
**Douglas**
**Isle of Man, IM1 5EP**
Tel: **+44 (0) 1624 687179**
Email: **development@gov.im**
Website: **www.gov.im/dti**

# Property challenges for growing companies

*Be flexible about property to keep growing, advises Howard Good of Fraser CRE, otherwise costs can start to spiral*

## Introduction

Property can be a minefield for any company at any stage of its development. It generally represents a fixed cost that has a long-term commitment with little opportunity for getting rid of the liability. Many large companies find themselves with properties they no longer want but they are unable to free themselves from the burden of the surplus property costs.

Research undertaken by Fraser CRE[1] reveals that the average estimated FRS 12 liability for surplus property for a mid-range to FTSE 100 Company is £22.6 million. (FRS 12, Financial Reporting Standard 12, also known as Accounting Standard 37, sets out how property should be accounted for on the balance sheet.) If this scale of liability were replicated across the whole of the FTSE 100, the liability would total £32 billion. If this figure were then extrapolated across corporate Britain, the FRS 12 liability for UK plc business as a whole could be well in excess of £100 billion.

As you can see, property represents a huge liability on a company's balance sheet.

## The start-up phase

When a business starts up, the issue of premises is a vital one. There will be a number of options to consider which will vary according to the amount of funding the business has been able to secure. Not surprisingly, a cash-rich company will be better positioned to find properties in the absence of a business track record.

Irrespective of the cash situation, every business should adopt a flexible approach in all its arrangements and especially in any commitments that are made on property. The one thing a new business can bank on is that its development will not mirror its business plan. The rate of growth may be more rapid or the business may flounder very quickly. It is essential, therefore, that the managers ensure that the business can respond to those changes, avoid long-term commitment and retain flexibility.

The property requirements will depend on the nature of the business. For an office-based operation, there are many more flexible options than in retail and industry. This is, in part, as a consequence of operators such as Regus developing the concept of flexible office space where rooms, suites or floors can be hired for days, weeks, months or years. There is now a wide range of service providers from offices in industrial units up to the high quality and expensive service provided by Regus. Industrial start-up units do exist – often provided by Local Authorities – but, by their very nature, the time commitment is generally longer and is usually a minimum of six months.

At one end of the spectrum, retail can offer considerable flexibility but that tends to be for poorer locations or in niche speciality shopping areas where the flexibility also allows the landlord to remove under-performing retailers.

## The growth cycle

After a year or so, when a business has achieved some degree of stability and cash flow is still positive, thoughts turn to expansion. It is at this point that the heady excitement of a growing business and anticipation of global domination interfere with good judgement. In this over-enthusiastic state of mind, businesses easily persuade themselves that they need to acquire premises that are much larger than their current ones (to accommodate growth), considerably more up market (to provide the right impression), and usually on a 10-year or longer lease (we need stability and we will be around for a long time). That is when the wheels will start to wobble – or totally fall off – as costs spiral and flexibility is lost.

It is essential that growth is controlled on the property front. Once a 10-year lease has been signed, the liability remains for 10 years and, possibly, beyond if occupation has generated any environmental issues. Examples abound of changes to businesses that have resulted in a surplus property. There was a company that took on a 10-year lease on the strength of being awarded a two-year Local Authority contract. The managers expected the contract to be renewed, but when it wasn't they spent eight years paying out rent that was far more than the profits they had made in the two years of occupation.

Another example is a world-leading IT company that took leases on buildings in the Thames Valley before the properties were built because that was what the development plan showed and they blindly followed the plan. Their marketplace changed, fewer employees were needed, and hence space requirements shrank. As soon as the buildings were completed, they had to find tenants for space that they had never occupied. Unfortunately, it was at the same time as demand in the Thames Valley collapsed.

Of course, there are positive examples. After a couple of years of steady trading, a company took a building, its business boomed, and it soon needed a bigger and better property. The longish lease it had taken as a small business meant that it had surplus space, which, despite the continued growth of the business, was a long-term drag on profits. The flexibility to accommodate changing circumstances has to be retained. Occupiers do not price the benefit of this flexibility and should be prepared to pay more rent or a penalty clause to allow them to break leases.

A fundamental question for any business of any size is: 'How confident is the management team that the business plan will be achieved?' In general, a three-year strategy is generally redundant after one year and, even if the three-year strategy is accurate, it is still only a three-year one, so do not take a 10-year lease.

## Financial impact

At the moment, the accounting for leasehold property is fairly straightforward while the property remains in use, and the impact is on the profit and loss account as and when the expenditure is incurred. This is likely to change as the IASB[2] is looking to introduce an accounting standard that will require all businesses to show property leases as liabilities on their balance sheet. That liability already exists in part with FRS 12 for leases that are now surplus to requirements.

Don't underestimate the substantial costs of vacating a property. The provision that has to be made should reflect the net cost of the liability, which is determined by the gross costs to expiry – rent, rates, service charges, etc, less any likely income. The longer the lease, the greater the net cost and, therefore, the bigger the provision and, with it, the bigger the adverse impact on the balance sheet.[3] Short-term leases will mitigate that risk and the effects that provisions will have on the business, such as raising finance, etc, as well as the cash flow impact of paying for a property that is not needed.

In summary, always seek maximum flexibility and short-term lease arrangements and, if in any doubt, don't sign anything.

## Notes

1. CORE Report 2004 by Fraser CRE.
2. International Accounting Standards Board.
3. For a more detailed explanation of FRS12, see the Fraser CRE booklet on the subject.

Howard Cooke is Managing Director of Fraser CRE, a London-based real estate management and consulting firm dedicated to the corporate occupier market. For further information regarding any of the issues raised in this chapter, please contact Howard, tel: 020 7312 1957; e-mail: hc@frasercre.com.

# Test Valley is open for business!

## Starting up

Thinking of starting your own business? Then you will be looking for all the support that is available. Test Valley Borough Council can help you. We offer a wide range of services including free expert advice from enterprise agencies, grant-aid and easy in-easy out accommodation in a host of centres across the Borough. Supporting new businesses is one of many economic development services offered by Test Valley Borough Council. Business is important to the character and vitality of Test Valley, whether Chilworth Science Park or community village shops. Promoting Andover and Romsey town centres, the growing tourism industry and attracting new businesses to Andover are also key objectives.

## Town Centres

One of the Council's key priorities is to promote Andover and Romsey town centres. Both have recently experienced major environmental improvement schemes. This £2.5m. public investment is a sign of the Council's commitment to strengthening our town centres and making them safer and more attractive for local people and visitors alike.

## Tourism

As a predominantly rural district tourism is slowly and quietly growing in importance. The attractive rural charm of our Conservation Area villages which sit alongside the River Test and the many attractive features have created an industry which generates £125m. and supports more jobs than farming.Test Valley's tourism is intimate in character – Farmers Markets and B & Bs.

## Andover

Andover is a thriving commercial centre with a population of over 40,000. It boasts excellent road communications and is on both the A303/M3 London – West Country route and A34 which connects the south coast ports and the Midlands. On Walworth Industrial Estate, global investment bank, UBS are making a long term investment to upgrade 250,000 square feet of industrial premises to suit modern industrial needs.

**Inward investment is** key to Andover. New businesses are moving in every week but there is a wide range of serviced sites and premises from small offices to high bay warehousing. For the future, outline permission for a 750,000 square foot Andover Business Park has the go-ahead subject to agreements and will cater for the town'ps economic needs for some time to come.

**So whether you are starting-up, investing in an established business or considering re-locating to Test Valley we are here to help you and support our local economy.**

# Business locations

*When a company is expanding or relocating its business units, either nationally or internationally, selecting the right location is critical. Optimizing business location decision making undoubtedly has a major and positive strategic influence upon companies' future commercial success. Tim Heatley, of GVA Grimley, explains why location strategy should be at the heart of all business decisions*

The rapid pace of globalization is providing increasing opportunities for all types of business. This trend can only accelerate, with increasing harmonization between different economies and new opportunities emerging for all types of business to operate in the international arena (through either new market expansions, or the increasing trend of off-shoring low cost business units, such as contact centres and back office functions, to more cost-competitive locations, such as Central and Eastern Europe, India and China). In addition, substantial infrastructural improvements in communications technology and international transport links have also had a major contributing impact in allowing companies ever greater options of where to locate their business. However, the flipside to these accelerating trends is that the growing choice of business locations further increases the chances of making either a sub-optimal or, in extreme cases, a wrong location decision, which can and often does have damaging commercial repercussions for individual companies.

Given the strategic importance of selecting the right location, it is perhaps surprising that many companies often do not take more care during the location assessment to ensure that they get it right. Whilst companies are understandably focused on their core business, increasingly with the current global competitive environment, they must look objectively upon their future location options and the implications that location strategy has for both their business and their business sector. Indeed, just about any factor that is important to the success of a business can be related to location, such as optimizing international tax systems; understanding the political and economic risk of specific country locations; assessing suitable transport links; and, perhaps most important, analysing the long-term availability of suitable skilled staff (the demographics of local populations, including skills, labour costs, labour laws and any other factor that might impact upon a future workforce). A common misconception about business location is that it is all about property, acquiring the right building at the right price. However, real estate is just one factor in the full range of location criteria that each needs to be carefully assessed both from a strategic and a commercial perspective.

There are a great number of issues and tasks to be tackled, often by someone who already has a full-time role in running the business. Often, individuals tasked with bringing about a successful outcome have limited previous experience of the complexities of location decision making and may, in any case, have difficulty dealing, *in situ,* with what can be highly sensitive and confidential issues. A person in charge of relocation may have to make major decisions on a wide range of vital policy and operational areas. Those who overlook a comprehensive location strategy, with a clear chain of decision making supported by the latest independent location intelligence, in favour of a more reactive approach, often struggle with a variety of operational issues. These can include retention of key staff or recruitment problems that can lead to more serious concerns regarding constraints on growth and a potentially increased cost base.

Moving business units, whatever their size, is a daunting task. It is an emotive and often fraught experience, with different people within the organization having very differing opinions as to the best course of action. It needs to be approached with an organized plan to maximize the benefits and reduce any possible negative effects, on both customers and existing staff. Some tough decisions will almost certainly have to be made in arriving at the best solution, and for those without any previous experience, it can be an intimidating task to select the most suitable long-term location in which to expand. It is an old adage that you can't please all of the people all of the time, but it certainly applies to almost any relocation project. Indeed, a key issue is often the lack of understanding of the impact of location change upon a company's stakeholders, such as senior management, staff, the customer base, shareholders and, indeed, overall public perception. How many companies stop to think carefully about what their operating locations say about their company? The right choice of location can give a real competitive edge and can also reflect the response of customers in terms of what your location says about your company.

In addition, it is crucial not to neglect other critical priorities related to a new location. These can include consultative programmes for all those who will be affected and advice to management on both internal and external communication during the relocation process. The supply of key information can make all the difference to the morale of key workers and major clients who will need reassurance in a time of change. By adopting a well thought out and structured approach to selecting a location, this can help, to some extent, to 'future proof' the balance sheet against known expenditure and substantially reduce the potential risks to a company and its future performance. At the same time, it maximizes the opportunity for capitalizing on the potential benefits that can be found in a new location and a new working environment. The key is to centre the location decision firmly at the heart of the business plan and assess the pros and cons of any move against what is ultimately best for the organization and its bottom line.

If you do not have the necessary in-house expertise to take on the full process of appraising and selecting new locations, it is worth looking at outside help to provide you with expert and independent advice to assess the key factors required for successful business location decision making. These include:

■ potential strategic risks to the business and any impacting regulatory issues;
■ detailed assessment of preferred locations across all the key location decision-making factors;
■ advice on staff retention, recruitment and redundancy initiatives and any union negotiation;
■ detailed assessment of the local labour market (including available skills and costs);
■ identifying any available government grants and financial incentives; and
■ financial analysis to support the business case.

Every company and every location decision is different depending on the objectives of the business. There are location checklists and 'what to do' guides available, but a 'one size fits all' formulaic approach simply does not work. Indeed, the one thing that all businesses do have in common is that they are all unique. There is no such thing as the perfect location – what might be a solution for one company may not be right for another. Companies are recognizing the importance of optimizing location decision making, that it should not be viewed as a daunting distraction from the core business, but an excellent opportunity to gain a real competitive advantage.

Tim Heatley is lead partner at GVA Grimley international property advisers for GVA Locations, a specialist team helping companies to find the right national and international locations to base their business units. GVA Locations has assessed over 175 locations within the UK and over 700 worldwide.

# The Netherlands: one of Europe's major business hubs

The central geographical position of the Netherlands, combined with good accessibility and excellent infrastructure, are among the reasons why numerous European, American and Asian companies have established their facilities in the Netherlands – whether it be a European headquarters, a shared services centre, a customer care centre, a distribution and logistics operation or an R&D facility.

The country's pro-business environment creates a gateway to Europe that helps international

hubs with over 100 international awards to its credit. The country is also classified among the most 'wired' in the world – and is a dynamic force in electronic commerce, communications and outsourcing. Over a decade of investment in high-speed Internet, cable and digital communication systems – and the rapid adoption of state-of-the-art computer and mobile phone technologies – yet further pre-qualifies The Netherlands as a base for companies.

The Netherlands has one of the most highly

companies succeed throughout the continent. An international outlook and openness to foreign investment is firmly engrained in the Dutch culture, and this has yielded a wealth of world-class business partners who know how to deal with the global business challenges in today's economy.

The Netherlands' port of Rotterdam ranks as one of the world's largest while its Schiphol Airport is recognised as one of Europe's major business

educated, flexible and motivated workforces in Europe. Dutch professionals are also among the most multilingual in the world, enabling them to successfully operate in companies across any industry serving customers throughout the continent.

The Netherlands has a high standard of living with lower costs of housing, education and cultural activities than in most Western European countries.

*For more information on the Dutch business climate go to* **www.nfia.co.uk**

# 8

# Corporate finance

# Accounting and reporting requirements

*By choosing the right path today for your growing business's reporting requirements, says Steven Brice of international accounting and advisory firm, Mazars, you can save time and money tomorrow*

Even those with only half an eye on the accounting press cannot have failed to notice that accounting and reporting requirements are changing rapidly. The last few years have seen an unprecedented number of changes to both accounting and legal requirements and that trend is only set to continue.

Companies that have good corporate governance and transparent financial reporting are valued at a premium by investors in relation to their competitors. Anticipating future changes in reporting requirements and making sure that your business is on the correct path to either take advantage of them or mitigate their effects is therefore key to ensuring the success of your company in the future.

## The knock-on effects of IFRS

Of the recent spate of financial reporting requirements that have been issued, one of the main driving forces has been the impending move to International Financial Reporting Standards (IFRS) for listed companies in Europe. The International Accounting Standards Board (IASB) has clearly been driving in the fast lane of the motorway for a while now and listed entities have had no choice but to get into the slipstream of this juggernaut or get left behind.

Many companies outside the listed sector are no doubt discounting the importance of these developments, but this is not necessarily the right approach to take. Smaller companies should note that the IASB has a massive influence on other standard setters, not least our own standard setter in the UK, the Accounting Standards Board (ASB).

The IASB's plans are having a knock-on effect that is threatening to cause tailbacks for non-listed UK entities for years to come. Without doubt, UK accounting is changing and there is no better time to plan the best route for your business than now.

# The routes available to growing businesses

A number of routes are possible for growing UK businesses, ranging from continuing to account under the UK's own accounting standards at the one extreme, to voluntarily adopting IFRS at the other.

## UK Generally Accepted Accounting Principles (GAAP)

Cautious companies may well see the continuing use of UK GAAP to be the safest and therefore the best option. While some convergence of UK GAAP with IFRS is inevitable, the ASB may hold out against adopting some of the IASB's more radical proposals such as fair valuation of all contingent liabilities. In addition, where convergence does occur, there will be the benefit of having been able to see the problems that listed companies have had in implementing these issues in practice and being able to learn from their experiences.

## The FRSSE

UK GAAP also has the benefit of allowing smaller companies to take advantage of reduced disclosure requirements by applying the provisions of the Financial Reporting Standard for Smaller Entities (FRSSE).

The FRSSE allows UK companies qualifying as small to apply a single stand-alone accounting standard rather than taking account of the disclosure requirements of each individual accounting standard. Given that there are over 20 individual UK standards and that the number looks likely to increase further, this is not an inconsiderable advantage. Furthermore, the ASB has recently extended this principle to the reporting requirements of company law, producing in its own words a 'one-stop shop' standard for smaller entities. There is currently no equivalent of the FRSSE for companies applying IFRS, although see the comments below about the possible introduction of one.

## Voluntary adoption of IFRS

At the other extreme lies the option of voluntarily adopting IFRS. Non-listed UK companies are permitted to prepare their individual and consolidated accounts under IFRS, and many will no doubt choose to do so. For growing companies there are clear advantages in doing so should they be planning to float on a stock exchange in the future. Although there are no requirements to adopt IFRS, it is likely that IFRS will be seen as best practice and, as such, companies voluntarily adopting it are likely to benefit from the valuation premium referred to above.

The decision to go down the road of voluntarily adopting IFRS should not be taken lightly, however. For one thing, the IFRS route is seen as a one-way option: once a company has started down this road it will only be able to reverse where (in the Government's words) it has 'good reason' to do so.

The cost should not be underestimated either. Changing accounting policies and restating financial statements can be a costly task for any business, but companies that will suffer in particular are those with financial instruments (a term that is widely defined), those engaged in hedging activities, and those with defined benefit pension schemes or which have granted share options to employees.

Companies should also be aware of the increased volatility that will result from the greater use of fair values in the balance sheet and the recognition of the resultant gains and losses in the income statement under IFRS. An associated issue that has not as yet been fully addressed is the extent to which 'mark-to-market' accounting will create realized profits and losses and so affect distributable profits. Until guidance is finalized on this matter, companies should pay heed to the risks of finding themselves in a dividend trap on transition to IFRS.

## International FRSSE

As mentioned above, there is currently no equivalent under IFRS to the FRSSE. There are, however, plans afoot to change this.

The IASB is currently consulting on the possibility of introducing such a standard for small and medium-sized enterprises (SMEs). Readers should be aware, however, that the term 'SME' as used overseas does not equate to what we in the UK understand by it. Instead, it denotes what we in the UK would consider to be mid-tier companies, and will not cover companies that are designated by UK company law as small.

This mid-tier solution may be appealing for many companies, but the project still has a long way to go and the final outcome, in particular whether there will also be different measurement rules as well as reduced disclosure, is still uncertain at this juncture.

## Starting down the road

It is more important than ever that finance directors keep abreast of changes in financial reporting and ensure they are starting from an informed position. Certain issues that are currently on the IASB agenda awaiting resolution may just sway the ultimate decision one way or another for a company.

Whatever route your company decides upon, you should remember that having the confidence of your investors in your financial reporting is seen as a critical factor in a company's success.

In today's age of increasingly modern business, transparent financial reporting that allows the reader to see through the complexity has never been more valued.

Steven Brice is a partner and Head of the Financial Reporting Advisory Unit for Mazars, the international accountancy and advisory firm. He devotes the majority of his time to technical consultancy for large corporate clients across the world, specializing in International Financial Reporting Standards (IFRS). Steven is currently Vice-President of the London Society of Chartered Accountants (LSCA) and Chairman of their Technical Committee.

Mazars' clients include a wide range of owner-managed businesses (including some of the UK's fastest growing entrepreneurial businesses) as well as international corporate groups and listed companies (15 per cent of the FTSEurofirst 100), public sector bodies and numerous private individuals.

For more information, tel: 020 7377 1000; e-mail: steven.brice@mazars. co.uk; website: www.mazars.co.uk.

# Acquiring a business

*It is a good time to be making acquisitions, says Andrew Millington, a corporate finance partner with Mazars, but the risks remain high*

In many ways the current financial climate is ideal for making acquisitions – a broadly stable economy that continues to grow at a manageable rate; low interest rates and inflation; availability of targets; ready access to finance; and a knowledgeable, developed M&A business community.

In many industries and sectors the drive for acquisitions continues to reflect the need to consolidate, develop critical mass, take advantage of market opportunities or react to the world economy. A well prepared management team able to take advantage of the acquisition opportunities that exist not only substantially strengthens the core business, but can also add significant shareholder value.

Whilst financial climate and market dynamics are a useful backdrop, they are not enough to guarantee a successful acquisition. To improve the chance of success or in reality minimize the risks, any team needs to:

■ be properly prepared with a cohesive and adaptable workforce who will work to integrate a new member of the group;
■ have a clear acquisition strategy;
■ have a well communicated integration plan;
■ have a strong core business;
■ have a robust financing structure behind the plan.

In general terms, larger entities attract higher valuations. Size does matter. It is associated with a stronger market proposition, security of revenue and underlying earnings stability, strong management and infrastructure, and often with potential. This is demonstrated by the higher price earnings multiples attributed to reported transactions for large private companies and also to publicly quoted companies.

The market usually expects unquoted companies to sell at a multiple of, perhaps, up to half that of a quoted competitor. The discount factor reduces for larger entities where aspects such as scale or market position can be demonstrated. It also leads to one compelling aspect of many well considered acquisitions. If a business can acquire on a p/e below its own current rating, it will enhance shareholder value even before savings or other benefits of an acquisition.

## Rationale for acquiring a business

Research into M&A activity continues to show that the majority of acquisitions fail to meet their original objectives, or indeed fail.

To avoid the pitfalls and to fulfil shareholders' expectations it is imperative that proper planning is carried out both before a search process is undertaken and then before the acquisition is completed. Even if an acquisition is being contemplated as the result of an opportunity that has arisen unexpectedly, it is important that, before moving forward, it can be justified as part of a clear strategy for the future.

An acquisition is usually the riskiest investment a company can make, often compounded by the use of borrowed money to finance the deal. The consequences of getting it wrong can mean destroying shareholder value, significant diversion of management time and resources and, in extreme situations, even the collapse of the whole company.

## Fundamentals

Before embarking on an acquisition, fundamental questions to answer include:

- Where can an acquisition deliver improved shareholder value?
- How could it enhance earnings?
- Is there potential to improve in the future?

## Vision

In whatever circumstances an acquisition is being contemplated, it should be part of the overall 'vision' of the purchaser, whether shareholders or senior management, and a number of questions need to be addressed:

- Where is the existing business heading?
- What are the aims of the shareholders and management?
- What is the exit strategy?

Once agreement has been reached by the shareholders and management on these fundamentals, the question of an acquisition in this context can be considered. This collective process should be committed to paper (one side, no more!). If a formal business planning process is undertaken this document should provide the context for the plan.

If significant funding is required for the acquisition, the answers to these questions will be tested by the investment managers or bankers before deciding whether to invest.

## Resources

For any investment, assessment of existing resources will be required:

∎ How is the funding to be raised?
∎ Do you have sufficient management and personnel with spare capacity to cope with the deal, both during and after completion?
∎ Do you have sufficient expertise to assess and then run the new company?
∎ Can any existing resources be diverted to help the acquisition? For example, you may need to withdraw from a particular market or to sell off under-performing sectors of the existing business.
∎ Who will be responsible at senior level, post acquisition?

It will also mean that during the acquisition process you are more prepared, present the acquirer in a more professional and considered manner, and improve your chance of winning any competitive auction. It also can make the negotiations process easier to conclude.

## Structure

Although the ultimate structure of the deal will often be driven by the outcome of negotiations with the vendor and, separately, the financiers, it is important to have an initial understanding of the preferred structure of the acquisition and what is likely to be achievable in the prevailing market conditions:

∎ Legal structure: Will the new company be a subsidiary or is its business going to be brought into an existing business? This may affect what is purchased – shares or assets.
∎ Day-to-day running: Is it going to be a stand-alone company with its own management? Will new management be required? Can it be safely managed using existing resources?
∎ Treatment of any associated property – ideally do you wish to acquire or lease?

Identify the likely key issues and ensure the planning process investigated these aspects early, otherwise significant time can be wasted.

Preliminary consideration should also be given to effective legal protection by use of warranties and indemnities in the sale and purchase agreement, as well as retentions, earnouts and due diligence.

## Organic growth

In acquisitive groups it is often ironic how much time and value will be invested in discrete acquisitions and, in comparison, how little is set aside for investment focused on organic growth. It is usually more cost-effective and less of a risk to invest in the existing business than it is to buy a company. A joint venture or purchasing a minority stake as a prelude to an acquisition may also be appropriate.

From an outsider's perspective it is important that growing turnover and profit should be derived from organic growth and suitable acquisition opportunities. Most acquirers will, at some stage, also need to consider an exit: just as they will seek growth potential when buying businesses so they will have to demonstrate it when putting their own company up for sale if they are to maximize value.

Andrew Millington is a corporate finance partner with Mazars, the international accountancy and advisory firm. He has more than 14 years' experience and has led a large number of M&A and MBO transactions for companies of varying size in a wide range of industry sectors. Andrew is in charge of corporate finance in the firm's Midlands region and head of private equity nationally. Prior to joining Mazars, he was an investment director at Barclays Private Equity.

Mazars acts for some of the fastest-growing entrepreneurial companies in the UK, offering a complete range of accountancy and business advisory services, including audit and assurance, tax advisory and compliance, corporate recovery and insolvency, consulting, forensic and investigations, corporate finance and financial services for private individuals.

For more information, tel: 0121 212 7711; e-mail: andrew.millington@mazars.co.uk; website: www.mazars.co.uk.

# Grooming a company for sale

*Failing to plan a company's life cycle can have a negative effect on value, says Adrian Alexander, a corporate finance partner at Mazars*

It is a fundamental 'given' in every boardroom that the directors should have a clear idea of the company's economic position and its likely development. Like humans, companies follow a fairly typical life cycle – they are created, flourish, grow and mature, or they may founder and, in the long run, expire. Ultimately every company is at some point in their life cycle a buyer or a seller and as such should be planning ahead for either eventuality.

Many businesses undertake little planning, which can result in the sale process becoming far more arduous and complicated than necessary, can have a negative effect on value and, in some cases, may mean that a sale is not achievable.

If selling the company is the most likely outcome, undertaking a properly planned 'grooming' exercise is essential.

## Commercial planning points

There are a number of commercial, accounting and legal aspects that can be planned for which will help maximize value at the point of exit. In addition, taxation planning is normally an important consideration in any sale.

The key for all prospective purchasers will be the quality of the underlying maintainable earnings and future growth prospects.

Areas that should be considered in the planning process include:

- Maintainable earnings should be as high as possible. To achieve this:
  - Cease any loss-making activities, divisions or speculative development work which has a long-term payback period.
  - Review any major supply or sale contracts which underpin the business going forward. Any contracts about to end should be renewed or extended.
  - Ensure that any acquisition programme is complete at least a year before the planned exit.
  - Review overheads, but be careful not to cut out anything that will damage the long-term health of the business, as this will be identified by purchasers when they carry out their due diligence.
- Growth should be demonstrated in the period preceding the sale and in a justifiable forecast with increasing profits, ideally from improving market share.
- Reduce the gearing as much as possible and increase the net asset value. The potential increase in value will have to be assessed against remuneration and dividend policy, although most purchasers will discount 'proprietorial' remuneration in their valuations.
- Review items such as freehold properties. Are they to be sold as part of the company or excluded from the deal? The position relating to property needs careful consideration before the deal; property can be a major issue to prospective purchasers. Many purchasers will be attracted (or not put off!) if there is flexibility within the property portfolio.
- Unless the business being sold is property-based, the purchaser may find that a short lease is preferable so that parts of the business can be closed and savings made. Alternatively, the purchaser may have unutilized space which they want to fill or have ambitious expansion plans which will require a move of premises. If the vendor has a particular requirement, then the necessary action needs to be made in advance of the sale.
- Sell off any surplus assets or subsidiaries not required for the core trading activities. These will be discounted anyway in future valuations.
- Identify surplus cash and a mechanism to realize this additional shareholder value.
- Avoid any unnecessary capital expenditure as this may not be fully reflected in the purchaser's valuation.
- Consider legal, VAT and PAYE/NIC audits to make sure there are no hidden problems.
- Does the business have reliable management information? The reliability of management information is more likely to be an issue for smaller businesses. However, being small is not a valid excuse when the time for the sale approaches. Potential purchasers will quite rightly ask for fairly detailed management information including forecasts. Just because the vendor has successfully run the business for 25 years without producing a single set of management accounts or forecasts, it is unreasonable to expect other businesses to act in the same way. Many owner-managed businesses are sold to listed plcs that have stringent reporting methods. They are likely to be more impressed if the quality of management information is

good. This issue must therefore be addressed as soon as possible in the planning process.

∎ Ensure that there is a suitable management structure with the right individuals in the key roles. This is particularly important when it is not a trade sale or the vendor is seen to be key to the running of the business. However, beware of increased costs in the short term without increased revenue, as this will reduce the maintainable earnings.

∎ If the vendor is an owner-manager and closely involved in the day-to-day running of the business, certain key questions need to be addressed:
  – Does the owner wish to remain involved on a medium- to long-term basis after the sale?
  – Is the owner fulfilling a vital management function not performed by anybody else?
  – After the sale will he or she retain the motivation to carry on working?
  – Can the business function without the owner-manager?

∎ If part of a business, for example a division or a subsidiary of a larger group, is being sold you should identify whether it can be sold as a stand-alone entity:
  – Can group functions be easily replaced?
  – Are the buildings, assets and employees separate from the rest of the group?
  – Is the accounting information on which valuations are to be performed accurate? Does it reflect all the costs and identify inter-group items?
  – Will inter-group pricing policies be maintained after the sale?

∎ Address matters with dissenting shareholders and ensure they all want to sell. If not, action needs to be taken to ensure they will not hold up any deal.

∎ Finally, give the factory a coat of paint to improve the image. Every little helps!

## Conclusion

Companies that are most likely to sell at the best price are those that have planned properly, on a timely basis and where the owners have become 'investors' in their own companies and are not involved in day-to-day management. Prospective purchasers will be looking for well run, profitable companies with future growth prospects and good quality management and employees. To ensure the company is well placed to achieve maximum value for the vendor, the importance of forward planning and meticulous grooming should not be overlooked.

Adrian Alexander is a corporate finance partner with Mazars, the international accountancy and business advisory firm. Based in the firm's Brighton office, he acts for owner-managed businesses, supporting them through major transactions and is active in all the main corporate finance disciplines: mergers and acquisitions, sales, raising finance and investigation work.

Adrian is the author of several articles on selling and acquiring businesses in Institute of Chartered Accountants publications.

Mazars acts for some of the fastest-growing entrepreneurial companies in the UK, offering a complete range of accountancy and business advisory services, including audit and assurance, tax advisory and compliance, corporate recovery and insolvency, consulting, forensic and investigations, corporate finance and financial services for private individuals.

For more informatiion, tel: 01273 206778; e-mail: adrian.alexander@mazars.co.uk; website: www.mazars.co.uk.

# 9

# Managing growth

# Entrepreneurial management for the ambitious business

*Capitalizing on potential demands different skills from creating an enterprise, says Dr Philip Vale at Durham Business School. No wonder so few SMEs make it past this stage*

Successful new businesses capitalize on a business idea that has the potential to generate profit. It is critical that attention is focused on generating profit from the idea as effectively as possible in the start-up phase. Unforeseen obstacles and delays can all too easily jeopardize success if attention shifts from the immediately pressing issues. The generic skill sets required to introduce and manage a new business include:

- commercial acumen;
- project management;
- statutory administration;
- business management.

A minority of owner-manager directors will have all the management and administration skills necessary for the new venture. Some skills can be bought in; administrative skills can be bought from accountants and solicitors, while the project management skills and commercial acumen are harder to sub-contract or develop in a timely and relevant way that reflects business needs.

Establishing a new SME and generating appropriate profit is a large task and a major challenge: the time and money invested by the founders represent a major commitment. On its own, establishing a new business can be an engrossing and exhausting process that is only achieved after years of hard work and sacrifice.

The disappointing news is that establishing a new business is only step one: directing a growing business that simultaneously captures the potential for growth and creates the potential for sustained growth, is over and above business management. The two tasks of capitalizing and creating potential on an ongoing, systematic basis, have different skill and time requirements. The new skills needed have to be developed or acquired while maintaining the core business. The generic skills sets include:

- strategic insight;
- portfolio management;
- investment appraisal;
- risk appraisal.

Given the demands of running the core business it is easy to see why such a small proportion of new and small firms develop to become significant and influential operations.

The growth stage of development is the point at which entrepreneurial management is critical. This stage of development does not require an entrepreneur – the business is already established, running and profitable. The growth stage does not require overly bureaucratic or professional procedures associated with large, publicly quoted companies. What is required is:

- maintaining a profitable and stable core business;
- the ability to establish and manage a portfolio of innovative initiatives;
- establishing and engineering a process to progress initiatives in a structured and economic way.

There is scope for disaster at every turn, with so many new projects being considered, developed and instigated at the same time.

To maximize the chances of success the managing director will need to keep two areas of the business in managed harmony; see Figure 9.1.1.

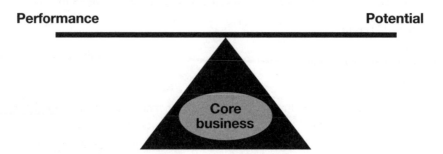

**Figure 9.1.1**   Managed harmony

# Performance

Managing the performance of the core business is critical: the performance achieved during the life of the business is a good pointer to the performance that will be achieved in the future. Approaches to monitoring and controlling key performance metrics are well known. Performance includes more than just financial performance and the most critical areas to monitor for any particular business should reflect the particular characteristics of that business. The Balanced Score Card approach can be helpful for more established businesses. For smaller businesses, performance measured by key metrics in the four key functional domains will normally be adequate.

# Functional performance domains

1. Finance.
2. Operations.
3. Markets.
4. People.

For each one of the domains above there will typically be three or four critical metrics.

## 1. Finance

■ Profit to sales percentage provides an indication of trading efficiency.
■ Profit to capital employed provides an indication of financial efficiency.
■ Working capital to sales provides an indication of operating efficiency.

## 2. Operations

■ *Utilization* of resource as measured by space, plant and people.
■ *Efficiency* focusing on in-bound and out-bound logistics together with resource use.
■ *Quality* measured by returns, complaints and re-works.

## 3. Markets

■ Sales growth – year-on-year and relative to competitors.
■ Market growth – by turnover, geographic region and consumer.
■ Price maintenance – in real terms.
■ New sales – on top of repeat business.

## 4. People

■ Commitment – to the task, team and business.
■ Competence – for current and future operations.
■ Cost-effectiveness – profit per pound of wages.
■ Communication – within and between teams, from top to bottom and side to side.

# Potential

The idea of actually engineering potential is becoming more widely recognized in established organizations. There will always be unforeseen opportunities that present themselves to a more flexible and responsive management. These opportunities may come along in a timely way that allows the fortunate business to grow and prosper.

In the entrepreneurial and managed business, opportunities will be cultivated: time and money will be invested to ensure an appropriate array of opportunities that can be developed in a structured and strategic fashion.

## *Potential bias*

Most trading organizations that recognize the requirement to be continually developing new income streams have a propensity to focus on one area of potential to the exclusion of other legitimate areas; for example, some organizations have sophisticated and energetic R&D departments that focus exclusively on up-grading the products offered to customers. These firms operate 'business as usual' policies elsewhere in the organization and thereby overlook the full range of opportunities.

Other organizations focus on the removal of costs from their internal processes so that the value for money proposition is continually being improved. The sophistication of these continual improvement processes can be impressive, but their development often takes place at the expense of other legitimate areas of opportunity.

In the entrepreneurially managed business the key domains for growth potential are purposefully identified and researched as part of a strategic process; see Figure 9.1.2.

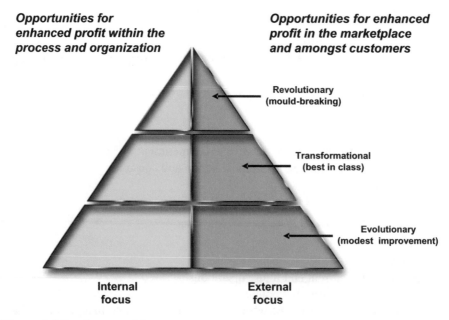

**Figure 9.1.2** Opportunities

## Key domains of potential

### The internal focus

Within any organization there will be opportunities for projects and change that make the organization more efficient and effective and thereby a more significant force in a competitive arena. Trawling the opportunities that exist within the organization requires a structured and disciplined approach if the full potential is to be exploited in a coherent way. Some organizations are exemplary and have sophisticated, well documented procedures, to ensure maximum value is achieved. One such approach is the Six Sigma method.

### The external focus

The customers and markets served by the products and services of a business will always be changing and reconfiguring to produce the prospect of new products that either 'bundle' a new set of benefits or 'de-bundle' existing offerings so that the customer's needs are more precisely met. Simultaneously, there will be advances in technology, changes in fashion and in the legislative environment, all of which create additional external opportunities. Some organizations have invested heavily to trawl the environment for developments and opportunities for new offerings. Whole teams are brain-storming and creating scenarios so that new products and services can be developed to satisfy emerging needs.

## Degrees of potential

Whether the opportunities have been trawled from the internal or external environment they can be further classified by the level of investment and time taken to develop and by the risk and magnitude of the potential return. It is useful to think of these business opportunities as falling into one of three groups.

### 1. The evolutionary

Small changes to existing processes and products.

Efficiency oriented, tailoring of product or service more closely to customer requirements or the refining of logistics and processes more effectively, so that greater resource use efficiency can be achieved. Evolutionary or refining activity produces incremental improvements and are now widely recognized as critical for sustained existence in a dynamic marketplace. Many manufacturing operations have operated continuous improvement programmes of one form or another for over two decades. More energy and focus seems to be applied to the production/operations functions than to other internal functions, although there is no reason why this should be so. Refining events by their very nature are low risk. The market or process is well known, the development is relatively modest and potentially informed by reliable cost or market data. The corollary is that the potential profit from this activity is also modest and short lived.

## 2. The transformational

A significant shift in product or process that aligns the business offering with that of the 'best in class'.

Development oriented; a discrete movement away from what has gone before. The origins and path of progress are there to be seen, however. Accommodating shifting preference patterns, the activity is more than incremental, it involves greater risk and investment but does offer the prospect of enhanced profit streams with longer life cycles.

## 3. The revolutionary

A mould-breaking shift in process or product that has no precedent and provides the prospect of achieving industrial or commercial leadership.

Mould-breaking: new and without precedent, opening the way to further activity and opportunities. These opportunities are high risk and potentially require large amounts of investment. There is the real prospect that the revolutionary opportunities can produce substantial levels of profit over long periods of time and introduce the prospect of the growth business becoming a leader in its industrial or commercial sector.

# Summary

For the established business to be entrepreneurially managed and for it to achieve levels of growth that exceed those of competitor firms will require that key strategic performance metrics are defined, measured and managed in an orthodox and professional way. In the past this would have been described as 'good management' and if the performance metrics did provide a comprehensive, or holistic, assessment of the organization, the management would have been described as 'exemplary'. For today's growth business this level of management is the minimum starting point.

The additional requirement for the fast growth firm is that there continues to be an adequate pool of potential that can be harvested to create new profit streams in the future. This is an area of activity that can be overlooked in the frenetic, high paced, action packed, daily management of the firm. Progress and effort developing potential can be overlooked for one or two years without there being any apparent impact on performance. The directors of successful growth companies, however, recognize that it is the potential for future performance that determines the value of the business and hence the amount of wealth being created. They will allocate the required time and ensure the performance/potential balance.

Increasingly directors of all companies will be expected to achieve the balance between potential and performance and when this expectation has become ubiquitous, new and differentiating demands will be placed on the directors of new growth companies. In the meantime, there continues to be scope to outperform and outgrow the competition.

Philip Vale is Director of Executive Education and Head of the Department of Executive Education and Enterprise at Durham Business School. The school is an internationally recognized, research-led provider of undergraduate, postgraduate and post-experience programmes for students, companies and executives from around the world.

Philip has over 25 years' experience with entrepreneurial organizations from the private and public sectors, representing small and large organizations in many countries. Prior to joining Durham, Philip established the Centre for Entrepreneurial Development at the University of Glasgow and has been involved in a private capacity as an investor, consultant and director to numerous organizations around the world.

Durham Business School offers executive education and enterprise development programmes for organizations at all stages of their development; from start-up companies, through the mid-corporate sector, through to the national and international corporates, and also offers programmes and consultancy for local and national government and not-for-profit organizations. The school has a full portfolio of MBA degrees, specialist masters, PhDs and doctorates in business administration, and is accredited by AMBA and EQUIS. It is recognized to be one of the top UK business schools.

For further information, tel: 0191 334 5311; e-mail: director.execed@durham. ac.uk

**Process Management International**

# Managing a growing business

For small and medium businesses, one of the biggest conundrums they face is how to grow whilst maintaining and developing the quality of the services/products that made the company successful. This is where Process Management International Ltd can help you grow successfully.

PMI has been a leader in applied process improvement since the 1980s, working in all aspects of change, across every organisational size and sector. We can work with you to jointly develop and implement a programme that will include your existing methods and competencies, enabling lasting change at the right pace. Whether you attend our open seminars or engage us for your own comprehensive programme, your achievement will be our driver.

Not only do we provide consultancy, project support and training for top management, but also for all levels within the company. Our consultants have a great depth of experience which they bring from their current and previous careers.

To help SMEs in particular with the development of their people, we have an impressive selection of on-line learning programmes combined with classroom training which can be tailored to meet your needs. This brings many benefits:

- Reduction in time off the job for classroom training
- Adaptability and convenience
- Efficiency and cost reduction
- Ability to monitor progress

For further information visit our web site: www.pmi.co.uk

# We will guide you to your goal

Contact: Process Management International Ltd • Argent Court • Sir William Lyons Road • Coventry CV4 7EZ
tel: 024 7641 9089 • e-mail: sales@pmi.co.uk • web site: www.pmi.co.uk

# Joined-up leadership in SMEs

*Lead your growing organization as a system, advises Jan Gillett and Jane Seddon of Process Management International*

In this chapter we propose a set of philosophies and methods that provide a robust foundation for managing a growing business as a system. Leaders who develop their skills in managing in this way can satisfy the increasing demands of large customers and improve their own profits at the same time.

## Managing the consequences of success

Many business leaders find growth to be a treadmill of having to respond to never-ending challenges of how important this year is, how unique this set of targets is, maybe their very fortune is on the line if this customer walks away or that project does not perform. Developing businesses often reach a crisis point in their growth when the great idea that has generated the products, services and customers is no longer enough to overcome the difficulties resulting from extra customers, staff or service and product problems. Such crises can lead to the business failing. Leaders have three choices to make in response.

One is maybe to retrench, concentrating on cost reduction or cash generation, regardless of the longer-term consequences. The business survives another year while someone else gets the bullet, but it's a gloomy approach to take for very long. And at the end of it all, the business itself may not have that vital spark of innovation or reputation that attracts real value when the time comes to sell.

Or maybe the founder recruits professional management in the hope that they will be able to get things organized and methodical. The well known risk here is that the newcomers don't understand the culture, or the uniqueness that created the demand in the first place, and the cost to the individual employees, both existing and new, can be huge. And the reader will no doubt know of many cases where the founder felt forced to move back in to rescue his or her own company.

The best choice is to take on the task oneself and learn how to think and act in systemic terms – joined-up management. This involves ensuring that everyone is making connections across the organization, not ploughing a lone and counter-productive furrow, enabling them to focus on the opportunities as the wood grows not just the obvious figures from the trees they happen to be standing next to. Such characteristics have always marked successful, growing businesses, but now at last we have a rigorous philosophy and methodology to underpin the entrepreneurial skills that get a new venture off the ground.

## Some background to validate the ideas

From 1950, Dr W Edwards Deming taught the benefits of joined-up thinking to leaders of companies in Japan. He proposed that they consider their organization as an interdependent system, not just in departmental or functional terms. The system should focus on its customers, not itself. We have all benefited from the revolution in quality and efficiency that followed.

Deming also introduced the Plan, Do, Study, Act (PDSA) cycle that has become the heart of Toyota's and others' approach to improvement (see Figure 9.2.1). It is a

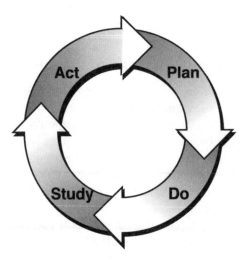

**Figure 9.2.1**   Deming's cycle

learning system, linking study of events to planning changes. Studying events provides data to compare with what was predicted. Learning comes from understanding the differences. It is the scientific method, so long the foundation for invention and innovation in the Western world, but hardly applied at all to management. Until now.

We have countless examples of small-scale application of this principle, in the form of process mapping, understanding variation, planning and project tools that are based upon PDSA. Two examples demonstrate the benefits of the thinking.

1. Take the case of a small business purchasing printing services for literature and promotional materials. The conventional approaches tend to be either to put each job out to tender, or to stay without thought with one company for many years. In the one case the drawbacks are inevitable from buying on price from people who don't understand you, whilst in the other you become dependent upon someone else's expertise.

The systemic leader joins up the processes. Recognizing the interdependencies, the person editing the materials spent a week working in the printer's office, designing wedding invitations, generating proofs – typical jobbing work. At the end of the week she understood all the operations that took place between sending the file for production and receiving the finished product back in the office. Most of all she could understand what the supplier could do best, and is able to take advantage of this to speed up her own processes.

2. Or consider the brief to be given to members of staff who purchase office consumables. Do they always buy the cheapest, or do they consider the best compromise between cost and performance? Only if they are trained to consider the whole system can they balance the appeal of cheap paper with the hassle of printer jams and smudgy results.

These are small examples, but together they amount to a revolution, truly enabling staff to be proactive in thinking on behalf of the company, but with structure and method.

Such thinking is becoming widespread in the car industry, which has seen dramatic improvements in cost and quality from which we all benefit. In particular it underpins the success of Toyota, which has been valued at more than Ford, GM and Chrysler *combined*.

In spite of our examples we can almost hear the reader commenting that such methods are all very well for multinational corporations, but surely it's all too much for SMEs. We believe that two reasons make them essential and applicable. The first is that many small businesses supply larger ones and will progressively find themselves having to achieve the targets of systematic business improvement, be it under the Six Sigma banner or some other name. The second is that since large business systems are simply a collection of smaller ones, the same principles and methods apply: they are just easier in smaller applications.

We are convinced that the case is made for all businesses to see themselves as a system, and understand how to get their processes stable, on the customer's target, and with minimum variation. More robust processes mean less cost, better products and customer service, and thus higher profits.

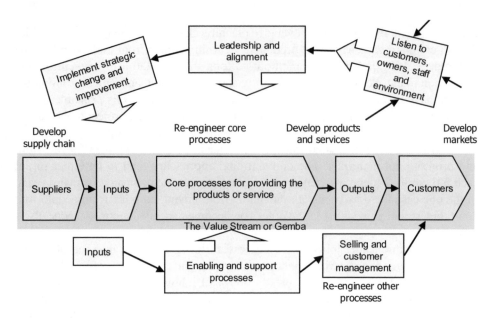

**Figure 9.2.2** PMI's system model

## How to go about improving your system

Everyone can learn how to understand their business processes and objectives, see their place in the system and be able to monitor and improve them in real time. As companies seek to realize gains across the whole organization, so all the disciplines become involved.

Managers start by creating a simple system model of the organization. They identify their customers and suppliers, then define those 'primary' processes that create value, their support processes and their feedback processes for listening to customers. They go on to develop processes for checking out the alignment of the team and others for implementing change.

They can then study their work in a logical and consistent manner. They map the process flow and join it to customers' needs and suppliers' capabilities. First identifying results measures that are meaningful for customers, they then link them to internal measures that they can manage. When these links are validated they gather and analyse data which they use to get the outputs on target with minimum variation.

## What does an improvement programme look like?

In companies employing less than 250 staff the job of leading change will rest with the top managers. Whilst this will seem a burden initially and will undoubtedly be time-consuming, it contains a major benefit. In large companies there is a tendency to start the learning process by delegating project leadership and change roles to middle or junior managers. Whilst this is practical, it has the effect of insulating the top managers from the experience of trying to change their own business.

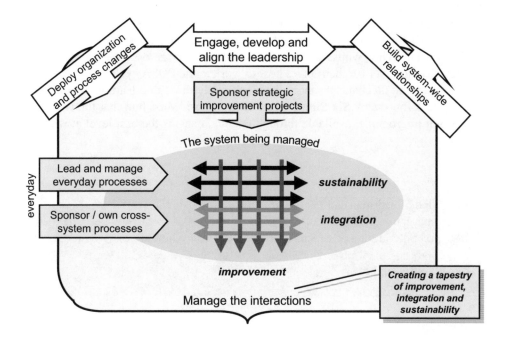

**Figure 9.2.3** Leading the organization as a system

These are the workstreams the top managers must lead:

■ Understand their organization as a system and clarify its purpose and priorities.
■ Identify a small number of initial improvement projects, get them to work and support their success.
■ Manage the interface with the outside: shareholders, financiers, etc, so they understand the investment, risks and benefits.
■ Train and educate the middle and senior managers in the principal methods so they can run the changed processes.
■ Redevelop the roles and jobs of people working in the new system.
■ Control and coordinate the programme as it develops.

All these workstreams come together to create real improvements that can be sustained and developed by your own staff.

## Learning how to understand and improve the system

The best people to lead and learn are the senior managers: indeed in a small business the only possible people. Although they find the time hard to reserve, they never regret doing so. They can see for themselves that the investment is worthwhile, that the issues they encounter are real not imagined, and they are able to lead by example, which is generally how they have been behaving in the development of the business so far.

They discover a robust way of relating their problems to specific processes. They learn methods for getting processes stable and on target, and use the knowledge to join up their own thinking, whilst starting to make connections across the system. In doing so, they also discover for themselves how to work to the PDSA cycle.

The learning mechanism ranges from self-study through e-learning modules, all the way to a four-week Six Sigma Black Belt course. Most find that the two-week Green Belt programme, available through open courses, is the best level at which to start.

Jan Gillett is chairman and Jane Seddon is managing director of Process Management International. Since its foundation in 1980, PMI's portfolio has extended from process and statistical techniques to facilitation, team skills, strategy deployment, and organization development. For further details, tel: 024 7641 9089; e-mail: info@pmi.co.uk.

# Strategic planning

*Failing to plan is planning to fail, says Nick Beech, Head of the Centre for Director Education at Leeds Metropolitan University*

Too many aspiring entrepreneurs' businesses fail because they simply do not devise a thought-through strategic plan, which results in them engaging in enterprises that are often ill designed to meet the needs of their customers or fails to prepare them for the backlash of their competitors.

Some hate the very idea of planning and see it as nothing more than an empty ritual that they escaped from when they left the world of employment. Others believe that strategic planning is something meant only for large corporations, too complex for their needs, that it has no relevance as it does not address the company's immediate business situation. Others feel that they are just too busy running their business to look at what might be around the corner.

However, today as the world becomes more and more competitive and cut throat, a strategic plan is an essential element for any small business that wishes to succeed in the long term.

## What is a strategic plan?

A strategic plan is often seen as an unnecessarily complex document. The problem here is that often SME entrepreneurs will have acquired a planning model that is designed for a major corporation and does not meet the needs of the average SME. The reality is that the magical and mystical strategic plan is nothing more than a thinking tool that allows you to see what you have got and devise a method to best employ it. The plan enables you to identify and then match the core strengths of your business to exploit the available market opportunities.

### Five good reasons to plan

1. Plans enable you to set milestones so that you can measure progress and your performance, enabling you to stay on track and correct mistakes.
2. If you know where you are going there's a good chance you will know when you have got there and can focus your resources on getting there.
3. Only by considering your future destination can you be sure that you are not going in the wrong direction.
4. The plan allows you to prepare for potential challenges en route.
5. A plan provides you with a tool to enable you to communicate your ideas to others.

## A thinking tool

The strategic plan is a thinking framework, a tool to focus the leader and his or her people on the critical issues for the business's growth and, where appropriate, survival. By instinct SME entrepreneurs are pragmatic activists who therefore tend to be more reactive to short-term events rather than focusing on the long-term aim. Producing a strategic plan reinforces a key leadership discipline and process, that of *critical thinking* and, at the top of the organization, thinking smart rather than working hard can pay big benefits.

Writing a strategic plan helps you to clearly identify and set out where you are now and where you could go. It requires you to identify, collect and analyse the key information about your internal and external business environment from which you can identify strengths and weaknesses, opportunities and threats and develop a clear mission and set supportive goals and objectives.

### Be cautious – the devil is in the detail

One major caveat here is that entrepreneurs often, by nature, get over-enthusiastic about the capabilities of their organization, can exaggerate return or not truly consider the practicalities of implementation. Here the word *critical* thinking is important and one must always ask, 'Do we have the resources and skill to implement this strategy in the timescale?' This approach is often difficult for people who live their business, and should not be underestimated. Therefore:

- Be realistic about your strengths and shortcomings.
- Distinguish between where you are today and where you could be in the future, and what impact this will have on you.
- Always consider yourself in context to the competition, both their current strengths and weakness and how they are likely to develop in the future.
- Be specific. Avoid grey areas and attempt to simplify complexity.

Two ideal and simple tools to support you with this is the PEST analysis, an acronym for Political, Economic Social and Technological, which can be used to assess your business environment and SWOT (Strengths, Weaknesses – internal focus, Opportunities and Threats – external focus) which can be used as a framework for evaluating your current strategy and position and help decide the future direction of your organization.

The PEST below provides a sound framework for you to identify which key external factors are likely to impact on your business. In this particular example you have the opportunity to rank the importance of each event by allocating it with a score of 1–10 across each of three criteria:

■ *probability* of occurrence – will it happen;
■ what *impact* it will have on your business; and the
■ *urgency* you give to addressing it.

From this you can identify and rank the important issues to address the needs of your business.

Completing a PEST analysis furnishes you with the critical information to feed in to the Opportunities and Threats in your SWOT analysis. Linked with your company's

| Political | | Probability | Impact | Urgent | Total | Economic | | Probability | Impact | Urgent | Total |
|---|---|---|---|---|---|---|---|---|---|---|---|
| 1 | | | | | | 1 | | | | | |
| 2 | | | | | | 2 | | | | | |
| 3 | | | | | | 3 | | | | | |
| 4 | | | | | | 4 | | | | | |
| Social | | Probability | Impact | Urgent | Total | Technological | | Probability | Impact | Urgent | Total |
| 1 | | | | | | 1 | | | | | |
| 2 | | | | | | 2 | | | | | |
| 3 | | | | | | 3 | | | | | |
| 4 | | | | | | 4 | | | | | |

**Figure 9.3.1** PEST analysis

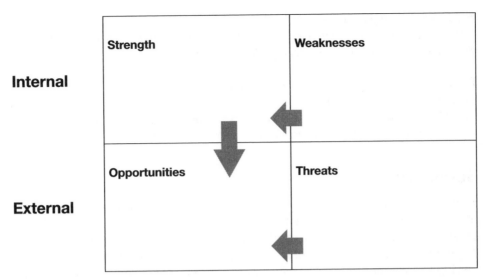

*Aim to turn all factors in to opportunities*

**Figure 9.3.2**   SWOT analysis

Strengths and Weaknesses, they will provide you with a more critical perspective on your capabilities.

When using a SWOT do not assume that all the boxes need to be filled to the brim. You often find that some boxes have more factors in them than others; the importance is the priority you apply to each factor. You may also find that an item will appear in more than one box. The key here is that you properly evaluate the factor, so use them as you find most helpful:

■ Where possible, match your strengths with external opportunities.
■ Weaknesses should be looked at in order to convert them into strengths and thereby provide a basis to develop new opportunities.
■ Threats should be converted into opportunities.

Once completed, the PEST and SWOT form the bedrock of the strategic planning process from which you can start to develop your long- and short-term planning strategy.

## The strategic planning process

■ Mission: *Why does the company exist? What are you in business for?*
■ External environment audit (PEST): *Where is the market going?*
■ Competition audit: *Who are your competitors, their strengths, and what are they doing?*
■ Summary of Opportunities and Threats (OT).

■ Market and product audit.
■ Internal audit: *innovation, financial resources, marketing and CRM capability.*
■ Summary of Strengths, Neutrals and Weaknesses (SW).

From this you can then set long-term objectives and devise and implement short/
medium- and long-term plans.

All that you need to do is to sell and resell the benefits to everyone involved,
secure and ensure the right resources are available and monitor its progress!

## Summary

Even at SME level strategic planning has become a vital tool for competitive advantage
and an essential competence in any business leader's personal skill set. Even though
rapid changes in technology and aggressive competition from home and abroad often
make the business environment less stable and less predictable, there is still a critical
need to know what markets and segments you are in, where the market is going and
what resources and capabilities you have to exploit it. An effective planning process
not only enables you to clearly see what you have but also helps you to optimize your
performance. But remember, a plan is only as good as the information you base it on,
so be critical when conducting your PEST and SWOT analyses.

The Faculty of Business & Law is the largest faculty of Leeds Metropolitan
University with over 5,500 students. Our courses are vocationally focused,
giving students the skills and experiences they need for the future. We have
strong connections with businesses and the professions in Leeds, one of the
leading financial and legal centres in the UK outside London, and the Faculty's
programmes reflect this dynamism. For further information, tel: 0113 283 7531
or visit www.leedsmet.ac.uk/businessandlaw.

Having had over 15 years running his own business, Nick Beech is now
the Head of the Centre for Director Education at Leeds Metropolitan University
where he is programme leader for a number of executive Masters programmes. He
further teaches on the Institute of Directors and Chartered Institute of Marketing
programmes. His specialist fields are governance, strategic management and
marketing.

# Directors' and officers' liability

_In an increasingly litigious and tightly regulated business world, problems for directors can materialize from a huge variety of sources, warns Nick Allen, Directors' and Officers' Liability Product Leader at Royal & SunAlliance_

The fact that company directors can be held personally liable for the decisions they make, or fail to make, in their official capacity is surprisingly little appreciated – especially among smaller businesses.

There is a misleading perception that accepting a directorship in a smaller company is somehow less onerous or leaves the individual less exposed to potential prosecution or investigation for alleged corporate wrongdoing. In practice the opposite is more likely to be the case, as directors of smaller companies tend to have less access to appropriate guidance, advice and support in avoiding the many pitfalls of modern corporate life.

Survey evidence suggests that only around 20 per cent of SME businesses take out directors' and officers' (D&O) liability insurance, which covers individual directors against such liabilities. This figure is worryingly low given the increasingly litigious business environment, and the fact that directors' personal liability is unlimited.

More surprising still are recently reported findings that as many as 30 per cent of SME directors are not sure whether they are covered by insurance, and that 60 per cent are unaware of what cover a D&O insurance policy provides. Many wrongly believe other corporate insurance, such as employers' liability or public liability will provide them with the cover they need.

Directors' liabilities tend to arise in one of four main areas: fiduciary duties, duty of skill and care, contract with authority, and statutory obligations. In each of these areas the director will have obligations to a wide range of other parties, including shareholders, employees, creditors, customers, regulatory bodies, insolvency practitioners, and the company itself. Keeping track of all of your responsibilities to all of these stakeholders, in relation to every area of the company's activities over which you could be considered to have exercised some influence, is no small undertaking.

There has been a huge amount of publicity recently about corporate governance. The Government is currently undertaking a major review of company law, which has already resulted in a number of significant changes and will lead to others in the near future. The key point to stress here is that the clear current trend is towards the imposition of increased duties on company directors.

Specifically, companies will in future be required to include a clear statement of directors' duties within report and accounts documents – making it easier for third parties to point to an alleged breach. A change in the wording of the law will oblige directors to actively volunteer information to auditors – increasing the likelihood of directors falling foul of audit reports.

At the same time, Section 310 of the Companies Act has been altered to broaden the scope for companies to reimburse directors for the costs of defending themselves against charges of wrongful actions on the company's behalf, previously not allowed. Directors should bear in mind, however, that this is an option rather than an obligation on the company's part. There are a number of circumstances under which the company may be unwilling (for example where the ownership or management has changed) or unable (most pertinently in cases of insolvency) to reimburse directors.

Where a company does choose to reimburse its directors, a D&O insurance policy can provide protection for the balance sheet through the Company Reimbursement coverage.

From the point of view of growing businesses, experience suggests that there are three main areas of concern: insolvency-related issues, investigations costs and corporate manslaughter.

The main point of reference on bankruptcy is the Insolvency Act 1986, which establishes directors' liabilities for trading while insolvent, and defines the standards of care required. This is an issue that comes up again and again with smaller businesses. Taking appropriate professional advice to ensure that directors understand their obligations is obviously essential. But things can and do go wrong – posing a significant risk of personal ruin for directors without appropriate insurance cover in place.

By way of illustration: two directors of a company recently placed in receivership were held liable by creditors for sums representing the total of two payments made to one of the directors prior to liquidation. The creditors argued – ultimately successfully – that these payments should not have been made whilst the company had not repaid its debts. D&O insurance paid out £800,000 in damages and costs sustained by the two directors – a burden few individuals would be able to shrug off.

In an increasingly tightly regulated commercial environment, company directors can find themselves under investigation with ever greater regularity by a range of bodies including the Financial Services Authority, the Serious Fraud Office, the Health

& Safety Executive, the Crown Prosecution Service, or any other of a huge range of regulatory authorities.

For a smaller business, such investigations – whatever their eventual outcome – can cause serious disruption over a period of perhaps 6 to 18 months. By ensuring directors have access to, and funding for, appropriate legal advice, D&O insurance can play an important role in minimizing this disruption and allowing the individual(s) concerned to concentrate on managing the business.

The third major area of concern for growing businesses is corporate manslaughter. This is a topic that has hit the headlines recently in connection with a number of major rail disasters – but is equally relevant to smaller businesses, where a prosecution can have a massive impact.

The best known example is probably still the 1993 case where the director of an outdoor activity centre in Lyme Regis was successfully prosecuted for corporate manslaughter and sentenced to three years in prison following a fatal canoeing accident involving children. But there are around 400 workplace deaths each year in the UK, and there is an increasing willingness to bring actions against directors for corporate manslaughter.

The directors of small companies are particularly exposed – because the emphasis in the relevant health and safety legislation is on identifying the 'directing mind' responsible. The simple and unambiguous structure of smaller companies makes it far easier to point the finger at a particular person or persons to be held to account.

Another significant trend we have seen in our experience as a D&O insurer is fraud. When one or more directors in a company is alleged to have acted fraudulently, they – and, unless the case is very clear cut indeed, their fellow directors – are likely to incur significant legal expenses in defending themselves against investigation and/or prosecution.

For example, the chairman and managing director of a UK firm were sued by its new French parent company by which they had recently been acquired. It was alleged that they had deliberately misrepresented the financial condition of the company during takeover negotiations – and specifically that they had overstated profit forecasts to secure an inflated sale price. The costs of their successful defence eventually ran into millions of pounds.

In another case, a full-time director of a company was found to have defrauded the organization concerned. Two non-executive co-directors were ordered to reimburse the company from their own personal assets on the grounds that they had paid insufficient attention to the management of the company's affairs. This provides a good illustration of the way the necessity to defend against allegation of fraud can spread beyond the individual(s) directly responsible.

Problems can also frequently crop up in areas such as employment practices liability (where, for example, a director might be sued for wrongful dismissal or for making improper advances, leading to significant defence costs) or breach of contract. One recent example of the latter involved a sales director becoming the subject of an action brought by an overseas retailer with whom he had negotiated an exclusive sales agreement – only for them to find that their competitors were also selling the product lines in question.

In an increasingly litigious and tightly regulated business world, it should be clear that problems can materialize from a huge variety of sources. No one should ever take on a directorship lightly, and directors should always do their best to keep abreast of the full range of their responsibilities. Equally, the importance of taking appropriate advice before problems arise should not be understated. Organizations such as the Institute of Directors have a lot of helpful advice available on their website. You can also seek advice from your solicitor or accountant.

Ultimately D&O insurance is certainly a good way of protecting the personal assets of directors. It ensures that appropriate legal representation will be in place to defend their interests and those of the company – in conjunction with a prudent approach to the responsibilities associated with directorship. As the range and scale of actions against individual directors, under both new and existing legislation grows, the issue is likely to become one of increasing concern to all employees and potential employees at board level. It's something UK companies of all sizes will need to address.

Royal & SunAlliance is one of the world's leading multinational general insurance groups focusing on all major classes of general insurance. Royal & SunAlliance currently transacts business in some 130 countries looking after 20 million customers and the group employs around 28,000 people worldwide.

# Growing better

*The tone set from the top is crucial as a business grows in size and influence in its market, says Philippa Foster Back, Director of the Institute of Business Ethics*

In growing a business to become a better business a key element is the tone set from the top – from the CEO and the Board. A definition of 'tone' is the qualities and style that characterize business behaviour. This will feed through to the tone that the company, through its employees, displays towards its stakeholders. This manifests itself in how the company undertakes its business. Does it endeavour to do the right thing or does it cut corners, getting the deal being the ultimate goal? There is a growing realization that an ethically bankrupt business risks becoming a financially bankrupt one.

So tone from the top is important. In a small company where the directors know everyone this tone is transparent, but as a company grows, and certainly once it has got to a size where not everyone knows each other, then problems can manifest themselves if there isn't any guidance given as to what is expected of individuals.

## Relationships and trust

A business should reflect the values, the core beliefs by which that business is to be conducted. At the start-up stage the values 'reflect' the entrepreneur or group of people who began the company. This reflection includes the individual's values, or ethics, being the way that they interact with others and build relationships. The best relationships are based on mutual trust and respect.

As the business grows, those relationships evolve and change. The one that is affected most by this is the relationship between the owner/directors and the employees.

**The Institute of Business Ethics (IBE)** was established in 1986 to encourage high standards of business behaviour through raising awareness of the issues and the sharing of best practice

- **Our vision is to be**
  ◊ *the leader in knowledge and practice of corporate business ethics.*

- **We seek to achieve this by**
  ◊ *raising the awareness of companies to the issues and by helping them to build relationships of trust with their customers, employees, suppliers, owners and the communities in which they work. We do this through the exchange and discussion of experience on issues relating to the conduct of business.*

- **We offer companies**
  ◊ *practical help and advice on business ethics matters relating to their organisation and the training necessary for their people to understand and solve business ethics dilemmas within the corporate context.*

- **Our work** is based on a programme of **research, publications** and meetings covering national and international issues of business practices.

- **Our team** apply their practical business experience of the issues that organisations face to fulfil the Institute's vision.

- Among our recent **publications** are:
  ◊ **Setting the Tone: ethical business leadership; Corporate Use of Codes of Business Ethics: 2004 Survey and Does Business Ethics Pay? – ethics and financial performance.**

- We run two training programmes on our premises: **Introduction to Business Ethics** and **Developing & Implementing a Code of Ethics.** We also provide tailor-made courses for companies.

- See our website for details of how to become a corporate or individual subscriber.

**www.ibe.org.uk**

**Institute of Business Ethics**
24 Greencoat Place   London SW1P 1BE
T +44 (0)20 7798 6040    F +44 (0)20 7798 6044    E info@ibe.org.uk
Charity No. 108014

At the outset the owner will know everyone and growth will be closely allied to the effectiveness of teamwork. As a company grows and employs more people, that closeness within the original team may begin to break down. New employees will bring different value sets, different concepts, and different aspirations to the business. These can be an important part of developing a business, of helping it to grow, but it does need managing in order to enhance the effectiveness of the bigger team (workforce). This underlines the importance of leadership to guide this growth.

Leadership is not just the person at the top; it cascades down the organization and manifests itself at many levels – the team leader, the project manager, the regional director and so forth. It is important for each person to recognize the example they are personally setting as a leader. The tendency in human nature is to emulate one's leader, so if someone sees that the boss is bullying or brusque in how he or she deals with people, the employees might copy this, the interpretation being that such behaviour is the way to advance in the organization. Examples can relate to dress code, interests, such as football or rugby, and so forth.

## How can this be managed?

The simple way is to put in a code of business ethics (business principles, statement of how we do business – there are many alternative names you can use). People work best when they are given a framework within which they are to operate. A framework is not prescriptive but it acts as a guide. The guide/code sets down 'how' the business of the company is to be undertaken. Implementation of course is still up to the individual. But individuals need to know that by following the guide/code they will be supported in their activities.

## How to put in a code

Follow nine steps for developing a corporate ethics programme.[1]

1. *Find a champion.* Unless a member of the board is prepared to drive the introduction of a business ethics policy, the chances of it being a useful tool are not high.
2. *Identify core values.* Ensure that your company has established core values. If not, identifying them must be the next step.
3. *Get endorsement from the chairman and the board.* Corporate values and ethics are matters of governance. The board must be enthusiastic not only about having such a policy but also about receiving regular reports on its operation.
4. *Find out what bothers people.* Merely endorsing a standard code or copying that of another company will not suffice. It is important to find out the topics on which employees require guidance.
5. *Pick a well-tested model.* Use a framework that addresses issues as they affect different constituents or stakeholders of the company (a 'stakeholder model'). The usual ones are: shareholders, employees, customers, suppliers and the local/national community. Some might include other interested parties such as competitors.

6. *Produce a company code of business ethics.* The code should be distributed in booklet form or included in a staff manual or on company websites. Existing policies, for example on giving and receiving gifts or the private use of company assets, can be incorporated. Include guidance on the use of the code.
7. *Try it out first.* The code needs piloting – perhaps with a sample of employees drawn from all levels and different locations. An external organization such as the Institute of Business Ethics will comment on drafts.
8. *Issue the code and make it known.* Publish and send the code to all employees, suppliers and others. State publicly that the company has a code and an implementation programme that covers the whole company. Put the code on your website and send it to joint-venture and other business partners.
9. *Make it work.* The policy needs to be endorsed and launched by the CEO and cascaded down to all levels and locations. Practical examples of the code in action should then be introduced into all company internal (and external) training programmes as well as induction courses. Managers should sign off on the code regularly and a review mechanism should be established. A code 'master' needs to be appointed.

## Further support

This can be given to employees in the growing business by giving them the opportunity to raise queries/concerns about corporate behaviour. In larger companies this can be done anonymously as well, but in all instances it should be handled confidentially. Public Concern at Work (www.pcaw.org.uk) offers a service to help smaller companies or individuals concerned by what they see at work.

## Why do this?

Putting in a code will support a growing business because it is an integral part of building a culture within the business. By following best practice and developing a code in consultation with employees, and based on core ethical values that are shared, it can become the glue that cements the company.

Core ethical values are interpreted as those key tenets underpinning 'how' the business operates. The most frequently used core ethical words identified by companies are:

| | |
|---|---|
| Integrity | Fairness |
| Responsibility | Transparency |
| Honesty | Openness |
| Trust | Respect |

## The business case

In the main, management recognize that doing business ethically is the right thing to do. They also recognize that it is not easy to achieve. It only takes one individual not behaving in the way the company would expect, for a customer to be lost – and in a growing business that is a real cost. So there is a 'defensive' business case to be made, along with the 'sustainable' business case. In this argument it can be shown that companies with this approach do tend to be better managed, have happier workforces and productivity and achieve better financial performance in the long run.[2]

There will be times, though, which are particularly pertinent to a growing business, when entering into contracts where (despite it being illegal either to demand or pay) there is an expectation that a bribe will be paid, in money or kind. To walk away will cost, and maybe dearly, but in today's environment, and with the 'voices' in your ears, can you afford not to? Those 'voices' are those of the public at large and the company's stakeholders (shareholders, suppliers, customers, employees). In the latter case they will want to see the company continuing to grow, but if it is charged with illegal practices this may lead to its bankruptcy, and they will lose financially.

## In conclusion

The tone from the top is crucial as a business grows in size and influence in its market. Such a growing business depends on its people as they face the challenge of a changed way of working in a small then a medium-sized business.

To help them and yourself as a business leader, so you can rest easy knowing that even when you or your management team are not around your employees are responding to your customers and suppliers as you would wish, you need to support them. A good way is to develop a code of business ethics.

## Notes

1. Taken from Webley, S, *Developing a Code of Business Ethics: A guide to best practice including the IBE Illustrative Code of Business Ethics,* 2003, IBE
2. See Webley, S & More, E, *Does Business Ethics Pay?: Ethics and financial performance,* 2002, IBE

Philippa Foster Back has over 25 years of business experience working as Group Treasurer in two FTSE 100 companies and as Group Finance Director of an SME business. She joined the IBE in August 2001 and has a number of non-executive roles.

The IBE was founded in 1986. The aims of the Institute are to emphasize the essentially ethical nature of wealth creation, to encourage the highest standards of behaviour by companies and to publicize the best ethical practices.

For more information, contact Philippa Foster Back, Director, Institute of Business Ethics, www.ibe.org.uk.

# Interim management

*Swallow your pride and bring in the interim, says Nick Robeson of Boyden Interim Management Limited*

It's a rare business that wants to stand still, but it's a rare business owner or manager who has already been where his or her vision wants to take that business – into uncharted territory.

So, if you haven't been there and done that then you may be understandably a little wary and cautious – but since when was an entrepreneur risk-averse? Vicious circle: you want to grow, you are wary of risk.

The way through? Swallow your pride, and no matter how big your ego, how focused and personally-developed your idea is, bring in somebody who *has* been there and done that.

Interim executives remain a mystery to many businesses – but those businesses that have discovered, understood and applied the skills and expertise of an interim manager to their organization are pioneering a management solution that is massively effective – but can appear to be too good to be true.

It's the shock of impact. An interim – correctly assessed, assigned, deployed and supported – will deliver with a speed and purpose that will astonish, especially so when the benchmark pace of a new permanent arrival can more often be described as measured.

There are a number of key issues to consider when interim management arrives on your agenda: Where do you find your interim manager? How do you deploy them and, indeed, is there a right time to bring an interim into play? Crucially, if growth is what you want – can you really let go? Can you provide them with an accurate brief?

Barely a day goes by without an organization announcing change, takeover, disposal, closure, growth, axe-wielding, brand re-positioning. Sectors rise and fall, everyone's in a race – some don't know why, they've simply been drawn in. But there's no option but to compete.

A strong economy, a skills shortage, an undoubtedly active growth culture amongst businesses – and the new-ish ethic of 'work–life balance' have encouraged experienced and expert people to forage for themselves instead of relying upon the corporate trough.

These are the people you should be looking to help grow your business. They are the interims: a secret army of business brains who have knowledge, experience and expertise.

But whoa there: it's not as simple as that. You have to be absolutely certain that you know what you're buying. I'm always intrigued to hear somebody's early definition of an interim. It's usually 'a temp'. That's unhelpful; in your mind's eye you conjure up the picture of somebody who awkwardly enters the office under curious stares, is plonked at a desk, given a cup of tea before somebody half-senior wanders over with a pile of end-of-financial-year paperwork nobody else really wants to deal with.

The industry's definition is vastly different: a highly-qualified professional, expert in their field, who can be brought in at short notice to take charge and control of a major issue involving crisis, disposal, acquisition, merger, turnaround – or opportunity. They perform against set objectives over a defined timescale, are apolitical – and they deliver.

Crucially, they have been there and done it; sometimes several times. That's what interims actually do.

You will be in no doubt as to who is in control when a proper interim comes in to land. They will be massively dynamic, your office upturned, your staff upended and your pace upscaled. Things will happen. These people are designed to drive change and growth.

So, who's hiring these interims? The answer is many FTSE 250 and major privately owned organizations. They generally tend to keep their interim hirings under their corporate hats, whether for secrecy – or for pride and ego. It's not necessarily in any specific sectors, it's departments or organizations involved in either attack or defence – change – whether in response to a problem or an opportunity.

There's something like 10,000 active interim managers in the UK. Those are the registered, assessed and highly capable interims that the key interim service providers are happy to recommend for assignment. There are many more purporting to be interims. If you're a business looking to hire an interim, ensure they are members of the IMA (Interim Management Association).

The IMA's principal aim is the development of interim management as a powerful and leading management resource based on the highest standards of professional service. Members work to a code of professional practice and good conduct backed up by a complaints and disciplinary process.

Of those interims currently in play, around 88 per cent are in the private sector, with the busiest sub-sector being accounting, banking and finance (18 per cent), while 17 per cent are involved with manufacturing companies.

Around a fifth of them are involved in internal change, 18 per cent in major new projects, 12 per cent in business development; 18 per cent are engaged to deal with a crisis, but only 2 per cent to manage a closure or disposal. Nine per cent are involved in acquisition or merger projects.

That's around a third involved in some way with fixed-term assignments involving growth or development – and the trend is upwards.

Expect to pay anything between £500 and £1,250 a day for an interim executive. Expensive? Well, it's all relative: they will arrive at your business knowing as much, if not more, about your sector or market as you do. They will have researched the extent of opportunity, they will be armed with intelligence about your products and services – and your competitors.

They will have had direct, relevant and recent experience in your sector or market – they will probably be genuine experts. They will assume a head of function or board level stance, role and approach.

In the time it would take you to stumble through phase one of your growth plan, they would be well into the next, or next-but-one, phase.

There are few elements of a business that want or need senior people with experience, expertise and proven ability more than the growth function. It is crucial to have as a guide somebody who knows all the potential perils, pitfalls – and pleasures – to be found in unknown territory.

From that perspective it is crucial that you look in the right place for your ideal interim. An IMA interim service provider will carefully identify and vet its clients, the roles and assignments offered and how realistic are the expectations of the client organization. The IMA is, therefore, your first point of call.

It is crucial that you understand and appreciate precisely where an interim should sit in the grand scheme of things, and what you can expect of them.

They will arrive with gusto, they will have researched your industry, your organization, your people, your reputation, your market, your competition and your potential.

They will assume a senior posture, they will take control of the environment; they will get under the skin and into the roots of your business very quickly; and they will make an assessment as to what, precisely, is the task at hand. They will discuss and agree timescales and objectives with the key people in the business – and they will launch themselves into the assignment with energy, agility and massive enthusiasm.

*They will then deliver.*

Nick Robeson is Chief Executive of Boyden Interim Management Limited.

**10**

# International growth

# Issues in global expansion

*Decide on how you are going to operate overseas, before the authorities do it for you, says David Sayers, Head of International Tax, Mazars*

One of the most difficult decisions for any growing business to make is when and if to start trading overseas. In the first instance, simply selling goods to an overseas customer might create significant issues in terms of increased credit risk, possible duties and tariffs and adherence to local laws. Nevertheless, a UK business with a sound product or service would be neglecting its true potential if it did not look overseas for different markets. Often such things happen completely by chance, by word of mouth, without the need for an aggressive sales pitch. On the other hand, many businesses will be dependent upon third-party sales agents at the outset, where a high degree of trust may need to be established before an effective working relationship is created. Finally, if adequate market research has already shown potential sufficient to justify you creating your own overseas office, then the business will be brought into a web of local labour laws and commercial and real estate issues. The purpose of this chapter, then, is to examine some of the potential pitfalls and opportunities inherent in overseas expansion and provide some guidance through what can be something of a minefield.

## Small acorns

It is important, in tax terms at least, to draw a line between trading *with* and trading *in* a country. In direct tax terms, it is only the latter scenario which will normally create a taxable presence. However, for VAT purposes, it is often the case that an obligation to register will come about well in advance of direct tax reporting, for example, under the distance selling regulations. Failure to register at the correct time can lead to overseas penalties in certain countries. In theory a taxable presence can be created by a travelling salesperson with no fixed base, if he or she can conclude contracts on behalf of his or her employer. In the same way, if a third-party agent acts exclusively for the home state business, then although he or she may be part of a completely distinct enterprise, he or she can unwittingly create a tax charge for the customer.

## Corporate structures

Once a decision is taken to set up a more permanent presence, then you need to choose your vehicle. Often this is tax driven, but it also depends very heavily on how the entity concerned will be perceived in the local market by the end consumer of the product or service. In most countries, customers will feel more comfortable dealing with a locally established, recognized entity rather than a nebulous branch of an overseas parent whose identity they can't confirm.

Even choosing a company can create unexpected tax and commercial consequences. In France for instance, there are many different kinds of corporate form, for example, non-trading companies designed specifically to hold real estate, vineyards and agricultural operations. Each entity needs to be scrutinized to determine its tax and legal status, both locally and in the home state, as often mismatches arise.

Setting up a company, too, can sometimes take months. Minimum share capital of €25,000 is not unusual – a far cry from the UK shelf company industry which provides a £2 company in 24 hours.

Beware also of allocating too much power to local directors: they can often find themselves in conflict with shareholders' wishes and be extremely difficult and expensive to remove.

## Code contradiction

For Anglo-Saxon businesses setting up abroad, one of the biggest differences to come to terms with is contradictory local codes. Much of continental Europe uses a civil law system based on written legal codes, rather than the Anglo-Saxon common law system, which is founded much more on precedents created by judicial decisions over time. Whilst the impact of EU law has diluted this to some extent, certain entities such as trusts and concepts such as the separation of legal and beneficial ownership are often alien to our continental colleagues.

As has been widely documented in the press in recent years, such systems are often highly protective of their workforce, offering a wonderful comfort blanket for employees, but a heavy social cost in terms of payroll taxes and redundancy packages. In certain countries, it is not uncommon for employers' national insurance to be almost 50 per cent on top of basic salary and for compensation for loss of office to be a year's salary or more.

# Financing the expansion

Building a business in a new market is likely to have a significant impact on working capital. Local banks will often be wary of new start-ups from overseas asking for credit facilities, even with a parent company guarantee. It will therefore usually fall to the parent company to fund the new overseas business through an inter-company account. If the loan is to exist for any length of time, the UK tax authorities will usually ask for interest to be charged, or make a corresponding adjustment to the parent company's tax computation. Moreover, if the subsidiary is inadequately capitalized, the local tax authority may seek to recharacterize some of the loan as equity and thereby deny a tax deduction for part of the interest. Therefore, whilst loan finance is often the first port of call, businesses may find that they are called upon to inject a significant proportion of equity in order to create a third-party lending scenario.

The same third-party test applies to inter-company pricing. Most tax authorities around the world will insist that prices charged between parents and subsidiaries are demonstrably arm's length, with often onerous documentation requirements and draconian penalty regimes.

# Making it more permanent

Prospective users of commercial property will also find that leases and acquisitions are subject to higher taxes than in the UK. A comparative analysis of stamp duty rates across Europe makes the oft-complained about UK rate of 4 per cent seem relatively modest. Most countries, unlike the UK, impose a capital gains tax on non-resident landlords holding investment property. Others will impose a penal tax rate on property held in a tax haven, some even taxing the sale of shares in foreign real estate companies rather than the sale of the asset itself.

# Bringing the cash home

Let us assume that your overseas business ventures have been successful and that you now have subsidiaries in a dozen countries. The key issue for any outward investor is successful repatriation of cash for use in the next venture. In order to do this, however, our successful entrepreneur may have to negotiate a myriad of exchange controls and withholding taxes, each of which is a potential cost of capital. In recent years China has attracted an immense amount of inward investment, not least because of low labour rates and attractive tax incentives. Nevertheless, it still has a restrictive exchange control environment and many of the tax incentives are geared around local reinvestment rather than repatriation of profits.

With some planning, a holding company jurisdiction will have been chosen at the outset that permits a free flow of funds back to the ultimate parent without withholding taxes. Such funds may then be recycled, perhaps without even having to go back to the ultimate parent, and used to reinvest in the next venture.

## Conclusion

Following the golden rules below will facilitate your global expansion and early investment will, hopefully, produce significant savings later on:

- Draw a line and establish your modus operandi overseas in advance, before the local authorities do it for you.
- Don't just accept the first corporate form that is offered to you. Make sure it meets your requirements both in the UK and the local jurisdiction. Take heed of what the taxman and your customers will think.
- Plan for culture changes and carefully calculate the on-costs of both setting up and closing down if it all goes awry.
- Look at your financing plans in advance. Don't be fearful of injecting too much equity – many countries will expect a much higher minimum than in the UK.
- Look out for onerous lease commitments and a higher overall tax burden on commercial property. Always add on at least 10 per cent to the sales price to allow for on-costs.
- Think about your outward investment structure at the earliest possible stage. It may seem expensive early on, but the investment is usually worthwhile in order to avoid future tax costs that might impact on profits at a later date.

David Sayers is Head of International Tax for Mazars in the UK. He has extensive experience in advising businesses on setting up new ventures all over the world through Mazars' international offices. His primary expertise lies in tax planning, but he is often involved in bridging the cultural and linguistic gaps that may arise. David is a regular presenter on international taxation issues both in the UK and abroad.

Mazars' clients include a wide range of owner-managed businesses (including some of the UK's fastest growing entrepreneurial businesses) as well as international corporate groups and listed companies (15 per cent of the FTSEurofirst 100), public sector bodies and numerous private individuals.

For more information, tel: 01582 700 700; e-mail: david.sayers@mazars. co.uk; website: www.mazars.co.uk.

# Efficiencies in international cash management and trade

*An end to overdrafts in the trading cycle? A pan-European direct debit scheme? Mark Davies, Director of International Product Management at The Royal Bank of Scotland, discusses where efficiencies can be made in international payments*

## Real time

Electronic payments are already a given for many international companies. The cost of making transfers online has come down significantly and the use of cheques is falling by 6 per cent a year. International business will increasingly be conducted in real time as the network for sending instructions between international banks, SWIFT, moves towards a more seamless processing of transfers and orders.

To view your accounts in different countries you no longer have to plug in software from each bank. Your electronic banking systems should show all your balances at any point in the day and you should be able to transfer money freely between all your different accounts.

You should also be able to query any payments online. For instance, you can display images of cheques or drafts on screen rather than having to go to your branch to check them.

More and more international sales are being made over the internet, so you should look to receive immediate payment by credit card. There are systems in place to accept payment from some 25 different countries and the use of cards will continue to grow, even with complications in the form of local credit cards and payment mechanisms.

Foreign exchange is easily wrapped into this technology. You no longer have to ring a dealer to obtain a rate. Instead, you can source competitive rates online, either on a proprietary system with feeds from Reuters or Bloomberg, or through a combined aggregator like FXAll.

## Secured terms

Technology does not affect whether you trade on open account or on secured terms, such as a letter of credit from your bank. Even though volumes of world trade have risen sharply, the broad split is still between 80 per cent on open account and 20 per cent on secured terms. In emerging markets such as China, Cambodia or Vietnam, most exporters or importers would not be happy to trade on anything other than secured terms.

However, technology does make letters of credit much easier to handle. Formerly extensive multi-page documents taking a long time to fill in, they can now be completed online, benefiting repeat traders in particular, who can easily repopulate fields. Or you can combine a number of purchase orders into a single letter of credit, which makes it easier to use but does not remove the need for it.

## Supplier finance

More can also be done on open account in areas like supplier finance. Large purchasers may have several small suppliers who would prefer to trade on letter of credit, because it is an instrument on which they can seek finance. But dominant buyers can improve their payables and extend their terms without spoiling their supplier relationships. They can allow trusted suppliers to benefit from their balance sheets and use their credit standing to receive finance on better terms as the risk moves from supplier to buyer.

## Trade cycle

Banks are also knitting together products to support customers through the trading cycle. For example, they can offer you a letter of credit on imports, then provide a loan to cover the period of converting raw materials into finished goods, and arrange the invoice discounting when you finally sell the goods.

Trade cycles can last 225 days or even longer, particularly if goods have been sitting on a ship before reaching the factory, and there are financing needs at every stage. With the help of technology, banks are better placed to understand the ebbs and flows of what is happening. As a result, smaller companies are able to plug a gap that would once have been covered by an overdraft or another source of more expensive lending. Tracing the flow of goods, banks are happy to offer more structured lending because they know they are guaranteed payment.

## Single European payments

Alongside these efficiency gains, the EU is seeking to move towards a Single European Payment Area (SEPA). Initiatives to improve payment methods, infrastructure and pricing are all likely to be carried forward in the next few years. So instead of cross-border payments and collections, there will be clearing systems allowing you to make credit transfers across borders as if you were in one country. Therefore, a pan-European direct debit scheme and a pan-European credit transfer scheme will soon be possible. At some point in the future we might even see a European-wide equivalent of BACS.

At the moment, if you want to start trading with 10 countries in the EU you have to work out how to collect the money. Do your buyers send money back to the UK or do you open up a local collection account? For now, if you are selling to a French consumer it is much easier to be paid in France using a domestic transfer, rather than asking them to pay you in the UK.

In the future, you may well be able to have a single European account to manage your cash, collect your dues and pay your suppliers and employees. It will not happen yet, but you should already be able to see tangible differences, with more to come in 2006 and beyond.

For further information, visit: www.rbs.co.uk. The Royal Bank of Scotland plc, registered in Scotland no 90312, registered office: 36 St Andrew Square, Edinburgh EH2 2YB.

# Using trade statistics

*Who says statistics aren't rewarding, asks Roy Chegwin, Editor of Export Focus magazine*

Now, before you turn the page thinking 'statistics are not for me', consider this: HM Revenue & Customs has a plentiful amount of information on imports and exports that can really help you evaluate markets and put a shape on your future marketing activity. Plus there is a bonus – this information is readily available on the internet and totally free of charge!

Statistics are vital to any business. They are the confirmation of fact that takes commercial decisions beyond opinion. Very often statistics do that basic and valuable job – they confirm what is commonly believed – but it is still essential to have that information. However, sometimes statistics throw up surprises and challenge popular conceptions, and when this happens opportunities can arise.

## Sand to Saudi?

As an example of how statistics can surprise us, who would have thought that the UK exported more than 32,000 tonnes of natural sand in 2004 to countries beyond the EU, including Saudi Arabia? Apparently the effects of desertification and the demands of the construction industry may lead to a sand shortage in that country. This fact is interesting in its own right but also triggers off other thoughts about the potential for the UK construction industry in the Middle East.

## No bed of roses

On the import front, the UK bought £45 million worth of roses from other EU countries in 2004 – of which more than 90 per cent came from the Netherlands. Nearly 20 per cent arrived in February, proving what a romantic bunch we are in the UK, but also begging the question whether UK producers could do more to fill that gap.

The facts above are perhaps quirky, but knowing what is happening in their sector is essential for all businesses in this undeniably global economy. The HMRC website, www.uktradeinfo.com puts these statistics at your fingertips.

The information is gathered by HM Revenue & Customs as part of its remit to monitor and check all commerce in and out of the UK both in terms of volume and value for imports and exports. These statistics are comprehensive and are accessible via the dedicated website. The website really does have a lot of information for anyone in international trade, starting right from the Home Page where you are invited to click on a number of options including 'Latest News' and the intriguing 'Stat Facts'. This scrolling facility encourages investigation from a choice of subjects that can be topical, such as Easter eggs at Easter time, though on the day this article was written it also included such diverse sectors as garments, orchids, tin and tobacco.

## Drill down and gather

The ability to drill down to individual products is what anyone in business wants because it allows them to investigate the business they are in. Whereas the scrolling 'Stat Facts' facility is a novel gizmo, 'Trade Data' is a powerful and fundamental business tool. This allows you to look at trading over a period of time, against any product type, to and from any area of the world. The data goes back five years and the good thing about this website is that it is very flexible, allowing you to gather the information you want, to manipulate it as required, to download it to your own computer in spreadsheet format and to convert it into charts.

The first thing you need to do is go to the website and register. Using the website is straightforward and for the purposes of this chapter I have chosen air-conditioning systems for vehicles, with the idea of looking at the market in North America.

### How to use www.uktradeinfo.com

Having logged on you check:

■ 8 Digit Data, then
■ Public Reports, then
■ UK World Trade, and
■ 8 Digit Commodity Code.

You will then be given a whole list of choices; see Figure 10.3.1.

For the purposes of this chapter, 2004 was chosen, though any year from 1999 is available and ultimately every user can construct their own data set by combining the information as they want it. The next page shows UK World Trade in 2004 but our business interest is 'Vehicle air-conditioning'. Consequently, on the left-hand side we check:

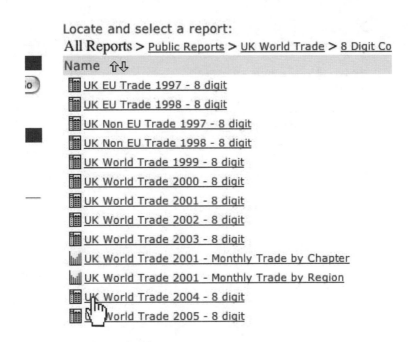

Locate and select a report:
All Reports > Public Reports > UK World Trade > 8 Digit Co

Name ⇧⇩

UK EU Trade 1997 - 8 digit
UK EU Trade 1998 - 8 digit
UK Non EU Trade 1997 - 8 digit
UK Non EU Trade 1998 - 8 digit
UK World Trade 1999 - 8 digit
UK World Trade 2000 - 8 digit
UK World Trade 2001 - 8 digit
UK World Trade 2002 - 8 digit
UK World Trade 2003 - 8 digit
UK World Trade 2001 - Monthly Trade by Chapter
UK World Trade 2001 - Monthly Trade by Region
UK World Trade 2004 - 8 digit
UK World Trade 2005 - 8 digit

**Figure 10.3.1** Choosing the year on uktradeinfo.com

■ *Units,* which presents us with further choices and the selections made are:
■ *Single Item,* and
■ *Pounds Sterling* (we could also have chosen *Quantity*).

Click on [Continue] and the next page presents us with a search facility box (see Figure 10.3.2).

In this box we entered 'vehicle air-conditioning'. Make sure that the [Single Item] box is checked and click on the [Continue] button. This will then bring up the product code and description. Check the box and click on [Continue].

The next window then confirms the period which, because we have already selected 2004, shows 'Year to date'; see Figure 10.3.3.

A click on this will bring up a new window allowing us to select any or all of the regions of the world. For this exercise we want to look at North America, where we think potential lies for our vehicle air-conditioning product.

Now you are given the option of choosing imports or exports or both. Select both and you now have the vital information you need in a very simple and understandable format.

Figure 10.3.4 shows imports and exports to North America, broken down by country. If we were looking at the United States in particular we could see that the total value of imports of these kinds of air-conditioning units is £136,071 and exports only £47,786.

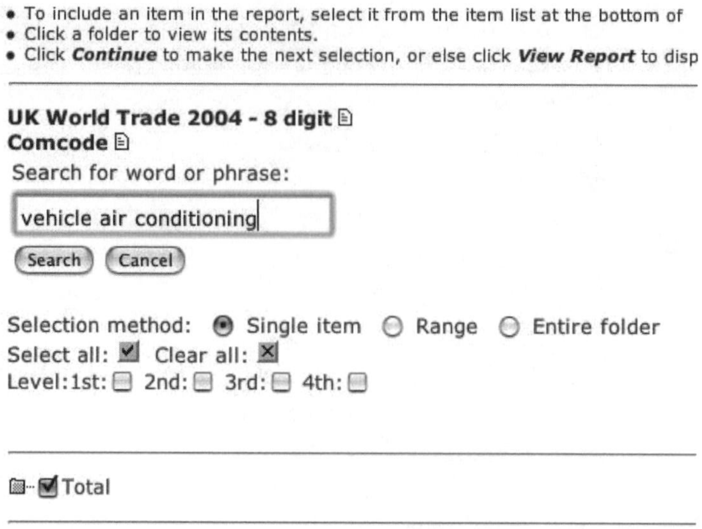

- To include an item in the report, select it from the item list at the bottom of
- Click a folder to view its contents.
- Click **Continue** to make the next selection, or else click **View Report** to disp

---

**UK World Trade 2004 – 8 digit** 🖹
**Comcode** 🖹

Search for word or phrase:

| vehicle air conditioning| |
|---|

( Search )  ( Cancel )

Selection method:  ● Single item  ○ Range  ○ Entire folder
Select all: ✔  Clear all: ✖
Level:1st: ▣  2nd: ▣  3rd: ▣  4th: ▣

---

🗀‑‑✔ Total

---

**Figure 10.3.2**  Choosing the search item

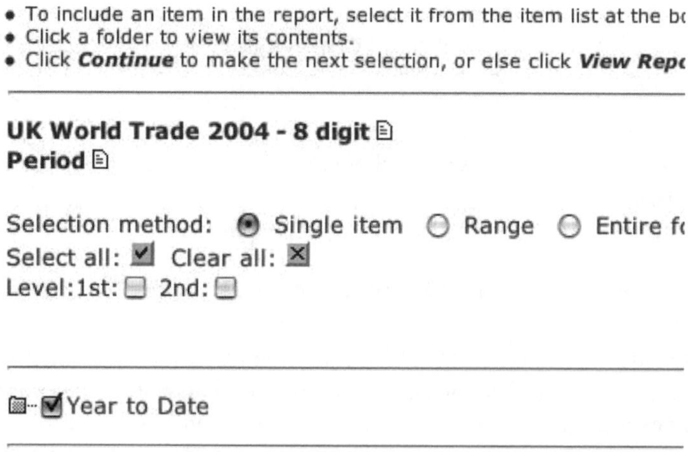

- To include an item in the report, select it from the item list at the b
- Click a folder to view its contents.
- Click **Continue** to make the next selection, or else click **View Rep**

---

**UK World Trade 2004 – 8 digit** 🖹
**Period** 🖹

Selection method:  ● Single item  ○ Range  ○ Entire fc
Select all: ✔  Clear all: ✖
Level:1st: ▣  2nd: ▣

---

🗀‑‑✔ Year to Date

---

**Figure 10.3.3**  Confirming the search period

| CANADA | 8,225 | - | - | - |
|---|---|---|---|---|
| GREENLAND | - | - | - | - |
| MEXICO | 4,500 | - | - | - |
| ST PIERRE-MIQUE | - | - | - | - |
| PUERTO RICO | - | - | - | - |
| USA | 136,071 | 47,786 | 10,031 | 2,808 |

**Figure 10.3.4**  Results for North America

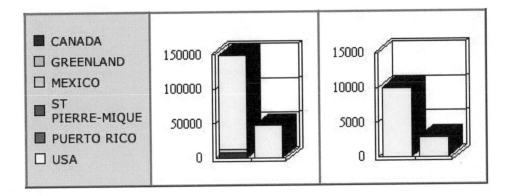

■ CANADA
□ GREENLAND
□ MEXICO
■ ST PIERRE-MIQUE
■ PUERTO RICO
□ USA

**Figure 10.3.5** The results in chart format

This information is very simply downloaded onto your own computer in spreadsheet format and can be converted into any one of nine types of chart. Figure 10.3.5 shows the data converted to chart format.

This exercise has illustrated a very simple example, but the key is that, when you get used to using the data available on www.uktradeinfo.com, you can begin to select the information you need in terms of product and period. You can, therefore, analyse import and export levels of any product to monitor and see trends over any period in the last five years. You can construct your own datasets and compile charts that help visualize the position. Clearly these charts can also be used in presentation material.

For some companies, the statistics available from www.uktradeinfo.com are an essential part of their business planning – but many UK companies have not been aware that this information is there for the downloading and available free of charge.

## You'd be nuts not to use it

Whether you use the website to evaluate your share of an existing market, to prospect for new business, or simply to be better informed about the global market your company operates in, you will not be disappointed with the ease of use and the breadth of information. Or you could just use it to find out interesting facts for that next dinner party – like of all the 4,894 tonnes of Brazil nuts we imported in 2003 only 0.6 per cent came from Brazil.

Further details can be found on www.uktradeinfo.com.

# 11

# Enterprise systems

# Always-on business

*Always-on communication is now a reality – so why are so few businesses making use of this opportunity for real-time communication with customers, suppliers and partners, asks Martin Taylor, Managing Director, Impact Applications*

The mobile environment has changed and always-on networks are now a reality. But the truth is that real-time communication between the mobile device and head office requires a new 'zero-client' software model, which the industry is struggling to adopt. For once, the IT vapourware model has been turned on its head: businesses can see quantifiable benefits for a technology that few vendors seem prepared – or able – to offer!

In an always-on world, this is the only way forward. 'Zero-client' systems that are low cost, easy maintenance and deliver real-time communications are providing businesses with a critical 5, 10 or 15 minute head start that can mean significant competitive advantage and financial benefit.

## Why settle?

Despite the much vaunted benefits of mobile computing, many organizations have eschewed the technology, perceiving the cost of implementation and ongoing maintenance as far outweighing the potential benefits.

Yet GPRS coverage is now at 98 per cent, and the networks are in place to deliver always-on communications – offering businesses the chance to improve response times to customers, reduce administrative overheads through direct, real-time server-to-mobile information provision and minimize stock holdings through intelligent purchasing and deployment.

So why settle for 'sometime soon' information when today's robust network infrastructure supports always-on communication?

The prevalent excuse is that organizations cannot risk the 2 per cent of time when the network is not available – an excuse that plays well to an audience of IT Directors but cuts little ice with senior business executives who will take the benefits of real-time mobile communication over occasional lapses in network coverage every time.

## Measured benefits

The truth is that always-on communication is a new way of working and, as such, requires a different approach. There is no need for any client-side software. Using a standard web browser the user connects directly to the server – just as in the days of the dumb terminal.

The benefits of this approach are significant, and not only for organizations in time-sensitive businesses. With no client-side software, the implementation is simple – users require just a user name and password to get access. There is no problematic synchronization of information between client and server and, critically, there is no expensive upgrade process.

And, without resource-hungry client software, users can be given standard mobile devices. Furthermore, with no data held on the device, there is little danger of business or customer-sensitive information falling into the wrong hands. Instead, using SSL, the connection between mobile web browser and server is completely secure, overcoming one of the major headaches associated with deploying technology to a mobile workforce.

## New model

Yet even the mobile network operators seem reluctant to push always-on networks to the business community for anything other than e-mail. Why? How can a technology that can undoubtedly transform business communication and performance to improve competitive edge be ignored by its providers in favour of encouraging bored teenagers to send each other pictures?

Are they waiting, perhaps, for full 3G networks before pushing the business button? If so, the wait may be a long one. 3G-enabled devices may now be available but, quite frankly, the quality of the network and the design of the software are so deplorable that the technology is unusable – by teenagers and businesses alike! It will be maybe 12 months or more before 3G has anything to offer. But with excellent GPRS coverage and zero client technology, always-on connectivity is available today at a price point and simplicity of solution that appeals to even the smallest business.

Take, for example, two organizations in a time-critical business – the emergency repair building services and maintenance industry. Wolverhampton-based Response Maintenance and Building Services has deployed this software model and achieved total visibility of the location of its workforce, the job status and the materials used. Job information is available in full, and in detail, immediately – reducing delays, miscommunication and errors. Customer response is faster, resource management slicker and administration costs reduced. Furthermore, problems such as illness can be flagged and addressed immediately, allowing rescheduling on-the-fly to ensure customer commitments are met. As a result, the overall profitability of Response Maintenance's business has doubled.

Midlands-based Northern Gas – a central heating and gas services supplier – has also implemented a similar system. The efficiencies within this system mean that the time from the initial enquiry to installation has been reduced by 20 per cent, and sales capacity and productivity have increased dramatically. The overall cost of sale has been reduced by 10 per cent through automation and reduced paperwork; mistakes in the ordering process have reduced by 50 per cent and the profitability of sales increased by 5 per cent.

Both organizations are now looking to build upon these systems to provide text message reminders to their customers, reminding them the morning of their appointment, or sending alerts when field engineers are en route to a job with names, contact details and the estimated arrival time, thereby significantly enhancing the relationship and reducing the administrative overhead associated with the customer update process.

## Why compromise?

Of course, not every business will feel confident to invest in a solution that leaves mobile workers completely in the dark should network congestion or failure occur. As a result, they may opt to retain the traditional thin client approach (see Figure 11.1.1), irrespective of cost and a delay in communication.

But, for many companies, the 10 or 15 minute delay of 'nearly now' software means the difference between winning and losing business, making or breaking a Service Level Agreement. For any organization juggling people and resources to get to the customer in time, real-time communication adds up to significant commercial advantage. Can you afford to compromise?

Martin Taylor is Managing Director of Impact Applications (www. impactapplications.com), an award-winning e-business and mobile solutions provider delivering effective, value-driven software solutions for the back office, website and mobile workforce. From operations management systems with live access in the field to unique e-commerce solutions that integrate with leading retail channels, Impact Applications' products and services deliver maximum productivity, lower costs and fully integrated business processes.

## Thick client

Server

Client

- A substantial software application is installed on the mobile device.
- Usually a different version of the mobile application is required for each type of device.
- The application is usually too large to load into permanent memory requiring it to be reinstalled if the device is reset.
- If the application is updated, each device will need to be recalled or connected to a PC to reload the software.
- All data processing and analysis is done on the mobile device requiring a well-specified PDA.
- Data is synchronized with the server periodically requiring complex data synchronization rules to cope with conflicts.
- If a device is reset, fails or is lost between syncs, all data modified since the last sync is lost. No new data is available on the device until the next sync.
- If a device fails or is lost, a replacement device will need to have the mobile application installed prior to use.
- The mobile device can be connected to the server in any number of ways, usually via a base station connected to a host PC.
- Usually the application requires a high level of custom security features to protect data on the device and during sync to the server.

## Thin client

Server

Client

- A small software application is installed on the mobile device.
- Usually a different version of the mobile application is required for each type of device.
- The application is often too large to load into permanent memory requiring it to be reinstalled if the device is reset.
- If the application is updated, each device will need to be recalled or connected to a PC to reload the software. Some applications may be self-updating.
- The application is normally a front-end (or graphical user interface) used to access the database on the server.
- All data processing and analysis is done on the server.
- If a device fails or is lost, a replacement device will need to have the mobile application installed prior to use.
- The mobile device is permanently connected to the internet using GPRS on the mobile phone network – currently with 99% UK coverage.
- Usually the application requires a high level of custom security features to protect data on the device and during transit to and from the server.

## Zero client

Server

- No new software is installed on the mobile device, so there are no data protection issues if the device is lost or stolen.
- The standard web browser built-in to the mobile device provides a familiar graphical user interface and is used to access the database on the server.
- If the device is reset, the web browser is automatically reinstalled by the device setup program.
- As the user interface is updated, all users automatically see the new interface on their mobile device without reinstalling the software or returning the device to base.
- All data processing and analysis is done on the server requiring only a basic specification for the PDA.
- If a device fails or is lost, the replacement device requires no additional software installation or configuration prior to deployment.
- The mobile device is permanently connected to the internet using GPRS on the mobile phone network – currently with 99% UK coverage.
- A high level of widely used security is already built into the web browser.

**Figure 11.1.1**  Always-on networks

# Enterprise reporting

*Keep your data and lose the paper with the best report mining software, says Rob Graham of Datawatch Europe*

In life, we are sometimes only limited by boundaries that we erect around ourselves. The same can be true in business. You are a smaller business either because you think or know you are or because others perceive you as such. This can result in your becoming marginalized when innovation comes knocking at the door of larger organizations.

Imagine yourself as a larger enterprise with access to better resources. Take corporate governance as an example. Whatever your size, you have a business to manage and care for, risk assessment, probably some compliance issues, internal and external audit, etc – the list can become quite long. Now imagine that you are an organization with instant and accurate data on demand, where everyone who needs them has access to the latest, correct reports in Windows format, where there is no need for expensive paper reports to be circulated. When you invest in report mining software, you acquire a new resource with enough scope and power to make a real difference to your organization.

Imagine you are an organization where anyone who needs to can quickly respond to customer enquiries or complaints; where actions are planned and tracked into a central database; where those actions may be monitored against user-defined criteria.

Imagine you are an organization with an integrated reporting system. Imagine you are maintaining compliance to multiple standards and requirements; where risk assessments, customer surveys, audits, action plans and much more are integrated via one software application.

All management systems, whatever the size of the enterprise, need the same certain core elements for:

- dealing with problems or opportunities for improvement;
- setting objectives and planning how to meet them;
- controlling the reports in use within the organization;
- review and audit to verify that the system is working.

Report mining software's ability to quickly and easily import, analyse and combine data from almost any data source makes it a powerful business intelligence solution for everyone. You can bring the analytical firepower of report mining software to bear on data mined from ASCII/ANSI files (such as reports), HTML files, data from spreadsheets, database files, delimited text or ODBC data sources. Report mining software's unique modelling technology allows even non-technical users to effortlessly build a collection of filters, summaries and charts and apply them to different data sets.

So easy to use, report mining software is the ideal solution for managers, analysts, accountants and auditors who want to access and manipulate data from trusted reports and other data sources, quickly and easily, without programming. IT professionals use report mining software as well, to help reduce demands for custom database queries and report writing jobs.

Report mining software should include all the standard features of industry benchmark products, as well as the ability to import and analyse data from XLS, MDB, DB, DBF, WKx, delimited text and HTML files, as well as any ODBC-compliant data source, including SQL Server and Oracle. All report mining software should read and mine data from report files commonly known as print files, spool files, TXT files, formatted ASCII files, PRN files and SDF files.

Society expects your organization to comply with an ever-increasing range of standards and legal requirements. Managers are also being expected to achieve greater efficiencies – providing better services while using fewer resources. To consistently achieve those aims and produce evidence of compliance activities, effective management systems need to be in place. Leading report mining software provides the infrastructure to assist any compliance or business management system. With such software, you can now afford to imagine yourself larger. Your staff and customers as well as business partners will have to view you in a different light. Report mining has developed over many years and versions, and will support all the items mentioned above. It's your one-stop solution for streamlining your business process for less than the cost of some temporary clerical activity.

You are probably already aware that there is a trend towards the integration of systems – reducing duplication and other inefficiencies. Formal management systems tend to be insular – focused on quality, safety, environment or another aspect of business management. However, they all have certain core elements in common: the need to control and understand data, the need to perform audits and reviews, the need to record nonconforming events and plan action to deal with them. The best report mining software allows for full or partial integration. Separate existing systems may be integrated gradually as the level of business maturity makes it most suitable. Data and report mining allows users to see information that matches their interest. For example, a compliance officer could exclude all other records from a search by simply selecting the filter tool in the best product.

As systems get larger and more complex, component inefficiencies and their lack of integration cause unproductive work. In most management systems, there are various separate components used, lists and registers, Excel workbooks, and perhaps various databases. Although these components may 'do the job' to some degree, there is usually no link between them. Imagine you can afford a system that offers sophisticated data and report mining and an unparalleled level of integration. Such sophisticated merging of data assists the auditors, both internal and external, to find a problem. It can then be referred back to the responsible person or department.

Report mining software provides the infrastructure for operating a one-stop compliance management system utilizing your existing system. The best software can merge up to nine different data sources. It removes the need for an expensive new system. It will help organizations of all sizes to learn about compliance and risk management, and implement them more effectively and efficiently. It can be used to address a whole range of compliance issues such as reporting and operational risk assessments. In short, it provides better control over and management of data without recourse to expensive IT time, and prolongs the value of your investment in an existing system.

Management without information is not management. The best report mining software solution may be the only data access and analysis tool you ever need. There's no need to flip through thick printed reports, re-key data into spreadsheets, or struggle with complex SQL data analysis tools. Instead, Monarch transforms your report files into data, without programming. Work smarter, with report mining software!

Like all powerful data analysis tools, report mining software lets you easily sort, filter, summarize and graph report data, export to Excel, Access, etc. Additionally, it can access additional data sources: Excel, Access, ODBC, HTML, etc.

As your organization grows, you will find uses for the automated version of such software. Gartner Group estimates that workers spend at least 10 per cent of their time just looking for the information they need to perform a business task or make a decision. *CIO Magazine* once noted that the average executive wastes up to 82 minutes per day searching for needed information.

Too often, workers must wait for IT department assistance to correctly work with a complex database access tool to provide customized data. Others resort to re-keying data from existing paper reports into MS Excel or Access in order to work with the data; a cumbersome and error-prone process. Either way, valuable work time is wasted, deadlines are missed, and opportunities are lost.

Organizations have invested heavily to collect data with enterprise systems, such as ERP systems, HR/payroll systems, and information systems designed for specific industries, such as healthcare and banking. Delivering such enterprise data to the right person at the right time, customized for specific business needs, will improve business performance and enhance competitiveness. But how can your organization easily create and deliver customized enterprise data, without a long, expensive and complex technology implementation?

Rob Graham joined Datawatch Europe in 2003 and directs a team that covers Europe, The Middle East and Africa. Graham commenced his career on the Stock Exchange servicing institutional investors. He later joined an international merchant house and spent five years on Wall Street, building a global business. On his return to the UK, he founded a corporate finance concern, which provided him with considerable experience of focusing on the particular problems of enterprises spread across the commercial spectrum. After selling his business, he joined a Middle East investment firm and gained valuable local knowledge of the region. His broad experience qualifies him to have an opinion on corporate governance and compliance. He is much published and a sought-after speaker on such issues.

Monarch Data Pump Version 8 (MDP8) combines Datawatch's latest Monarch Report Mining/Data Mining engine with the Microsoft.NET framework to provide a highly scalable and easily administered enterprise solution to acquire, combine and monitor customized data, and deliver that data in a wide variety of formats, on an automatic, scheduled basis. MDP8 can access, combine, customize and publish data mined from 'unstructured' data sources, particularly existing reports, along with 'structured' data sources, such as databases and spreadsheets, to fulfil your organization's ETL and enterprise information delivery needs. For further information, e-mail: rob.graham@datawatch-europe.com.

# Using technology effectively to support a growing business

*Business planning is a dynamic process, so make sure you have a real-time view of your entire business, says Tony Speakman, General Manager, FileMaker International*

As with most things in life, there are benefits and challenges associated along every step of the way for a growing business. Just getting a business off the ground is a major task in itself. But once the business is moving forward, rapid growth can bring with it a whole host of other issues. For example, it's great if your business is growing in line with your business plan, but as it expands and you take on more people, you'll inevitably have less direct control. It's therefore vital to put in place processes that will allow you, and your managers, to keep tabs on how different parts of the business are performing, and to spot potential problems early on.

One of the areas that can trip up a growing business is technology. Even the most well prepared business that has planned ahead in terms of its technology requirements can sometimes fall foul of a lack of flexibility in the systems originally invested in. In the area of software, most businesses will utilize standard office productivity packages such as word processing, spreadsheets and presentation packages to take care of typical administrative tasks. In terms of finance, an accounting package such as Sage

will be used. Beyond that, depending on the type of business involved, companies may well look to develop bespoke applications to handle specific aspects of the business, such as new business development, customer relationship management, etc.

The challenge here for companies is twofold. Whereas basic office packages are well designed for individual productivity, they tend to be limited in terms of their ability to share information. And bespoke packages more often than not cannot be modified easily (or cost-effectively) to take account of rapidly changing business demands.

One area where this can have a big impact is in adapting your business plan to focus on the growth potential of the business and your strategy for achieving this. For example, the new plan could explain how you intend to grow your market share, how to improve operational efficiency and how to produce more of your product/service or widen the range of products you sell. It is worthwhile setting new goals based on your experience so far. So while you may have had good insight into what was originally required to create your business plan, this is only the beginning of your journey to success. Once the revised plan is written, you need to communicate the plan – both to those who must agree its implementation and to those who will implement it. Failure will inevitably ensue if you don't communicate the plan properly. Not only this, your plan needs to be flexible and dynamic in order to allow for inevitable changes and adjustments in relation to both internal and external business conditions.

As mentioned previously, many people will use a presentation package such as Microsoft PowerPoint to share the initial plan. Relevant financial information may well be conveyed using a spreadsheet, such as Microsoft Excel. For most growing businesses, spreadsheet software is the standard for crunching numbers. These tools are entirely appropriate at the original planning and communication phase. However, some important considerations need to be taken into account when moving into the execution phase of the business plan.

All too often people make the mistake of trapping information in a spreadsheet that could better be used in other ways. For example, they may want to put spreadsheet data on the web that can also be updated by other browsers via the internet. This is particularly relevant when the people you need to communicate your business plan to may be widely dispersed geographically. Or you may want to easily include other information from other software packages such as word processing documents, images or PDFs. None of this is really possible with a spreadsheet – so the key point to bear in mind when executing your business plan is to realize that it is a dynamic process. Spreadsheets, word processing and presentation software are essentially static tools. With the plan agreed and communicated, you really need to be able to monitor, analyse and report on the progress you are making. Ideally, you want to have a near real-time view of your entire business. You need to be aware as soon as possible of any activity that will have a material impact on achieving the objectives laid down in your plan.

Let us take an example. When you created your original business plan, you will have made certain judgements and assumptions about your business and the marketplace in the future. However, the likelihood is low that all of those assumptions will in fact occur. Perhaps you are planning to launch a major new product in six months time, allocating a lot of time and resources to support your activity. Your assumption is that your competitors will not be launching a similar product in the same timeframe. But what if they do?

At best, you will have to spend considerable time reworking the plan and communicating the revised version to all necessary participants. At worst, your entire business plan may be thrown into disarray through your inability to realign the business appropriately.

So what is the solution? Fortunately, there is a type of software package that lends itself very well to providing a dynamic means of monitoring, analysing and reporting on the progress of your plan. And because of its inherent flexibility, reworking your plan to take account of changing conditions is easy to achieve in minutes rather than weeks.

The other good news is that database software doesn't need to cost the earth. Using modestly-priced database software, you can really have a very tight handle on the health of your business. For example, with easy-to-use database software, it's simple to convert spreadsheet information into a database format that gives new life and possibilities to the information you've already entered. In seconds, spreadsheet information is transformed into a friendly, easy-to-use and easy-to-view database. With the information in a database, you have far more flexibility in terms of sharing and communicating your business plan – within minutes and without re-entering your original information.

Perhaps the most important part of the business planning process is how the plan is to be implemented – and how the implementation is to be monitored and measured. Unless you have a very firm grip on who is responsible for doing what and when, as well as whether you are achieving the objectives you set yourself, the best written business plan in the world will fail.

Ultimately, writing the business plan is merely the start of an ongoing iterative process. Even though you may have created the plan in a Word document and your financial information in a spreadsheet, it can be difficult to ensure that the information contained in both is synchronized – as well as ensuring that everyone involved in the plan is working from the very latest information. For example, you may have set certain sales targets – but you may be using a different software package for day-to-day sales monitoring. The ideal solution would be to have a software package that not only encompassed the plan, but your day-to-day sales figures and customer information, allowing near real-time monitoring of the business plan.

This is a very important point for growing businesses. While the overall plan may set strategic goals, these are unlikely to be achieved unless specific targets have been set that everyone in your business understands and a system has been put in place to measure their achievement.

Targets give clarity to everyone within a business – whether owner-manager, departmental manager or employee – of what they need to achieve and when they need to achieve it.

Proper measurement indicators also enable those running a business to monitor the performance of a particular division, a new product or service or individual employees or teams. Indicators can be:

- sales figures over a given period;
- milestones in new product development;
- productivity benchmarks for individual team members;
- market-share statistics.

Targets make it clearer for individual employees where they fit within an organization and what they need to do to help the business meet its objectives. Setting clear objectives and targets and closely monitoring their delivery can make the development of your business more effective.

Another example is product pricing and costing. By its very nature, it encompasses a variety of variables such as personnel resources, volume and capacity, and delivery times. The ability to maximize the total resources available in order to meet demand has been a traditional headache for many growing businesses. Far too often, technology can be a hindrance to achieving the best results.

Any growing business in any sector can benefit from using technology appropriately. In summary, the key to success is being able to control and adapt to the inherently dynamic nature of the business environment. Such a context requires the use of a highly flexible, yet easy to use tool such as FileMaker Pro 7. Ultimately, it is the ideal tool for a growing business. Here are some examples.

## Up and down stairs

Graphic Facilities (GF) is now the parent company of a multi-million pound group and one of the largest reprographic companies in the UK. It produces work for many well-known titles, including the *Radio Times*, the *Telegraph, Maxim, Glamour, Autocar* and many more household names. The company processes and prepares more than 9,000 individual pages per month.

GF has a team of 30 people in its booking department (where each page gets initially booked in) – 20 on a day shift and 10 on a night shift. After booking, the page elements are checked and the job bag is sent downstairs to the production department, where another team of 30 people work on putting the pages together.

GF's old booking processes were entirely manual, with job numbers coming from a red book. Each page element was priced manually with each page 'managed' by writing details or ticking boxes on an A3 sheet which stayed in the job bag. No one ever knew where a job bag was, except by shouting from upstairs to downstairs: 'Has anyone got job number 12345 for the *Sunday Telegraph?*' There were two full-time employees, whose main job was to run up and down the stairs finding job bags and ensuring they were flowing through the system at the correct speed. Sometimes a job bag had to be found because the client had sent in an updated image or changed the text, at other times because it had to be at the printers within an hour.

A FileMaker-based solution dramatically improved this situation. With FileMaker in place, GF took on a number of new clients and brought in additional revenue to the tune of approximately £250,000. This was because booking staff no longer needed to know the price of each page or page element for every publication as these are all controlled in a prices module of the database. Now, whenever they book in a page or page element, the price agreed with that client is automatically added to the page total. At the end of every week, the department manager clicks on a button labelled 'Generate Invoices' and the database automatically summarizes and generates the invoices for each completed publication. Each invoice provides a high level of detail for the client, made up of two parts – a 'pages' invoice and a 'corrections' invoice that details the many elements on each page.

## Special places to stay

Alastair Sawday Publishing (ASP), the company behind the well-known travel guide-book series *Special Places To Stay*, has saved thousands of pounds a year by managing its book production process with FileMaker. *Special Places to Stay* is a collection of travel guidebooks covering most of Europe and now India and Morocco. Nearly every edition published (over 50 books) has been compiled with the help of FileMaker. Over the years, the use of FileMaker has become more and more elaborate, as the firm continues to mine FileMaker's built-in flexibility and versatility.

According to Russell Wilkinson, IT Manager for ASP, 'Our whole business is run on FileMaker. We all work to the same agenda, making the company a more productive and integrated one.'

## Live data

The leading secondary care home group, Forest Healthcare, has used FileMaker-based solutions to create an integrated management control system that brings together core aspects of the business – accounting and payroll, staff management, and patient care – and helped deliver significant benefits in terms of improved resident care and bottom line impact.

Forest has grown to become a well-established company currently employing over 250 staff including specialist physicians, GPs, qualified nurses, care assistants and domiciliary staff. Two of the Forest Group's care units in particular have benefited from a FileMaker solution developed by IT specialist Softcare Medical – Ash Court, a purpose built 62 bed dual-registered home in Central London, and Borehamwood Care Village, a purpose built 94 bed dual-registered home in North London.

As Andy Macdonald of Softcare Medical explains, 'The FileMaker system generates customized, individual resident care plans based on assessment data and on each resident's specific condition, and comes with a standard Care Plan Library. The Library contains problems, goals and disciplines, and is customized to meet Ash Court's specific needs. Having used the system, the home added nearly £50,000 in the first six months to the bottom line through improved efficiency, while at the same time raising the quality of care received by residents.'

According to Margaretta Hammond, Director at Borehamwood Care Village: 'I was a complete "technophobe" at the beginning of the project and resisted it wherever possible. However, since the system started going live and data started to be produced, I have become more and more reliant on it. I now cannot imagine how I would be able to operate without it.'

See for yourself how FileMaker Pro could make a real difference to the success of your business plan. You can obtain a free 30-day trial version from www. filemaker.co.uk, or call for more information on 01628 534158.

# How do you keep your business growing?

As widely as growing businesses vary, they do generally share two common goals: containing costs and improving services. Many of these have discovered the answer to both challenges with FileMaker software. No matter what size of business, FileMaker can manage all your information in one place, gaining organisational efficiencies and saving costs.

FileMaker is the world's best selling easy-to-use database, supporting both the Windows and Macintosh operating systems. As you grow you can store, find, manage and share virtually any electronic file type between any computer – on a network or over the web.

Simplify your office tasks by organising your contacts, time, schedules and projects. How about automating your invoicing and standard communications such as memos and status reports. Or perhaps track products and orders.

With FileMaker you'll have all your information at your fingertips, securely stored with access privileges that you set, so you can share what you want with who you want.

No doubt, your success lies in having the right systems in place so that you can focus on what you do best – the business. With FileMaker supporting you we wish you well, growing!

# FileMaker.

Telephone: 01628 534 158    **www.filemaker.co.uk**    uk_sales@filemaker.com

# Offshore outsourcing

*Offshore outsourcing is growing in the middle market, reports NIIT Smartserve's Rajiv Dey*

The internet has redefined the way in which global business is run. High-speed fibre optic links and efficient telecommunication channels have broken down geographical boundaries. Nowhere has this impact been more keenly felt than in the supply chain of services. As businesses look to focus more on their core competencies there arises the need to contract-out peripheral activities to external vendors. Thanks to cheaper communication networks, organizations outsourcing services today have the option of 'going offshore' in their search for the supplier that can deliver the greatest value to their business.

Offshore outsourcing comprises two elements – IT Offshoring (ITO) and Business Process Offshoring (BPO). ITO involves the outsourcing of elements of the IT organization such as application development and maintenance, legacy system modernization, package implementation, network support, technical helpdesks and IT infrastructure/operations management.

BPO involves the outsourcing of business services like back office processing, call centre services, finance and accounting, HR, etc to remote suppliers located in other parts of the world, often thousands of miles away from the home country. This allows organizations to benefit from the laws of comparative advantage by obtaining services from the most competitive sources in the world.

According to a recent report by Ovum Holway, the UK BPO and ITO market is as shown in Table 11.4.1.

The BPO adoption level is far from saturation and growth rates are sustainable for years to come.

# A SMART PLAYER
## ...at the core
### of your business

## NIIT SmartServe... Your Indian Partner for Business Process Outsourcing (BPO)...

→ **Back Office Administration**
→ **Transaction Processing**
→ **Accounting**
→ **Customer Service**
→ **Call Centre - Inbound / Outbound**
→ **Technical Help Desk**
→ **Compliance Services**

## We deliver

→ **Highly skilled manpower and quick ramp ups ensured by the training heritage of NIIT**

→ **Improved service levels and turnaround times, high quality and productivity**

→ **Customised solutions**

→ **Great pricing**

**For more details, visit** www.niitsmartserve.com **or** www.niit.com
**Contact Rajiv Dey at** rajiv@niit.co.uk **Tel: 01494 539 333**

**UK**: NIIT Technologies Ltd, Westfields, London Road, High Wycombe Bucks, HP11 1HP, UK. Tel: +44 (0) 1494 539 333, Fax: +44 (0) 1494 539 444
**USA**: NIIT Technologies Ltd, 1050 Crown Pointe Parkway, Floor 5, Atlanta, GA 30338, Tel: +1(770) 551 9494, Toll Free: +1(888) 454 NIIT, Fax: +1(770) 551 9229
**India**: 230, Udyog Vihar, Ph-I, Gurgaon (Haryana)-122002, India. Tel: +91 124 5002702, Fax: +91 124 5002701

**niit smartserve**
the remote business process management company

MWIPL/05/05

**Table 11.4.1**   The UK BPO and ITO market

| £ Billion | 2002 Market size | CAGR 2002–07 | 2007 Market size |
|---|---|---|---|
| BPO | 3.55 | 12.7% | 6.45 |
| ITO | 6.27 | 6.0% | 8.38 |

India is a leading destination for offshore ITO and BPO. Organizations like GE, American Express, Prudential, AVIVA, Dell and others have all established significant BPO operations in India. Whilst the initial driver for offshoring to India was a 40 to 60 per cent cost advantage, India has also been able to deliver significant productivity increases resulting in a definite win–win for both the client and the offshore service provider.

The Indian offshore BPO services industry is one of the fastest growing segments of the Indian market. From a level of US $1 billion in 2001 the industry is expected to touch $21 to 24 billion by 2008.

## The need for offshore outsourcing

CEOs of Western companies have been coming under increasing pressure to deliver shareholder returns in mature markets characterized by low growth rates. The task is not easy. To deliver 8 to 10 per cent annual returns consistently when the broader economy is growing at 3 per cent per annum requires constant innovation when organizations are faced with the following challenges:

■ market saturation limiting significant top line growth potential;
■ a mature customer base constantly expecting higher value for money;
■ ever increasing competition threatening to erode margins and the customer base.

Due to these reasons organizations' growth strategies have tended to focus on the demand side by constant product innovation, better value for money, enhancing the customer experience, customer retention through better customer service and customer acquisition through better customer profiling and target marketing.

On the supply side, the growth strategies have focused on aggressive cost cutting and rationalization, productivity improvements, improved time to market, etc.

Businesses have also started relying heavily on technology to deliver competitive advantage on both the demand and supply sides. Technology has now become an 'enabler' and a critical component of business strategy, whereas previously it was a support function.

As a first step, companies started re-engineering their processes and consolidating their service operations into shared service centres that support multiple locations. Having achieved this, the next level of cost reduction was achieved by relocating the shared service centres to offshore locations.

Due to these reasons the market for both IT offshoring and business process offshoring has been growing significantly in recent times as both IT and BPO have become essential ingredients of corporate growth strategies.

## The offshore market

Multinational organizations were the first to sense this opportunity to harness the low-cost, high-skill workforce available in India and other offshore destinations. Early adopters like GE set up captive BPO operations in India in 1996. American Express, Standard Chartered, British Airways and others soon followed.

Given the initial success of these organizations, we are now witnessing the second phase of this market development where more and more mid-sized European organizations are actively starting to use offshore outsourcing.

## What can be offshored?

The types of BPO work that can be offshored include voice and back office processing and can be broadly categorized as follows:

- *Front office* – telesales, customer service.
- *Middle office* – vertical specific rule-based transaction processing, eg banking and insurance back office processing.
- *Back office* – finance and accounts, HR, etc.

As the market for offshore services continues to mature, more and more high end processes have started getting offshored, like market research, equity research, engineering design, compliance, investment analysis and knowledge-based services like analytics. A new phrase – Knowledge Process Offshoring ( KPO) – has been coined to recognize this shift.

The IT offshore market is relatively more mature and most elements have already been offshored successfully.

Of late there has been a shift towards BPO-cum-ITO contracts in the market and most vendors today can offer a mix of BPO and IT offshoring.

## Where can we offshore?

Quick to seize on this emerging opportunity, a number of countries have emerged as potential destinations for ITO and BPO. Whilst India by far leads the field in both ITO and BPO due to its vast base of low-cost skilled resources, other countries that have made an imprint in the BPO space are the Philippines, Mexico, China, Brazil and South Africa.

Around Europe we have other strong contenders with a 'near shore' offering, like Russia, the Czech Republic, Romania, Hungary and Ireland. Whilst these may not offer the same level of cost savings as the original offshore destinations, they have the benefit of being closer to Western Europe and offer advantages in terms of multilingual capability and cultural affinity.

Western European organizations can therefore look to blend an onshore service with a near shore or offshore operation and thereby create geographical redundancy and a 24-hour service by operating in different time zones.

## Types of offshore service providers

The early adopters like GE started by setting up captive operations offshore as shared service centres. Sensing the direction in which the market was moving, a whole host of offshore service providers have emerged. These can be broadly categorized as follows:

- *Western outsourcers* – international outsourcers like IBM, Unisys, EDS, Accenture and others have set up offshore operations to support their clients.
- *Third-party vendors* like leading Indian global IT companies such as Wipro, Infosys, Satyam and NIIT have all set up offshore BPO operations.
- *Captives* – multinational banks and insurance companies like HSBC, Prudential, Allianz Cornhill have set up their own captive operations.
- *Shared service centres going to market with a third-party offering* – traditional shared service operations like GE and British Airways are now offering their services to the wider market.

Most of these service providers can provide multilingual and multi-shore offerings to their Western clients and are able to work across different time zones. The stage is now set where service providers have begun to differentiate themselves by developing areas of competence and vertical specific niche offerings.

## Engagement models

Companies looking at offshore outsourcing often have very different objectives driving their strategy. Developing the correct engagement model is key to ensuring those client objectives are met and paves the way for a long-term partnership. Some of the more common engagement models are:

- *Captive* – where the client sets up a wholly owned subsidiary. Typically used when the client has strong local experience and feet on the ground and control and security are key objectives. Widely used by multinational banks and insurance companies.
- *Build, operate and transfer* – where the client wants a third party to take the risk of initially building the operations and wants an option to take over the ownership once steady state operations have been achieved. Typically used by clients who do not have any local experience but ultimately want a long-term presence.
- *Joint venture* – combines the clients' domain capability with the knowledge and experience of a local partner. Both parties have a stake in the success of the project,

but problems could develop in the relationship between the partners over a period of time.

■ *Third-party vendor* – arms-length vendor. Used when client wants minimal local presence, quick exit, or benefits from a centre of specialization already created by the vendor.
■ *Captive going to market* – where a captive offers its specialization to the market in competition with a third-party vendor.

Apart from this, *hybrid models* have developed where clients use a mix of captive and third-party suppliers to minimize risk and take advantage of vendors with niche areas of expertise. *White label services* are another option, where a third-party service provider becomes an extension of the client organization and the client brands the service.

## Problems faced

Whilst offshoring has generally been successful in delivering significant cost savings as well as productivity gains, clients embarking on this for the first time need to be aware of certain pitfalls:

■ *Cultural issues* – cross-cultural issues can impact the effectiveness with which teams work together and understand each other.
■ *Potential brand dilution* – there is the potential for brand dilution if customer-facing interactions are not handled with appropriate skill and empathy.
■ *Transitioning and domain knowledge transfer* – clients often underestimate the management resources that are needed and the amount of 'hand holding' required to migrate a process effectively.
■ *IPR* – some countries do not have adequate laws to protect patents and intellectual property.
■ *Data protection and data security* – there are operational risks in this area that need to be mitigated.
■ *Compliance and governance* – weaknesses in this area can result in significant operational risk.

None of these issues is a showstopper and most of them can be overcome through proper due diligence, project planning, project management and training. The benefits far outweigh the additional cost and effort involved.

## Conclusion

The world is becoming a smaller place. The future lies in networked organizations that can retain their competitive edge by developing a supply chain that reaches out to the far corners of the world to source the most productive resource in the most cost-effective manner. Technology is even more important now as an enabler, and is driving business to meet growth strategies. Welcome to the world of offshore outsourcing.

NIIT is a global IT and BPO services provider, with a footprint that spans 14 countries across the world. It has been working with global corporations in the United States, Europe, Japan, Asia Pacific and India for over two decades. It has state-of-the-art offshore development facilities to meet the demands of British Airways, ING Group, Toshiba, and SEI Investments, among others. Customers can also leverage the company's intrinsic strengths in the areas of IT education and global software solutions using its 3,000 learning centres, more than 250 of which are outside India. To stay at the cutting edge of technology, NIIT has set up Centres of Competence in multimedia, netcentric computing, software R&D and manufacturing solutions.

Rajiv Dey is Senior Vice President and Head of Business Development, BPO. He has experience of both offshore operations and business development in the UK, working across a wide range of verticals including financial services, insurance, direct marketing and telecoms.

He joined NIIT soon after its BPO business was set up and has played a major role in building the UK business, which currently accounts for more than 90 per cent of the BPO/call centre revenues. Projects currently running at NIIT Smartserve include closed books life insurance processing, FSA regulatory compliance, consumer lifestyle surveys, B2B directory cleansing, telesales, lead generation and appointment setting across many industry verticals.

For further details: Rajiv Dey, Senior Vice President and Head of Business Development, NIIT Smartserve, Westfields, London Road, High Wycombe, Buckinghamshire HP11 1HP; tel: 01494 539333; e-mail: rajiv@niit.co.uk; website: www.smartserve.com or www.niit.com.

# Software...

## are you managing the risk?

27%* of software in the UK is being used illegally.

Do you know what software is installed in your organisation?

Do you have sufficient software licences? - if not, your organisation is at risk.

If anyone in your organisation is caught using under licensed or pirated software your company Directors are liable and they could face unlimited fines or prison sentences.
FAST Corporate Services can help you manage that risk.
Our software compliance programme educates and advises you on how to achieve excellence in software and IT management.

The FAST Standard for Software Compliance FSSC-1:2004, a private standard developed in collaboration with BSI, is the essential first step on the path to a legal IT environment. Registration to the FAST Standard helps:

- identify and eliminate the risks relating to software management
- maximise your software and hardware investment
- set up purchasing and installation procedures and educate staff

Find out how many organisations have benefited from the FAST Programme by visiting the case studies section on www.fastcorporateservices.com. Alternatively for more information call 01628 622121

## FAST
Corporate Services

*Business Software Alliance/ IDC Global Software Piracy study 2004

# Software licensing for SMEs

*Ignorance is no defence, so don't get caught out by illegal use of software, says Geoff Webster, CEO, FAST Corporate Services*

Most people wouldn't watch TV or drive without a licence – so why are so many businesses, from large corporates to SMEs, using software without one? The answer in the majority of cases is ignorance. But, as software publishers crack down on piracy, businesses would do well to remember that ignorance is no defence in a court of law.

## Why worry about software licences?

According to research recently carried out by IDC and the Business Software Alliance (BSA), about one-third (27 per cent) of software in UK businesses is illegal or pirated, costing UK technology firms over £1 billion a year. However, many company directors are still unaware that they face uncapped fines and up to 10 years imprisonment for software theft, as stated in the Copyright Designs and Patents Act 1988 (section 107). Even when a case is not pursued in court, an out of court settlement could damage a company's reputation.

Fortunately there is a relatively simple process that smaller businesses can put in place to manage software licensing and ensure that the organization is legally compliant.

# Software compliance process

## Setting boundaries

The first step in the software compliance process is to ensure that the appropriate policies and procedures are implemented so that employees know what they can and can't do when it comes to software purchase, installation and use. This should include obtaining authorization from the appropriate member of staff before downloading or installing anything on the organization's computers.

Naturally, users should be made aware of new policies and procedures, and this can be done via posters, newsletters and notice boards. Employees should sign a document to say that they understand them and will follow them to the letter. A disciplinary process should also provide reinforcement, and should be used if staff are found to be contravening the new policies and procedures.

Having procedures in place for downloading and purchasing software is vital for the growing business. Even if a company only has one or two PCs now and is aware of all the installed software, having policies in place will ensure that company directors can still retain control over software licensing as the business grows.

## Getting your house in order

Next up is to audit all software assets to find out exactly what is already installed and, more important, what is actually used. Many businesses find they are over-licensed and are wasting money on buying more copies of software than required or paying maintenance on unused applications. The money wasted on these could be channelled into other areas.

The audit process can either be done using an electronic network auditing tool or via a manual walk-round audit. There are advantages and disadvantages to both, and it may also depend upon the size of the organization and how many PCs it owns.

Collecting data via an electronic tool is much quicker, but it is practically impossible to obtain all the information required for the audit. Information on the user – name, department, physical location, etc – as well as details of standalone PCs or laptops that may be off-site, cannot be collected via an electronic audit. A physical walk-round is very time-consuming, but ensures that these details are not left out of the audit. It also takes into account peripherals such as printers, plasma screens, scanners and external modems. Once each item has been audited, it should be marked with a unique identification sticker.

## Ensuring compliance

The third step in the process is reconciliation of the audited assets with relevant software licences, to ensure that the organization is correctly licensed. An asset register should be devised, listing the unique asset number identified during the audit process with the licence number. Many software publishers now allow invoices to be used as proof of licence purchase, so it is worth reconciling software to invoice numbers as backup.

The organization should then ensure it has the correct number of licences. This is likely to involve purchasing licences for software that is under-licensed and deleting any unlicensed software that is not needed. Licences should also be stored in a fireproof safe once the reconciliation has taken place, to avoid potential loss or disasters.

## Ongoing management

The last, and perhaps most difficult task is ongoing management of the compliance programme. As the IT and business environment is constantly changing and evolving, so too does the use of assets.

Policies and procedures should therefore be reviewed frequently and updated as necessary, with regular communication sent out to all staff to remind them of their existence. A full audit should be carried out at least once a year, as well as an interim audit every quarter of between 5 and 10 per cent of the organization's PCs. This will ensure that the organization is as compliant as it can be.

---

### Six-point guide to software licensing for the SME

1. All software is copyright material and must be licensed correctly. You never own the software, regardless of how much you pay: you are only buying the right to use it.
2. Licence agreements are often printed on single sheets of paper that may or may not come with the boxed software. It is important to keep them in a safe environment, such as a fireproof safe, as they can often be the only proof of the organization's right to use the software.
3. If a licence agreement genuinely cannot be found, the receipted invoice can often be accepted as proof of purchase. It is therefore advisable to reconcile the invoices as well as licence agreements with the software installed on your system.
4. Shareware, freeware, games, screensavers, fonts, music, video and pictures are all copyright materials and should be treated in the same way as any other software, with careful consideration of the licence details.
5. Smaller businesses cannot always afford the wide range of technology on the market for controlling computer use. Often a cost-effective way to address this issue is with robust policies, which help staff to understand the implications of incorrect computer use.
6. Policies should include obtaining authorization from the appropriate person before downloading or installing anything onto computers.

Geoff Webster is CEO at FAST Corporate Services. The company offers a membership programme that provides advice and training to help businesses understand the various areas of effective IT and software management. The FAST Standard for Software Compliance, a private standard developed in collaboration with the British Standards Institution, is now widely recognized as the 'benchmark' in the software management arena. For more information visit www.fastcorporateservices.com.

# Index of advertisers

# Further reading from Kogan Page

*Business and the Beautiful Game: How You Can Apply the Skills and Passion of Football to be a Winner in Business*, 2005, Theo Theobald and Cary Cooper

*The Business Plan Workbook*, 4th edn, 2005, Colin Barrow, Paul Barrow and Robert Brown

*The Company Secretary's Handbook: A Guide to Duties and Responsibilities*, 3rd edn, 2004, Helen Ashton

*The Corporate Finance Handbook*, 4th edn, 2006, Jonathan Reuvid

*The 18 Immutable Laws of Corporate Reputation: Creating, Protecting and Repairing Your Most Valuable Asset*, 2004, Ron Alsop

*The Employer's Handbook: An Essential Guide to Employment Law, Personnel Policies and Procedures*, 3rd edn, 2005, Barry Cushway

*Going Public: The Essential Guide to Flotation*, 2nd edn, 2006, Jonathan Reuvid

*A Handbook of Management and Leadership: A Guide to Managing for Results*, 2005, Michael Armstrong and Tina Stephens

*The Health and Safety Handbook: A Practical Guide to Health and Safety Law, Management Policies and Procedures*, 2005, Jeremy Stranks

*How to Be an Even Better Manager: A Complete A to Z of Proven Technologies and Essential Skills*, 2004, Michael Armstrong

*How to Grow Leaders: The Seven Key Principles of Effective Leadership Development*, 2005, John Adair

*How to Invest in Hedge Funds: An Investment Professional's Guide*, 2005, Matt Ridley

*How to Understand the Financial Pages: An A to Z Guide to Money and the Jargon*, 2005, Alexander Davidson

*IT Governance: A Manager's Guide to Data Security and BS 7799 / IS 17799*, 2005, Alan Calder and Steve Watkins

*Making Sense of Change Management: A Complete Guide to the Models, Tools and Techniques of Organizational Change*, 2004, Esther Cameron and Mike Green

*Managing Business Risk: A Practical Guide to Protecting Your Business*, 3rd edn, 2006, Jonathan Reuvid

*Marketing Communications: An Integrated Approach*, 4th edn, 2004, P R Smith and Jonathan Taylor

*The Handbook of Personal Wealth Management: How to Ensure Maximum Return and Security*, 2005, Jonathan Reuvid

*Raising Finance: A Practical Guide for Starting, Expanding and Selling Your Business*, 2004, Paul Barrow

*The Sustainable Enterprise: Profiting from Best Practice*, 2005, Christopher Brown

*Venture Capital Funding: A Practical Guide to Raising Finance,* 2005, Stephen Bloomfield

The above titles are available from all good bookshops or direct from the publishers. To obtain more information, please contact the publisher at the address below:

Kogan Page
120 Pentonville Road
London N1 9JN
Tel: 020 7278 0433
Fax: 020 7837 6348
www.kogan-page.co.uk